Bengt Nyström

Rörstrand

Jugendstil-Porzellan aus Schweden

Das weiße Gold des Nordens

Art Nouveau Porcelain from Sweden

The White Gold of the North

Collection Hans Schmidts

ARNOLDSCHE Art Publishers

Inhaltsverzeichnis
Contents

Vorwort
Preface

Anders als die Erzeugnisse der Königlichen Porzellanmanufaktur Kopenhagen und ihres am selben Ort tätigen Konkurrenten Bing & Grøndahl begegneten die Kunstporzellane der schwedischen Manufaktur Rörstrand in den Jahren um die vorletzte Jahrhundertwende in Deutschland nur einer verhaltenen Aufnahme. Das Standardwerk „Moderne Keramik" von Richard Borrmann bildet zwar eine Auswahl von Arbeiten ab, merkt aber in Bezug auf deren typische Gestaltungsmerkmale mit leichtem Tadel an: „Rörstrand verbindet mit der Unterglasurmalerei im Stil von Kopenhagen eine äusserst feine, vielleicht zu zierliche Blumenplastik." (Leipzig 1903, S. 94) Und zwei Jahrzehnte später konnte Borrmanns Nachfolger Otto Pelka bereits abschließend resümieren: „Im allgemeinen hat man den Eindruck, daß die Kunst in Rörstrand der Vergangenheit angehört. Selbst sein erster Künstler Alf Wallander, der in zukunftsreich scheinenden Anfängen stand, ist zu keinem Fortschritt mehr gelangt." (Keramik der Neuzeit, Leipzig 1924, S. 93).

Auch in der Folgezeit setzte sich diese Einschätzung zunächst fort. Die Frankfurter Ausstellung von 1955, mit der die Wiederentdeckung und Rehabilitierung des bis dahin verpönten Jugendstils in Deutschland begann, ließ die Jugendstil-Porzellane aus Stockholm unbeachtet und beschränkte sich auf eine noch ganz historisierende Kanne von 1876. Der Bestandskatalog des Berliner Kunstgewerbemuseums von 1966 zeigte immerhin drei 1897 erworbene Vasen, und in der 1968 in Kassel gezeigten Sammlung des Münchener Kunsthistorikers Gerhard P. Woeckel war auch eine Tierplastik vertreten. In der 1974 vom Düsseldorfer Hetjens-Museum unter dem Titel „Europäische Keramik des Jugendstils" veranstalteten repräsentativen Gesamtschau wurden die gezeigten Arbeiten den entwerfenden und ausführenden Künstlern zugeordnet. Bereits fünf Jahre zuvor hatte der Berliner Sammler Karl H. Bröhan neben seiner Kollektion von Berliner Porzellanen auch eine repräsentative Auswahl von 55 Rörstrand-Porzellanen vorgestellt, in der neben Zierobjekten aller Art auch figürliche Arbeiten in größerer Zahl vertreten waren, ergänzt durch eine Firmengeschichte,

Unlike the china made by the Royal Copenhagen Manufactory and their competitor based in the same city, Bing & Grøndahl, the art porcelain produced by the Swedish Rörstrand factory met with only a muted response in Germany during the years shortly before and after the turn to the twentieth century. A selection of Rörstrand pieces is pictured in the standard work Moderne Keramik by Richard Borrmann but the author remarks rather disparagingly on the stylistic features typical of them: 'Rörstrand unites extremely fine, perhaps too delicate, floral sprigging with underglaze painting in the Copenhagen style' (Leipzig 1903, p. 94). And two decades later, Otto Pelka, Borrmann's successor, felt he could write Rörstrand off: 'In general, one has the impression that art at Rörstrand belongs to the past. Even their premier artist Alf Wallander, who seemed to be at the start of a promising career, has not managed to make any further headway' (Keramik der Neuzeit, Leipzig 1924, p. 93).

This appraisal persisted for quite some time. The 1955 Frankfurt exhibition heralding the rediscovery and rehabilitation of Jugendstil/Art Nouveau, which had until then been frowned on in Germany, passed over the Stockholm Art Nouveau porcelain and limited itself to a jug dating from 1876 that was still entirely historicising in style. Still, the 1966 inventory catalogue of the Berlin Applied Arts museum did feature three Rörstrand vases acquired in 1897. Moreover, Rörstrand was represented by an animal figurine in the collection amassed by the Munich art historian Gerhard P. Woeckel that was shown in Kassel in 1968. The Rörstrand works shown at Europäische Keramik des Jugendstils [European Art Nouveau Ceramics], the historical retrospective mounted by the Hetjens Museum in Düsseldorf in 1974, were duly attributed to the artists who had designed and executed them. Five years previously, the Berlin collector Karl H. Bröhan had, along with his collection of Berlin porcelain, also shown a representative selection of fifty-five Rörstrand pieces that included not only all sorts of ornamental objects but also quite a number of figurative works, supplemented by a

Künstlerbiographien und Auszüge aus der zeitgenössischen Literatur. Im zweiten Band des Bestandskataloges „Porzellan" des Bröhan-Museum (Berlin 1996) wurde der schwedischen Manufaktur ein von Dieter Högermann erarbeitetes fünfzigseitiges Kapitel gewidmet, das neben farbigen Wiedergaben von 74 sorgfältig beschriebenen Objekten eine Firmengeschichte, zahlreiche Wiedergaben zeitgenössischer Texte sowie eine sorgfältig recherchierte Bibliographie enthält und damit den bislang umfangreichsten Beitrag zum Thema darstellt. Eine deutschsprachige Monographie zu den Rörstrand-Porzellanen des Jugendstils fehlte allerdings noch immer.

Diese Lücke wird durch die jetzt vorgelegte Publikation geschlossen. Ihr Autor, der schwedische Kunsthistoriker Bengt Nyström, der mit zahlreichen teilweise auch in englischer Übersetzung erschienenen Veröffentlichungen zur angewandten Kunst in Schweden und insbesondere zur schwedischen Keramik des 19. und 20. Jahrhunderts im allgemeinen und zu den Kunstporzellanen von Rörstrand im besonderen hervorgetreten ist, gibt auf der Grundlage von Originalunterlagen und zeitgenössischen Quellen eine fundierte Darstellung der kunstkeramischen Aktivitäten bei Rörstrand von den in dem letzten Viertel des ausgehenden 19. Jahrhunderts zu registrierenden Ansätzen zu einer stilistischen Erneuerung bis zu dem durch die Aufgabe der historischen Produktionsstätten in Stockholm im Jahre 1926 markierten späten Abschied von der Epoche des Jugendstils. Anders als in den angeführten Beiträgen zu Rörstrand, die sich im wesentlichen auf die zeitgenössische Rezeption in Deutschland und den Nachbarländern stützen, behandelt Nyström nicht nur die Porzellanarbeiten und die an ihrer Gestaltung und Ausführung beteiligten Künstlerinnen und Künstler sowie die keramtechnischen und materialspezifischen Voraussetzungen ihrer Herstellung, sondern auch die kunst- und kulturgeschichtlichen Entwicklungen und Zusammenhänge konsequent aus zeitgenössischer skandinavischer Sicht. Das führt zu ungewohnten Akzentsetzungen, macht aber beispielsweise auch die zeitlichen Verschiebungen im Vergleich zu den dänischen Manufakturen und damit auch deren Popularitätsvorsprung in Deutschland verständlich. Die von ihm gewählte Methode, sich dabei dem Thema aus verschiedenen Richtungen anzunähern, stellt die begleitenden Umstände und die beteiligten Personen unter jeweils unterschiedlichen Aspekten dar und gibt überraschende Einblicke in die Randbedingungen, unter denen die beeindruckend schönen und in ihrer Art unvergleichlichen künstlerischen Porzellane entstanden. So erfährt man nicht nur etwas über das soziale Engagement des leitenden Künstlers Alf Wallander, sondern nimmt auch zur Kenntnis, daß er gleichzeitig mit seiner Tätigkeit für Rörstrand Geschäftsführer eines renommierten Kunstgewerbehauses war. Der Bildhauer und Keramiker Waldemar Lindström und sein als Maler und Keramiker tätiger Cousin Karl begegnen einander in gemeinsamer künstlerischer Arbeit, aber auch als Mitglieder einer über drei Generationen dem Unternehmen

history of the Swedish porcelain factory, artist biographies and excerpts from literature of the period. In the second volume of the Bröhan Museum porcelain inventory catalogue (Berlin 1996), a fifty-page chapter by Dieter Högermann is devoted to the Swedish factory. Featuring seventy-four objects pictured in colour and meticulously described, the catalogue contains a history of Rörstrand, reproductions of numerous contemporary texts as well as an exhaustively researched bibliography and therefore represents the hitherto most comprehensive work on the subject. A monograph in German devoted to Rörstrand Jugendstil/Art Nouveau porcelain was, however, not yet on the books.

This gap has now been filled by the present publication. The author, the Swedish art historian Bengt Nyström, has distinguished himself with numerous publications, some of them also in English translations, on the applied arts in Sweden, specifically Swedish ceramics of the nineteenth and twentieth centuries, with a focus on Rörstrand art porcelain. Nyström gives us a grounded survey of art ceramic-related activities at Rörstrand in the closing years of the last quarter of the nineteenth century based on original documents and contemporary sources, ranging from evident approaches to stylistic renewal to the belated farewell to the Jugendstil/Art Nouveau era marked by the closure of the historic Stockholm workshops in 1926. Unlike the above listed writings on Rörstrand, which are essentially based on the contemporary response to it in Germany and the neighbouring countries, Nyström deals not only with the pieces and the artists who designed and executed them as well as the technical and materials-related aspects of ceramic production but also consistently places his subject matter in the context of art history and cultural developments as seen from the contemporary Scandinavian viewpoint. This approach has led to unusual shifts in focus but also clarifies why Rörstrand lagged behind Danish porcelain factories and why Danish porcelain has been so much more popular in Germany. The method Nyström has chosen for approaching the subject from different angles shows the attendant circumstances and the persons involved from various perspectives, providing astonishing insights into the wider context in which these impressively handsome and, in their way, peerless pieces of art porcelain were created. Hence readers not only learn about the social commitment displayed by the leading Rörstrand artist Alf Wallander but also discover that, while working for Rörstrand, Wallander was the managing director of a reputable applied arts firm. Waldemar Lindström, a sculptor and ceramicist, and his cousin Karl, who worked as a painter and ceramicist, are frequently mentioned as collaborating on art projects as well as being members of a family that was linked with Rörstrand for three successive generations. Their story reveals the importance of a significant religious affiliation as the basis for dutiful conduct in a penurious life. 'Tales of an old Porcelain Painter' are instructive on those difficult lives, linking them with the

Rörstrand verbundenen Familie. In deren Geschichte wird die Bedeutung einer ausgeprägten religiösen Gebundenheit als Grundlage der Pflichterfüllung in einem kargen Leben deutlich. Die von diesem kargen Leben berichtenden „Erzählungen einer alten Porzellanmalerin" schlagen den Bogen zu den mehrfach zitierten sozialethischen und sozialästhetischen Reformbestrebungen von Ellen Key und ihrer Bedeutung auch für die schwedische Kunstkeramik der Zeit.

Das vorliegende Werk präsentiert einen Höhepunkt der europäischen Porzellankunst des Jugendstils; aber auch sein praktischer Nutzen für die Liebhaber und Sammler des schwedischen Porzellans und alle an der künstlerischen Keramik dieser Zeit Interessierten ist gar nicht hoch genug zu veranschlagen. Die Abbildungen und die Ausführungen im Text ermöglichen eine Einordnung, die zahlreichen neuen Biographien der an dem Entwurf und der Herstellung Beteiligten samt ihren Monogrammen und Signaturen eine Zuordnung eigener Objekte. Die für die skandinavische Malerei des Jugendstils geprägte Charakterisierung als „Licht aus dem Norden" war bereits in der Zeit häufiger auch auf die Porzellane von Rörstrand übertragen worden. Ein besonderer Reiz dieses Buches von Bengt Nyström besteht darin, daß es ihm gelungen ist, dieses hier durch die hervorragenden Belegstücke aus der Sammlung Schmidts repräsentierte Licht aus dem Norden in einer ebenso eigenwilligen wie beeindruckenden Sicht aus dem Norden nahezubringen.

Johannes Busch
Juni 2011

frequently cited attempts at reform in the field of social ethics and aesthetics made by Ellen Key and her relevance to Swedish art ceramics in her day.

This book presents a highlight of European Jugendstil/Art Nouveau porcelain. Its usefulness to lovers and collectors of Swedish porcelain and anyone who is interested in the art ceramics of the period cannot be overstated. The illustrations and explanations in the text facilitate classification of their own objects, and attribution to individual designers and ceramicists is made possible by a wealth of new biographies. The characterisation of Scandinavian Art Nouveau painting as 'northern light' was even then quite often applied to Rörstrand porcelain. One particularly attractive aspect of this book by Bengt Nyström is that he has succeeded so brilliantly at showcasing the northern light as represented by these superlative pieces from the Schmidts Collection in a view from the North that is as idiosyncratic as it is impressive.

Johannes Busch
June 2011

Rörstrand Firmengebäude im umgebauten Schlosskomplex, 1899 (Luftbild).
// The Rörstrand Porcelain Manufactory in the converted castle grounds, 1899
(aerial photo).
Photogravure from Eckert & Pflug Kunstverlag Leipzig. Rörstrand Museum.

Betrachtungen des Sammlers
Reflections of the Collector

Schon in jungen Jahren hatte ich ein ausgeprägtes Interesse für Kunst und Antiquitäten. Im Laufe der Zeit habe ich nach und nach einzelne Werke und Objekte erworben, die mich besonders angesprochen haben. Wenn mir auf meinen beruflichen Reisen ein wenig Zeit blieb, stöberte ich gerne auf Antikmärkten, z. B. in Berlin oder London, nach ausgefallenen und schönen Stücken. Es blieb aber beim Kauf einzelner Objekte, mehr Zeit blieb mir nicht für meine Liebhaberei.

Das änderte sich 1988 mit der Beendigung meiner beruflichen Tätigkeit. Ich fing an, mit großem Interesse und Vergnügen Auktionshäuser zu besuchen – in Hannover, Köln, Hamburg und Berlin –, nun aber weniger auf der Suche nach Einzelstücken als nach einem möglichen Sammelgebiet. In einem Auktionshaus in Köln sah ich 1989 zum ersten Mal bewusst eine Jugendstil-Vase von Rörstrand und war sofort fasziniert von der Ästhetik und Eleganz dieses Porzellans. Es handelte sich um eine ganz kleine Vase mit einem Reliefdekor aus Pilzen am oberen Vasenrand (siehe Objekt-Nr. 148). Mein Sohn, der sich als Antiquitätenhändler damals vor allem intensiv mit Glas, Keramik und Porzellan des Jugendstil und Art Déco beschäftigte, schätzte die Jugendstilvasen und -objekte von Rörstrand als besonders ausgefallen, schön und selten ein und meinte, sie seien als Sammel-Objekte für mich nicht nur aus diesen Gründen speziell geeignet, sondern auch wegen meines engen persönlichen Bezugs zu Schweden. Seit Jahrzehnten besaß ich dort ein Ferienhaus, in dem ich jedes Jahr mit meiner Familie den Urlaub verbrachte und mich mit einigen Schweden traf, die zu meinen Freunden geworden waren.

Ich erwarb also die „Pilz-Vase" in Köln und damit das erste Objekt meiner heutigen „Rörstrand-Sammlung". Es folgten Ankäufe auf Auktionen in deutschen und schwedischen Auktionshäusern sowie auf Antikmärkten und -messen in Deutschland, England und Schweden. Inserate in schwedischen Fachzeitschriften für Antiquitäten führten mich zu Händlern und privaten Sammlern in Schweden. Langsam wuchs die Sammlung und so füllten die Vasen und Objekte die Regale im Wohn-

Already in my younger days I had a lively interest in art and antiques. Over the course of time I gradually acquired individual works and objects that particularly appealed to me. Whenever I had a bit of time to spare on my business trips, I enjoyed browsing at antiques markets, for instance in Berlin and London, for unusual and beautiful pieces. However, I only bought a few objects since I had no more time than that for my favourite pastime.

All that changed in 1988 when I retired from professional life. I began with great interest and pleasure to visit auction houses – in Hanover, Cologne, Hamburg and Berlin – but by now I was not so much after individual pieces as I was on the look-out for a possible collection area. It was at a Cologne auction house in 1989 that I consciously saw for the first time a Rörstrand Jugendstil/Art Nouveau vase and I was instantly fascinated by the aesthetic and elegance of the porcelain. It was a very small vase, with relief decoration consisting of mushrooms on the upper part of the vase rim (see object no. 148). My son, an antiques dealer who at that time was primarily focused on Jugendstil/Art Nouveau and Art Déco glass, ceramics and porcelain, deemed the Rörstrand Jugendstil vases unusual and rare indeed and thought they would be especially suitable objects for me to collect, not only for those reasons but also because of my own close personal ties to Sweden. I had owned a second home there for years, where I spent holidays with my family and time with Swedes with whom I had become friends.

So I bought the 'Mushroom vase' in Cologne and thus it became the first object in what is today my 'Rörstrand collection'. It was followed by purchases made at auctions held by German and Swedish auction houses, and at antiques markets and fairs in Germany, England and Sweden. Advertisements in Swedish antiques magazines brought me into contact with antique dealers and private collectors in Sweden. The collection gradually grew so large that vases and objects filled the shelves in the living room and other rooms of my house. To display the collection in a way that seemed to me worthy of it I set up a sepa-

zimmer und in anderen Räumen des Hauses. Um für mich die Sammlung besser zur Geltung zu bringen, richtete ich einen gesonderten Raum mit großen eingebauten Glasvitrinen ein, in denen ein Großteil der Sammlung Platz fand. Damit habe ich die Objekte dieser längst vergangenen Epoche täglich vor Augen und kann mich an ihnen erfreuen.

Um an Hintergrund-Informationen über das Rörstrand-Porzellan und vor allem über die für Rörstrand tätigen Künstler zu gelangen, besuchte ich Museen mit einem großen Bestand an Jugendstil-Porzellanen (u. a. das Bröhan-Museum in Berlin) und natürlich auch das Rörstrand-Museum in Lidköping. Ich nahm Kontakt auf zu dem Kunsthistoriker und anerkannten Rörstrand-Kenner in Stockholm, Bengt Nyström. Aufgrund des gemeinsamen Interessengebietes und nach seinen beiden Besuchen bei mir entwickelte sich aus dem Kontakt bald eine freundschaftliche Beziehung. Ich freue mich ganz besonders, dass er sich als Autor für das gemeinsame Buchprojekt gewinnen ließ und möchte ihm an dieser Stelle ausdrücklich meinen herzlichen Dank aussprechen.

Ein besonderer Dank gebührt auch der ARNOLDSCHEN Verlagsanstalt, insbesondere Dieter Zühlsdorff, unter anderem für seine Bereitschaft, das Buchprojekt umzusetzen und vor allem für seine große Geduld in den nicht immer einfachen Zeiten während der Realisierung des Buches.

Hans Schmidts
Juni 2011

rate room with large built-in glass display cases, in which I had exhibition space for the bulk of the collection. In this way, I can look at these objects of a long-forgotten era every day and enjoy them.

To acquire background information on Rörstrand porcelain and especially on the artists who worked for Rörstrand, I visited museums that own large collections of Jugendstil/Art Nouveau porcelain (including the Bröhan Museum in Berlin) and of course the Rörstrand Museum in Lidköping as well. I also contacted the art historian and distinguished Rörstrand expert Bengt Nyström in Stockholm. After he had visited me a couple of times and since we shared an interest in the same field, the contact soon grew into friendship. I am delighted that he agreed to author all the background information on Rörstrand porcelain in this joint book project and therefore should like to express my grateful thanks to him.

Special thanks also to ARNOLDSCHE Art Publishers, in particular to Dieter Zühlsdorff for so many things, including his commitment to ensuring that this book project was carried out and above all for his unstinting patience during times that were not always easy while the book was coming into being.

Hans Schmidts
June 2011

Rörstrand Porzellanmanu-faktur um 1900
The Rörstrand Porcelain Factory ca 1900

Rörstrand in Stockholm –
Ein Rückblick auf die Geschichte

Rörstrand in Stockholm –
Looking back at history

Nach dem Ende des mehr als zwei Jahrzehnte währenden verlustreichen und kostspieligen Großen Nordischen Krieges (1700–1721) hatte Schweden große Teile seines Territoriums und damit seine Vormachtstellung im Ostseeraum verloren. Die Kriegszüge Karls XII. hatten das Land an den Rand des finanziellen Ruins gebracht. In der Regierungszeit seines Nachfolgers Fredrik I. wurden unter dem Einfluss der „Partei der Hüte" („Hattarna") und ihres mächtigen Anführers Arvid Horn[1] im Sinne des Merkantilismus Bestrebungen wirksam, durch den Ausbau der inländischen Güterproduktion und die Förderung des Ausfuhrhandels die Wirtschaft des Landes wieder zu beleben und die Staatsfinanzen zu sanieren. Als ein Teil dieses „Aufbauprogramms" wurde am 13. Juni 1726 das schwedische „Porcellainsvärket" gegründet. Unter dem aus Holstein stammenden deutschen „porslinsmakar" und „chemicus" Johann Wolff (auch Wolf oder Wulf) sollte im Erdgeschoss und in einigen Flügeln des im 17. Jahrhundert errichteten und nördlich von dem heutigen, um 1900 errichteten St. Eriksplan in Stockholm gelegenen Schlosses Rörstrand „Porzellan nach delftischer Art", also Erzeugnisse in der Art niederländischer Fayencen nach dem Vorbild ostasiatischer Importporzellane, hergestellt werden. Obwohl hier von 1729 bis 1733 auch der 1717 aus Meißen entflohene, mit den Geheimnissen des „Arkanums" vertraute Vergolder Christoph Conrad Hunger, der 1719 an der Gründung der Wiener Manufaktur mitgewirkt hatte, beschäftigt war, wurde noch kein „echtes Porzellan" hergestellt, und erst in den siebziger Jahren des 18. Jahrhunderts kam es zu der Umstellung der Produktion auf „flintware", ein in seiner Massezusammensetzung dem englischen Steingut ähnliches Material. 1782 wurde die seit 1758 bestehende Fayencefabrik Marieberg, der auch eine kleine Porzellanwerkstatt angegliedert war,

The Northern Wars lasted for more than two decades (1700–1721), entailing heavy casualties and expenses. By the time hostilities ended, Sweden had lost a great deal of territory and, with it, supremacy in the Baltic. The campaigns fought by Charles XII had brought the country to the brink of ruin. In the reign of his successor, Frederick I, The Hats' Party ['Hattarna'] and its powerful leader, Arvid Horn[1] promoted mercantilism with the aim of fostering the growth of domestic production and trade to revive the Swedish economy and replenish the depleted state coffers. Part of this 'reconstruction programme' entailed the granting of letters patent to make porcelain in Sweden (*Porcellainsvärket*) on 13 June 1726. Under the supervision of the German Johann Wolff, (also spelled Wolf or Wulf) who was a porcelain maker (*porslinsmakar*) and chemist (*chemicus*, meaning 'alchemist'), a porcelain manufactory was to be established in the cellar and wings of Rörstrand Castle in Stockholm, which was built in the seventeenth century north of where St Eriksplan stands today, to produce 'porcelain as it were made in Delft'. That meant imitating the porcelain the Dutch faiencemakers at Delft were assiduously copying from imported East Asian porcelain. Christoph Conrad Hunger, a gilder who was also conversant with the 'arcana' of porcelain making, had fled Meissen in 1717 and co-founded the Viennese Porcelain Manufactory in 1719. Although Hunger then proceeded to work at Rörstrand Castle from 1729 to 1733, no 'true porcelain' was made there during his stint at the Swedish manufactory. In the 1770s Rörstrand also took up making flint porcelain (*flintporslin*), with a paste that was similar to that of English stoneware. The Marieberg Faience Factory (est. 1758), which also operated a small porcelain workshop, was bought out by Rörstrand in 1782 but closed down only six years later. Röstrand became the

aufgekauft, aber bereits sechs Jahre später wieder stillgelegt. 1797 ging Rörstrand in den Besitz von Bengt Reinhold Geijer über; nach seinem Tod im Jahre 1815 wurde das Unternehmen in den folgenden Jahrzehnten unter der Bezeichnung „B.R. Geijers Arfvingar" weitergeführt und 1867 in die Rörstrand Aktiebolag umgewandelt.

Nachdem die Bedeutung der Fayence im letzten Viertel des 18. Jahrhunderts kontinuierlich zurückgegangen war, wurde ihre Fertigung kurz nach 1800 ganz eingestellt. Das Unternehmen produzierte jetzt Steingutwaren aller Art. Erst ab 1850 führte die Einbeziehung weiterer keramischer Erzeugnisse wie Majolika, Parian, Weichporzellan in englischer Art und seit 1880 auch Hartporzellan zu einer erheblichen Ausweitung des Programms, das nunmehr neben Gebrauchsgegenständen auch Zierartikel umfasste; außerdem wurden jetzt auch Kachelöfen und keramische Bauteile hergestellt. In der zweiten Hälfte des 19. Jahrhunderts hatte sich Rörstrand mit diesem umfassenden Angebot an hochwertiger keramischer Ware aller Art zu einem Großindustriellen Unternehmen entwickelt. Das Fabrikgelände war ausgebaut und um viele neue Anlagen und Einrichtungen erweitert worden, darunter Werkstätten und Labore sowie mehrere Dampfmaschinen, Mahlwerke und Brennöfen; deren Anzahl war 1890 auf 36 angestiegen (siehe Abb. 1). In den Jahren um 1850 haben hier etwa zweihundert Beschäftigte gearbeitet und einen Umsatz von 248.000 Kronen erwirtschaftet; 1899 hat sich die Zahl der Beschäftigten auf über 1.000 erhöht, und der Umsatz war auf 2.901.000 Kronen gestiegen. In den letzten Jahrzehnten des 19. Jahrhunderts war Rörstrand mit seinem Angebot, das mit keramischen Produkten von Haushalts- und Zierkeramik bis zu Kachelöfen und technischem Porzellan reichte, der führende Keramik-Hersteller in Schweden und nach dem Umsatz eines der zehn größten Unternehmen des Landes. In dieser Zeit waren nicht nur zahlreiche

property of Bengt Reinhold Geijer in 1797. After he died in 1815, the business continued to operate for several decades as *B. R. Geijers Arfvingar* until it was changed into a private company, Rörstrand Aktiebolag (limited company), in 1867.

The popularity of faience dwindled to such an extent in the last quarter of the eighteenth century that production of it at Rörstrand yielded to the making of ordinary stoneware from around 1800. Rörstrand did not start making other types of ceramics, such as majolica, Parian porcelain and soft-paste porcelain of the English kind, until the 1850s. By 1880 the making of hard-paste porcelain had greatly enlarged the Rörstrand product range, which now included, apart from utilitarian wares, ornamental articles as well as tiled stoves and ceramic building elements. Making such a broad range of high-quality ceramic wares of all kinds enabled Rörstrand to grow into a large industrial enterprise in the latter half of the nineteenth century. The factory premises were enlarged and a great deal of new machinery and new facilities were added, including workshops and laboratories as well as several steam-driven machines, grinding-mills and kilns. By 1890 there were thirty-six kilns (see fig. 1). In 1850 the workers numbered about two hundred and annual turnover amounted to 248,000 kronor. By 1899, however, the workers had grown to over a thousand and turnover had risen to 2,901,000 kronor. In the last decades of the nineteenth century, Rörstrand, which sold a range of ceramic products that included utilitarian household and decorative ceramics, tiled stoves and technical china, was the leading Swedish ceramics manufacturer and, measured by turnover, among the top ten largest businesses in the country. During that period of steady growth, numerous improvements in pastes as well as innovations in decoration design were introduced, including new colours, painting techniques and glazes. New materials and new manufacturing processes as well as increased output

Abb. // Fig. 1
Rörstrands Fabrikgelände //
The Rörstrand factory premises, 1904

Ab den 1890er Jahren befinden sich in dem dominierenden Gebäude verschiedene Werkstätten und Ateliers. Kachelwerkstatt, Malersaal, Brennöfen und Feldspatherstellung befanden sich in weiteren Bauten. Links der Giebel eines Magazingebäudes, rechts das lang gestreckte Mühlen- und Schlemmhaus. // By the 1890s there were various workshops and studios in the main building. A tile workshop, painting hall, kilns and a facility for working feldspar were housed in other buildings. On the left, the gable of a storehouse, on the right the elongated mill and slip-casting shed.
Photo: Private collection.

Verbesserungen bei den keramischen Massen, sondern auch technische Neuerungen bei der Gestaltung der Dekore eingeführt worden, darunter neue Farben, Maltechniken und Glasuren. Neue Materialien und neue technische Verfahren, aber auch eine verbesserte Produktion trugen zu Rörstrands schneller Entwicklung bei und ermöglichten die Herstellung von Ware in unterschiedlicher Qualität für unterschiedliche Kundenkreise. Die Objekte, die Formen und die Dekore entsprachen den internationalen Modetrends der Zeit, und man ließ sich auch von dem Angebot der englischen und der großen kontinentalen Fabriken inspirieren.

Nach der Erteilung des Privilegs (November 1873) hatte Rörstrand 1874 in Helsingfors das Tochterunternehmen *Arabia* gegründet, um über das dem Zaren gehörende Großfürstentum Finnland Zugang zum russischen Markt zu bekommen. Die Fabrik war in diesen Jahren de jure eine finnische Aktiengesellschaft; obwohl sie stilistisch eher die schwedische als die finnische Keramik repräsentierte. So gelang es ihr, sich erfolgreich in das finnische Unabhängigkeitsstreben gegenüber Russland einzugliedern; sie nahm an mehreren Weltausstellungen als finnische Firma teil. Auf der Weltausstellung 1900 in Paris konnte sie mit den dort gezeigten Porzellan-, Steingut- und Majolikagegenständen Finnland eine Goldmedaille sichern. Für Arabia waren ständig Mitarbeiter von Rörstrand tätig, und auch ein großer Teil des Sortiments ging auf Modelle und Muster aus Rörstrand zurück, u. a. die Standardmodelle von gegossenen Vasen für die Majolikaproduktion, die Dekore für die Unterglasurbemalung und die Lüster- und Kristallglasuren. Anregungen wurden aber auch von den Fabriken des Kontinents übernommen und man versuchte, sich von Rörstrand stilistisch zu emanzipieren.

Bis in das letzte Viertel des 19. Jahrhunderts war bei Rörstrand die Produktion von Haushaltsgeschirren, Kachelöfen und technischem Porzellan kontinuierlich gewachsen; ähnlich bei Arabia. Zum Ende des Jahrhunderts nahm der Anteil künstlerischer Objekte bei Rörstrand deutlich zu.

Hinter dieser Expansion standen zwei junge, begabte und energische Enthusiasten. Der 27-jährige Gustaf Holdo Stråle (1826–1896) hatte seinen Vater Nils Wilhelm Stråle als Fabrikdirektor 1853 abgelöst. Stråle, aber vor allem Robert Almström (1834–1911), der nach seinen Studien in England schon mit 21 Jahren die Verantwortung für die technische Entwicklung übernommen hatte, trieben die Expansion voran. Almström wurde technischer Disponent, übernahm 1893 die alleinige Leitung und wurde zum gleichen Zeitpunkt Haupteigentümer von Rörstrand (siehe Abb. 2, 3). Eine Bibliothek wurde aufgebaut, in der außer Literatur über keramische Technologie und Dekore auch Musterbücher und Veröffentlichungen über Kunst und Keramik aus anderen Ländern zu finden waren, neben französischer, englischer und deutscher Fachliteratur auch beispielsweise Werke über japanische Kunst und chinesische Keramik. Auch eine große museale Sammlung, die nicht nur Stücke aus

and quality standards contributed to Rörstrand's rapid growth and made it possible to target several market segments simultaneously with wares of varying quality. Rörstrand articles, forms and decoration kept up with trends in fashion at the time and inspiration was also drawn from the products made at the English and large continental European factories.

In 1874, Rörstrand founded a subsidiary, *Arabia*, outside of Helsingfors in Finland for the purpose of gaining access to the Russian market through Finland, which at that time was an autonomous Grand Duchy within the Russian Empire. The Helsingfors factory was by law a Finnish private company but its products were stylistically representative of Swedish rather than Finnish ceramics. Rörstrand successfully negotiated the upheavals of the Finnish strive for independence from Russia and even showed wares at several international exhibitions as a Finnish firm. The Finnish subsidiary won a gold medal for Finland for the porcelain, stoneware and majolica articles it showed at the 1900 Paris World Exposition. Rörstrand employees always worked for Arabia and most of the Arabia product line derived from models and patterns from Rörstrand, including the standard cast majolica vases, underglaze painted decoration and lustre and crystal glazes. Continental European inspiration was assimilated by the Finnish subsidiary, which strove to emancipate itself stylistically from the parent company.

Output in household tableware, tiled stoves and technical china continued to grow at both Rörstrand and Arabia throughout the last quarter of the nineteenth century. Towards the close of the century, the share of objets d'art and art ceramics in the Rörstrand range increased considerably. This expansion in the art line was propelled by two talented and energetic young enthusiasts. Gustaf Holdo Stråle (1826–1896) succeeded his father Nils Wilhelm Stråle as managing director of the factory in 1853 when he was twenty-seven years old. Gustaf Holdo Stråle and especially Robert Almström (1834–1911), who had studied in England and returned to assume responsibility at the age of only twenty-one for technological development, were the driving forces behind the rapid expansion in art ceramics at Rörstrand. Almström became technical manager and by 1893 was sole managing director and at the same time majority shareholder at Rörstrand (see fig. 2, 3). A library was built up, which contained specialised works on ceramic technology and decoration as well as sample books and publications on ceramics from other countries, such as France, England and Germany and even works on Japanese art and Chinese porcelain. A large museum collection, which did not consist solely of Rörstrand and Marieberg pieces but also featured ceramics from abroad, was housed in separate rooms in the Rörstrand office building, built after 1880. One of the largest specialist collections in Stockholm, the Rörstrand works museum, was also accessible to the artisans at the factory for study purposes.

The firm financial footing and high technical standards made it possible to drive forward the expansion of the art division, a

Rörstrand und Marieberg, sondern auch aus ausländischer Produktion enthielt, war in gesonderten Räumen in dem nach 1880 errichteten Verwaltungsgebäude eingerichtet worden. Es war eine der umfangreichsten musealen Spezialsammlungen in Stockholm, die insbesondere auch als Studiensammlung für die Künstler der Fabrik diente.

Die solide wirtschaftliche Grundlage und der erreichte technische Standard erlaubten es, den 1872 mit der Verpflichtung von Hugo Tryggelin (1846–1925) begonnenen Ausbau der künstlerischen Abteilung zu forcieren. Als „Chefdessinateur" und damit erster künstlerischer Ratgeber war er nicht nur für die Musterentwicklung im Tafelgeschirr, sondern auch für die Formgebung der Ziergegenstände und die Entwürfe der neuen Werkstatt- und auch Wohngebäude zuständig. Kurze Zeit nach der Kopenhagener Ausstellung von 1888 stellte man den Architekten Hugo Hörlin (1851–1894) als zweiten künstlerischen Berater ein. Ihm folgte der Maler Alf Wallander (1862–1914), Hörlins Schüler an der Högra Konstindustriella Skolan (HKS).[2] Unter der Leitung Wallanders, den eine enge Freundschaft mit den Söhnen Robert Almströms verband, vollzog sich nach Kopenhagener Vorbild eine Hinwendung zu neuen stilistischen

Abb. // Fig. 3
Robert Almström, Gedenk-Medaille // Commemorative Medallion, 1900

„Robert Almström zum Gedenken an 50 Jahre Tätigkeit in Rörstrand. Als Zeichen der Dankbarkeit von Rörstrands Aktiengesellschaft d. 25. Mai 1900." R. Almström zuerkannt von dem Vorsitzenden der Aktionärsversammlung, Mai 1900. // *"To Robert Almström commemorating 50 years of work at Rörstrand. As a sign of gratitude from the Rörstrand Corporation on 25 May 1900."* Awarded to R. Almström by the chairman of the shareholders meeting, May 1900.
Rörstrand Museum.

Abb. // Fig. 2
Robert Almström, Anfang der 1890er Jahre // early 1890s

National Library, Stockholm.

Tendenzen. In der Folge entstanden, unter Mitwirkung einer größeren Zahl selbständig arbeitender künstlerischer Mitarbeiterinnen und Mitarbeiter, für Rörstrand charakteristische Arbeiten. So rückte das Unternehmen – quasi über Nacht – in die erste Reihe der europäischen Porzellanmanufakturen von Weltgeltung. Die erste internationale Präsentation der neuen Kollektion auf der Allgemeinen Kunst- und Industrie-Ausstellung in Stockholm 1897 leitete eine Serie erfolgreicher Auftritte bei internationalen Ausstellungen ein. Die Blütezeit der Manufaktur dauerte knapp eineinhalb Jahrzehnte.

development which had set in when Hugo Tryggelin (1846–1925) was hired in 1872. As 'head designer', the top artistic consultant, he was responsible not only for developing tableware patterns but also for designing ornamental articles as well as new workshop facilities and employee living quarters. Not long after the 1888 Copenhagen exhibition, the architect Hugo Hörlin (1851–1894) was hired as a second art consultant, followed by Alf Wallander (1862–1914), a painter who had studied under Hörlin as a student at the Högra Konstindustriella Skolan (HKS).[2] Bound by close ties of friendship with Robert Almström's sons, Wallander was in charge of implementing the shift towards new stylistic trends in line with Copenhagen. Distinctive work was subsequently produced, a development that owed much to the numerous freelance men and women working for Rörstrand. Thus the business rose – almost overnight, as it were – to the first rank of internationally renowned European porcelain factories. The first international presentation of the new Rörstrand collection at the 1897 Stockholm General Art and Industry exhibition marked the beginning of a series of successful shows at trade fairs. However, Rörstrand's heyday only lasted for a decade and a half.

In 1909, Robert Almström's sons Harald (1871–1944) and Knut (1873–1955) succeeded their father as co-directors. Even before the First World War broke out, the economy was in decline so

1909 übernahmen Robert Almströms Söhne Harald (1871–1944) und Knut (1873–1955) die Gesamtleitung und behielten sie bis Anfang der 1920er Jahre. Schon in den Jahren vor Ausbruch des Ersten Weltkrieges und insbesondere in der Kriegszeit waren mit dem allgemeinen Rückgang der Wirtschaft auch die überfälligen Investitionen in die Stockholmer Anlagen unterblieben. Nach der mehrjährigen Suche nach einem passenden Ort für eine Neugründung bei Stockholm hatte man 1914 „Göteborgs Porslinsfabrik" gekauft. Nach der Konzernbildung zu „Rörstrands Fabriken" überführte man 1918 nach und nach Teile der Produktion in das Werk auf Hisingen in Göteborg. Göteborgs Porslinsfabrik wurde dort 1898 gegründet und war zur Jahrhundertwende die drittgrößte Porzellanfabrik des Landes. In Stockholm beließ man einen Teil der Produktion noch bis zum 200. Jahrestag. Im Oktober 1926 fand der letzte Brennvorgang statt und der Betrieb wurde in Stockholm eingestellt; Rörstrand war nun in Göteborg etabliert. Mit dem Umzug wurde die Mustersammlung und die umfangreiche Bibliothek verkauft. Schon 1916 wurde die Beteiligung an Arabia in Finnland verkauft. 1927 kaufte Rörstrand die 1911 aus einer seit 1900 existierenden Porzellanmalerei hervorgegangene *Lidköpings Porslinsfabrik* und begann 1932 mit der Verlegung der gesamten Produktion in die erneuerten und erweiterten Anlagen in Lidköping. Mit ihrer Schließung im Dezember 2005 ging die Geschichte der Porzellanfabrik Rörstrand in Schweden zu Ende.

Ein eigenes künstlerisches Profil

Um 1900 gelang es Rörstrand und seinen Künstlern, seinen Kunstporzellanen ein unverwechselbares Erscheinungsbild zu geben, das in der zeitgenössischen französisch-, englisch- und deutschsprachigen Presse Aufmerksamkeit erregte und eifrig besprochen wurde. Es war eine exklusive und kleine Produktion, ausgeführt von einer Handvoll Künstlern und Keramikern im neuen zeitgenössischen Stil – Art Nouveau oder Jugendstil – und mit Alf Wallander als führendem Künstler. Der Stil war international orientiert und knüpfte an die allgemeinen künstlerischen Trends und die Programme der Fabriken des Kontinents an, jedoch mit einem ganz eigenen Charakter. Unter Wallanders Leitung wurde Rörstrand zu einem der Betriebe, die die weitere Entwicklung beeinflussten. Schon seit 1896 verkaufte man bei Siegfried Bing in dessen neu eingerichteter Galerie L'Art Nouveau in Paris, die der ganzen neuen Kunstrichtung ihren Namen gab, Rörstrand Kunst-Porzellane. Die Kritik wies schon frühzeitig auf die Parallelen hin, die sich in der Motivwahl, der Farbgebung und der Behandlung des Lichtes zu der zeitgleichen schwedischen und nordischen Stimmungsmalerei erkennen ließen – eine Art „Licht aus dem Norden" im Porzellan.
Die nordische Malerei der Jahrhundertwende konnte man als eine besondere licht- und stimmungsgesättigte Naturmalerei

that much needed and overdue investment in the Stockholm Rörstrand factory failed to materialise and the financial situation deteriorated sharply during the war years. After a search that took several years for a suitable site near Stockholm on which to build a new factory, Rörstrand had bought Göteborg Porslinsfabrik in 1914. The company was restructured as Rörstrand Fabriken. After 1918 parts of production were gradually shifted to the factory taken over on Hisingen in Göteborg. Established there in 1898, Göteborg Porslinsfabrik had become the third largest porcelain factory in Sweden by the turn of the century. Some production remained in Stockholm until the Rörstrand bicentenary in 1926. In October that year, the last kiln ceased to operate and the Stockholm factory was closed down. Rörstrand was now established in Göteborg. The sample collection and the large library were sold before the move. The Rörstrand shares in Arabia in Finland were sold in 1916. In 1927 Rörstrand bought Lidköping Porslinsfabrik, which had grown out of a porcelain-painting business established in 1900, and began to move all production in the late 1930s to the premises in Lidköping, which had been renovated and enlarged. The history of the Röstrand Porcelain Factory in Sweden ends with the closure of the Lidköping factory in December 2005.

The distinctive Rörstrand style

Around 1900 Rörstrand and the artists working for the firm succeeded in lending its art porcelain a distinctive appearance that attracted a great deal of attention and discussion in the French, English and German-language press of the day. It was an exclusive, small product range, executed in the new contemporary style – Art Nouveau or Jugendstil– by just a few artists and ceramicists, of whom Alf Wallander was the most distinguished. The style was international in conception and linked up with the prevailing trends in art as well as the stylistic agenda of continental European makers while retaining a distinctive character of its own. Under Alf Wallander's artistic management, Rörstrand became a firm that exerted an influence on further developments in ceramics. Since 1896 Rörstrand art porcelain had been sold at Siegfried Bing's newly established Galerie L'Art Nouveau in Paris, which lent its name to the whole new art movement. Art critics soon pointed out the parallels between the mood created in the Rörstrand pieces and Swedish and other Scandinavian painting of the day in respect of the motifs and palette chosen and the handling of light – a sort of 'northern light' in porcelain.
Turn-of-the-century Scandinavian painting might be characterised as profoundly atmospheric nature painting suffused with a special light and mood, a unique blend of Symbolism and 'northern light', the term which was occasionally applied to it abroad. This special quality is perhaps most memorably

charakterisieren, einzigartig in ihrer Mischung aus Symbolismus und dem Nordischen Licht; international mitunter auch bezeichnet mit „northern light". Vielleicht kommt diese Besonderheit am deutlichsten in den Darstellungen des charakteristischen blauen Schimmers der nordischen Frühlings- und Sommernächte zum Ausdruck.

Die gleichen, wenn auch auf andere Weise ausgedrückten Stimmungen kann man auch in den Kunst-Porzellanen finden, die in den Jahren um die Jahrhundertwende bei Rörstrand entstanden. Diese Objekte, überwiegend Vasen in sehr unterschiedlicher Form- und Dekorgestaltung, wurden aus einer Porzellanmasse hergestellt, die einen dünnen und zarten plastischen oder figürlichen Dekor erlaubte. Die Motive sind überwiegend Darstellungen aus der schwedischen Natur, die in gelungener Weise den Gefäßformen angepasst und in sie integriert sind. Aus der Nahsicht werden Pflanzen, Blumen und Zweige betrachtet, ergänzt um Meeres- und Tiermotive, die – wie in der Malerei – zugleich Symbolträger sind. Es gibt große Ähnlichkeiten in der Malweise und der plastischen Gestaltung und nicht zuletzt in den fein abgestimmten, milden Nuancen der Unterglasurfarben mit ihren Abtönungen in Blau und Meergrün. Wie in der Malerei, sind es ein spezielles Licht und spezielle Farbtöne, die in diesen Jahren auch die erlesenen Exemplare des Rörstrand-Porzellans auszeichnen.

Etwa um die Mitte der 1890er Jahre hatte sich die Marke Rörstrand durchgesetzt, und die Objekte große Bekanntheit erlangt. Der Maler Richard Bergh, einer der führenden Künstler im Künstlerverband, hatte für das Plakat zur Stockholmer Ausstellung von 1897 den Titel „La lumière du Nord" gefunden. Und der Architekt Ernst Jakobsson, einer der führenden Köpfe im Schwedischen Gewerbeverein, notierte in einem Artikel über die Ausstellung, dass das beste Porzellan der Schau *„sich der Malerei anschließt; denn die neuen Farbzusammenstellungen und Stimmungen, welche die moderne Malerei entdeckt hatte, vermittelten ihre vertraute Bekanntschaft mit der Natur, und der erweiterte Blick der Künstler für die Eigentümlichkeit des Naturlebens brachte neue Ideen für Farbe und Form der Porzellandekoration."* Er würdigte die schwedischen Porzellanfabriken und deren neue Produkte: *„Eine diese auszeichnende, in der ausländischen Kunst- und Kunstgewerbeliteratur oft angeführte Eigenart ist die Behandlung der schwedischen Flora, die Wiedergabe der delikaten Farbzusammenstellung und der stilisierten Konturen und Biegungen in den Blattreliefs der nordischen Gewächse. Durch eine für das schwedische Porzellan charakteristische Kombination von Malerei und Plastik sind so Effekte von vorher unbekannter Wechselhaftigkeit und Lebendigkeit erzielt worden."*[3]

In der führenden englischen Kunstzeitschrift „The Artist" schrieb man über die Rörstrand-Ausstellung 1897 und speziell über Alf Wallanders Keramik *„the principal feature of whose is a keen observation of the poetry of nature, combined with a very skilful handling of his material. Various kinds of flowers, such as thistles, poppies, chrysanthemums and iris. As well as pine bran-*

expressed in the bluish shimmer characteristic of representations of northern spring and summer nights.

The same atmospheric qualities, albeit expressed in a different way, inform the art porcelain Röstrand produced in the years before and after the turn of the century. Most of those pieces were vases made of a porcelain paste that made possible thin, delicate applied relief or figurative decoration. Most of the motifs are taken from the Swedish landscape and are adroitly adapted to the vessel forms and integrated in them. Plants, flowers and branches are viewed in close-up. There are also marine and faunal motifs, which – as is the case in the Scandinavian painting of the time – are also vehicles for symbolism. Painting and sculpture are handled in a very similar way on Rörstrand porcelain, especially in the delicate tints of the mild underglaze colours shading into blues and sea-green. As in Scandinavian painting, a special light and distinctive colour tints distinguish the exquisite pieces of Rörstrand porcelain produced during those years.

By the mid-1890s Rörstrand had become a successful label with products that were widely known. The painter Richard Bergh, a leading light in the Swedish Artists' Association, was the author of the title 'La lumière du Nord' for the poster for the 1897 Stockholm exhibition. And the architect Ernst Jakobsson, an eminent intellectual in the Swedish Association of Applied Arts noted in an article on the exhibition that the best porcelain shown *'approaches painting, for the new colour combinations and the atmospheric qualities discovered by modern painting convey its familiarity with nature, and the artists' field of vision, enlarged in scope to appreciate the uniqueness of natural life, has brought new ideas on colour and form in porcelain decoration.'* Jakobsson had nothing but praise for the Swedish porcelain factories and their new products: *'One characteristic of this Rörstrand porcelain that is often mentioned in foreign [non-Swedish] publications dealing with the fine and applied arts is the treatment of Swedish flora, the reproduction of exquisite colour combinations and the stylised contours and curves of the leaves in northern plants. The combination of painting and sculpture characteristic of Swedish porcelain has created the effect of unprecedented variety and liveliness.'*[3]

The Artist, a leading English art magazine of the day, wrote as follows on the Rörstrand exhibition in 1897 and on Alf Wallander's work in ceramics in particular: "[...] *the principal feature of whose is a keen observation of the poetry of nature, combined with a very skilful handling of his material. Various kinds of flowers, such as thistles, poppies, chrysanthemums and iris as well as pine branches and mountain-ash are the objects he principally makes use of to decorate his vases, bowls and lamps. Especially charming is the ability of this artist to make material give the illusion of the movement of water and his mermaids are most delicately modelled and seem to glide along the waves.'*[4]

And the French periodical *L'Art Decoratif* waxed lyrical in spring 1898: *'I seek in vain in all ceramics a note as sweet, as*

ches and mountain -ash are the objects he principally makes use of to decorate his vases, bowls and lamps. Especially charming is the ability of this artist to make material give illusion of the movement of water, and his mermaids are most delicately modelled and seem to glide along the waves."[4] Und in der Pariser Zeitschrift *L'Art Decoratif* konnte man im Frühjahr 1898 folgende lyrische Sentenz lesen: *„Je cherche en vain dans toute la Céramique une note si douce, sie sauve que celles des porcelaines de Rörstrand (Stockholm). Dans leur genre, ces vases sont la perfection, et le genre est ce qu'on peut rêver de plus exquis. Dans les porcelaines de Rörstrand c'est au rose ou au mauve rosâtre que vise la grisaille des motifs; mais quelle rose! Si naissant, si pâle, qu'il est à peine un reflet sur la neige sur laquelle il gît. Sur ces vases, tout est fait comme par les doigts subtils d'une fée du Nord."[5]*

Die ganze Entwicklung lässt sich anhand der zahlreichen und großen internationalen Kunst- und Industrieausstellungen der Zeit verfolgen: der großen Marktplätze des späten 19. Jahrhunderts. Rörstrand nahm an den meisten Ausstellungen teil: Malmö 1896 und Stockholm 1897, dann Berlin, Kopenhagen, Paris, Gävle, Göteborg, Turin, Helsinki, St. Louis, Liège, Norrköping, Lund, St. Petersburg, wieder Stockholm 1909, Brüssel usw., bis Malmö 1914 und San Francisco 1915. Das geschah oft mit eigenen Ausstellungsständen oder im Rahmen der schwedischen nationalen Repräsentation, und einige Male auch in Verbindung mit Alf Wallanders eigenen Ausstellungsbeiträgen.

Die Resonanz in der zeitgenössischen Presse war positiv, sowohl in Hinblick auf die technische Qualität des Porzellans als auch auf dessen künstlerischen Ausdruck. In der internationalen Presse der Zeit und in der Literatur wurde das schwedische künstlerische Porzellan in der Zeit um 1900 sehr ausführlich behandelt, zuweilen im gleichen Umfang wie das aus Kopenhagen, Sèvres und Berlin. Es gibt viele Berichte über Rörstrands Präsenz auf den vielen Kunst- und Industrieausstellungen in einschlägigen Zeitschriften, neben *The Studio* und *L'Art Decoratif* auch in *The Artist, Art et Decoration, Sprechsaal, Dekorative Kunst, Kunst und Handwerk* usw. und in mehreren Fachbüchern, wie *Moderne Keramik* von Richard Borrmann und *Das Porzellan* von Georg Lehnert.

pure as those qualities in the Rörstrand porcelain (Stockholm). These vases are perfect for their genre and the genre is the most exquisite imaginable. In the Rörstrand porcelains, the grisaille of the motifs tends towards a pink or pinkish mauve but what a pink! So pale is this blush of dawn that it is scarcely more than a reflection on the snow on which it lies. It is as if everything on these vases had been done by the subtle fingers of a fairy of the North.'[5] [*"Je cherche en vain dans toute la Céramique une note si douce, si sauve que celles des porcelaines de Rörstrand (Stockholm). Dans leur genre, ces vases sont la perfection, et le genre est ce qu'on peut rêver de plus exquis. Dans les porcelaines de Rörstrand c'est au rose ou au mauve rosâtre que vise la grisaille des motifs; mais quelle rose! Si naissant, si pâle, qu'il est à peine un reflet sur la neige sur laquelle il gît. Sur ces vases, tout est fait comme par les doigts subtils d'une fée du Nord."*]

How things developed for Rörstrand can be traced through the many large international art exhibitions and trade fairs of the time: they were the great marketplaces of the late nineteenth century. Rörstrand participated in most of those exhibitions: Malmö (1896) and Stockholm (1897), followed by Berlin, Copenhagen, Paris, Gävle, Göteborg, Turin, Helsinki, St. Louis, Liège, Norrköping, Lund, St Petersburg, Stockholm again in 1909, Brussels, etc., on up to Malmö in 1914 and San Francisco in 1915. Rörstrand either had its own stalls or Röstrand pieces were shown as part of an overall exhibition representing Sweden at trade fairs. They were also exhibited several times at such shows under Alf Wallander's name.

The echo in the press of the day was positive about both the quality of the porcelain and the aesthetic side of these pieces. The international press and specialist publications devoted quite a bit of space to Swedish art porcelain around 1900, at least as much to it as to contemporaneous porcelain from Copenhagen, Sèvres and Berlin. There are numerous reports on Rörstrand's presence at the many art exhibitions and trade fairs in specialist periodicals; apart from *The Studio* and *L'Art Décoratif*, Rörstrand was written up in *The Artist, Art et Décoration, Sprechsaal, Dekorative Kunst, Kunst und Handwerk* and the like, as well as handbooks, including *Moderne Keramik* by Richard Borrmann and *Das Porzellan* by Georg Lehnert.

Ein neuer Stil
A new Style

Abb. // Fig. 4
Weltausstellung Paris, 1900 (Luftbild) // The 1900 Paris World Exposition (aerial photo)

Mit den einzelnen Ausstellungsarealen, so u.a. links der Invalidenplatz mit der schwedischen Kunstindustrie-Ausstellung und dem „Schwedischen Landhaus". Unten links Porte Binet, der Haupteingang.
// Showing the various exhibition venues, including, on the left, Place des Invalides with the Swedish Industrial Arts exhibition as well as the 'Swedish Country House'. Bottom left: Porte Binet, the main entrance.
Le Panorama. L'Exposition Universelle, Paris 1900.

Für das Kunsthandwerk bot „*L'Exposition Universelle*" in Paris 1900, wo der neue Stil „*L'Art Nouveau*" zum Durchbruch gelangte, ein Forum, auf dem man über *Le Style Moderne* in Kunst und „Decoration" ins Gespräch kam. Obwohl die Anfänge weit früher lagen, tauchten viele Neuheiten erst jetzt auf.

Im Hintergrund hatten sich viele Elemente der neuen Kunst – besonders eine neue Grundeinstellung, neue Sichtweisen, neue Motivkreise und neue Techniken – bereits in den 1890er Jahren bemerkbar gemacht. Die Malerei wurde von einer Reihe neuer „Ismen" bestimmt: Impressionismus, Japonismus, Symbolismus, und viele mehr. Als ein besonderes Beispiel hierfür auf dem Gebiet der „angewandten Künste" kann die Kunstkeramik der Zeit gelten. Hier wurden neue Impulse aus der Kunst, dem Kunstgewerbe und insbesondere der Keramik Chinas und Japans wirksam. Dazu kamen neue Techniken aus den führenden englischen Fabriken, Anregungen aus den Manufakturen in Kopenhagen, Berlin und Sèvres und nicht zuletzt auch von den französischen Steinzeug-Künstlern, um nur einige herauszugreifen. In Schweden bezog die breite Kunstkeramik-Produktion ihre Inspiration von den Auftritten der bedeutenden

The 1900 Paris L'Exposition Universelle, the forum at which Le Style Moderne in the fine and 'decorative' arts was discussed, brought about the breakthrough for the new style, Art Nouveau. Although its beginnings went further back, much that was new was not noticed until the Exposition.

Many elements of the new style – especially a new attitude to art, new ways of seeing, new motifs and techniques – had already made their appearance by the 1890s. Painting was in the throes of new 'isms': Impressionism, Japonism, Symbolism, and so on. Art ceramics are typically classified as belonging to the 'applied arts'. In ceramics, fresh influences came from both the fine and the applied arts, notably Chinese and Japanese pottery and porcelain. New techniques were learnt from the leading English china factories. Inspiration came from the porcelain factories in Copenhagen, Berlin and Sèvres as well as French artisans working in stoneware, to take just a few examples. In Sweden, the production of art ceramics on a broader basis drew inspiration from the works shown by major factories, workshops and individual ceramicists at the large trade fairs of the day.

The new style was so pervasive that it affected all fields of art, rapidly becoming widespread internationally although there was also a national side to all this: traditional themes and motifs taken from vernacular art came to dominate the movement in Sweden and other countries. Those years saw an explosion of aesthetic creativity – liberation from constraint and convention. Swedish art and the Swedish decorative and applied arts, which had just achieved international recognition, especially in the field of textiles and, most notably, Rörstrand porcelain, were caught up in the general trend. The new Swedish ceramics were shown at international trade fairs, including exhibitions in Berlin and Brussels. The high point, however, was the participation of Rörstrand and its domestic competitor Gustavsberg[6] in the 1900 Paris World Exhibition. That success was followed by the 1902 specialised trade fair devoted to design and the applied arts in Turin, which may be viewed as the high point for Jugendstil/Art Nouveau. At the same time, artisans were concentrating on more functional form. In Sweden itself, the 1897 Stockholm Exhibition marked the breakthrough for the new art ceramics produced by Rörstrand and Gustavsberg. Trade fairs at Helsingborg (1903), Norrköping (1906), Stockholm (1909) and Malmö (1914) represented later stages in this development.

Manufakturen, Werkstätten und Keramiker auf den großen Ausstellungen der Zeit.

Der neue Stil ergriff alle künstlerischen Gebiete und verbreitete sich schnell international, wenngleich unter nationalen Vorzeichen: Nationale und traditionelle Themen aus der Folklore wurden dominierend. In diesen Jahren vollzog sich so etwas wie eine höchst schöpferische künstlerische Explosion – oder Befreiung. Davon waren auch die schwedische Kunst und die Kunstindustrie ergriffen, die gerade jetzt internationale Anerkennung für ihre Textilkunst und eben das Rörstrand-Porzellan erlangt hatten.

In mehreren internationalen Ausstellungen wurde die neue schwedische Keramik gezeigt, u.a. in Berlin und Brüssel. Der Höhepunkt war allerdings die Teilnahme Rörstrands und seines inländischen Konkurrenten Gustavsberg[6] an der Pariser Weltausstellung 1900. Als spannende Fortsetzung folgte die Sonderausstellung über Design und Kunsthandwerk 1902 in Turin, die als Krönung der Entwicklung des eigentlichen Jugendstils angesehen werden kann; gleichzeitig konzentrierte man sich auf eine stärker funktionelle Formgebung. In Schweden selbst hatte die Stockholmer Ausstellung 1897 den Durchbruch für Rörstrands und Gustavsbergs neue Kunstkeramik gebracht; weitere Etappen waren die Ausstellungen in Helsingborg 1903, in Norrköping 1906, Stockholm 1909 und in Malmö 1914.

Kunst und Kunsthandwerk aus Japan und China waren zum ersten Mal auf den Weltausstellungen in London 1862 und in Paris 1867 gezeigt worden; in größerem Umfang waren sie nun auf den Ausstellungen 1878 und 1889 vertreten und erweckten auch auf der Pariser Weltausstellung 1900 mit einem großen eigenen Pavillon noch besondere Aufmerksamkeit. Ihre Bedeutung für die Geschmacksbildung und ihre Wirkung auf Kunst und Kunsthandwerk der Zeit können nicht hoch genug bewertet werden. Sie beflügelten das künstlerische Element in der Gestaltung der Formen, dem Umgang mit den Glasuren und der Steuerung der Brennvorgänge, und wurden so zu einem der Grundpfeiler des neuen Stils. Dazu kamen unzählige europäische Anregungen, insbesondere aus London und Paris, aber auch die Königliche Porzellanfabrik in Kopenhagen mit Arnold Krog[7] und seiner neuen Unterglasurmalerei wirkten stilbildend. Exemplarisch für die neue Keramik war besonders das neue leichte Porzellan mit Naturmotiven in Unterglasurmalerei, die Plastiken und das neue künstlerische Steinzeug, das in Paris und den anderen französischen Zentren seit den 1880er Jahren entstand. Alles war direkt oder indirekt, inspiriert durch japanische Kunst und Keramik, die auch die Entwicklung der schwedischen Kunstkeramik prägten.

„Schönheit für alle"

Im letzten Drittel des neunzehnten Jahrhunderts verbanden sich die Tendenzen zur künstlerischen Erneuerung in vielfältiger Weise mit sozialethischen und sozialästhetischen Reform-

Japanese and Chinese art and applied arts were shown for the first time in Europe at the 1862 international exhibition in London and the 1867 exhibition in Paris. More Chinese and Japanese works were shown at the 1878 and 1889 international exhibitions. Even at the 1900 Paris World Exposition, where they were displayed in a large pavilion of their own, Japanese and Chinese works were still a major focus of attention. Their importance to the formation of taste and the impact they made on the fine and applied arts of the day cannot be overestimated. They gave wings to the aesthetic side of design, the handling of form, the development of glazes and firing techniques and became a pillar on which the new style rested. In addition, there was a great deal of inspiration from the rest of Europe, especially London and Paris as well as the Royal Copenhagen Porcelain Factory, where Arnold Krog[7] and his new underglaze painting exerted a formative stylistic influence. The salient features of the new ceramics in Europe were a new, light porcelain body featuring motifs taken from nature in underglaze painting, figurines and the new art stoneware that was produced in Paris and other French ceramics centres from the 1880s. It was all directly or indirectly inspired by Japanese art and ceramics, which also shaped the development of Swedish art ceramics.

'Beauty for all'

In the last third of the nineteenth century, the trends towards aesthetic renewal were indissolubly linked in manifold ways with a drive for social reform. The leading exponent of this dual reform movement in social ethics and aesthetics was the English art theorist and critic John Ruskin (1819–1900). The primacy of art in all its forms as a basic human need and an indis-

Abb. // Fig. 5
L'Exposition Universelle Paris, 1900

Blick über die Seine auf die nationalen Pavillons, darunter das „Schwedische Landhaus" (3. von rechts).
// View across the Seine to the national pavilions, including the 'Swedish Country House' (third from the right).
Le Panorama. L'Exposition Universelle, Paris 1900.

bestrebungen, als deren Protagonist der Engländer John Ruskin (1819–1900) zu nennen ist. Die von ihm postulierte Bedeutung der Kunst in all ihren Erscheinungsformen als ein menschliches Primärbedürfnis und eine unabdingbare Voraussetzung für eine humane, individuelle und gesellschaftliche Entwicklung hatte weitreichende Auswirkungen auf das soziale Selbstverständnis der Gestalter und Entwerfer der Zeit von Emile Gallé (1846–1904) bis zu Henry van de Velde (1863–1957). Das für die schwedische Variante dieser Bewegung geprägte Schlagwort „Schönheit für alle" ist auf die sozialliberale Reformerin und Schriftstellerin Ellen Key (1849–1926) zurückzuführen. Ihr Ziel war es, das Bedürfnis nach neuen sozialen und ästhetischen Zielen auch in den unteren Schichten der Gesellschaft zu wecken. Sie verlangte deshalb nach einer neuen, modernen Formensprache und einer damit verbundenen neuen sozialen Zielsetzung. Die Umsetzung dieser Forderung ist auch in Arbeiten von Alf Wallander für Rörstrand zu erkennen.

International hatte der „Moderne Stil" eine reich variierte Formensprache mit unterschiedlichen Ausprägungen, die auch einen nationalen bzw. persönlichen Stil des Künstlers zuließ. In Schweden drückte sich dies durch ein großes Interesse für die eigene Flora und Fauna aus, die als Motive für die neuen Dekore genutzt wurden. Daneben gab es Bestrebungen, billigeres Material zu verwenden, um die Produkte – im Sinne der Devise „Schönheit für alle" – für breite Käuferschichten erschwinglich zu machen.

Die Werksleitungen bei Rörstrand und auch bei dem Konkurrenten Gustavsberg folgten der künstlerischen und technischen Entwicklung auf dem Kontinent. Sie waren wohlunterrichtet über die Produktion in den führenden keramischen Fabriken. Die patriarchalischen Direktoren standen den neuen sozialen Perspektiven, die während der 1880er und 1890er Jahre hervorgetreten waren, skeptisch gegenüber. Man nutzte aber die Veränderungen und setzte auf den neuen Stil und auch auf ein billigeres Steingut. Wahrscheinlich hoffte man auch auf die Entstehung eines neuen Marktes. Tatsächlich stiegen in den Anfangsjahren des 20. Jahrhunderts die Herstellungszahlen von Service- und Kunstware in billigerer Porzellanqualität und ebenfalls die Serienproduktion.

Auch die neuen Ideen fanden Verbreitung, so ist anzunehmen, dass Ellen Key mit ihrer Forderung nach ästhetischer Erneuerung auch die Umorientierung bei Rörstrand und Gustavsberg bewirkte. In der zeitgenössischen Debatte war sie in sozialen und ästhetischen Fragen und in der Auseinandersetzung um die Rolle der Frau tonangebend. In einem programmatischen Artikel „Skönhet i hemmen" (Schönheit im Heim), der 1897 zunächst in der populären Familienzeitschrift *Idun* erschien und 1899 in ihre vielbeachtete Schrift „Skönhet för alla" (Schönheit für alle) aufgenommen wurde, betonte sie, dass eine ästhetische Durchgestaltung von fabrikmäßig hergestellten Verbrauchsgegenständen für Wohnung, Heim und Alltag ein besseres und gemütlicheres Lebensumfeld schaffen könne. Das

pensable precondition for the development of humane individuals and a humane society as postulated by Ruskin had far-reaching effects on the social views of artists and designers of his day from Emile Gallé (1846–1904) to Henry van de Velde (1863–1957). The slogan coined for the Swedish variant of this movement, 'Beauty for all', goes back to the liberal and later socialist Swedish reformer and writer Ellen Key (1849–1926). Her aim was to awaken a need for new social and aesthetic goals in the lower classes as well. Hence she called for new social objectives accompanied by a new, modern language of forms. Her aims were attained, for example, in the works that Alf Wallander produced for Rörstrand.

On the international level, the 'Modern Style' found expression in a richly diverse formal idiom that produced distinctive stylistic variants, allowing for both national trends and artists' own individual styles. The Swedish approach to the Modern Style entailed a great interest in endemic flora and fauna, which were used for the new decoration. Moreover, there was a trend towards using more inexpensive materials to ensure that the products were affordable for all market segments – true to the slogan 'Beauty for all'.

Works managers at Rörstrand and the competition Gustavsberg, followed artistic and technical developments in the rest of Europe. They were well informed about what was being produced in the leading porcelain factories. Although the paternalist thinking of the Swedish factory managers made them sceptical of the new perspectives that emerged in the 1880s and 1890s, they nonetheless took advantage of the changes to capitalise on the new style and the cheaper material it called for ordinary stoneware. Presumably they were also hoping to develop new markets. In the early years of the twentieth century, the output of tableware services and art wares in porcelain of a less expensive quality did in fact rise and mass production grew.

The new ideas spread and it is safe to assume that Ellen Key with her call for aesthetic renewal was the driving force behind the turnaround at Rörstrand and Gustavsberg because she was the trendsetter in the social and aesthetic issues debated in her day, especially the role of women. She proclaimed her agenda in an article entitled 'Skönhet i hemmen' [Beauty in the Home], which was first published in 1897 in *Idun*, a popular family magazine, and reprinted in 1899 in her well-received work 'Skönhet för alla' [Beauty for All]. She emphasised that designing all industrially mass-produced utilitarian objects for everyday use in the home to a high aesthetic standard would create an improved, more pleasant home environment, which in turn would contribute to both the happiness of the individual and social harmony. She also proposed beautifying the homes of those living on lower incomes with affordable yet handsome objects of majolica and stoneware. Her suggestions did not go unheeded in the porcelain industry; in fact, they informed the designs Alf Wallander produced for Rörstrand. Some of his

wiederum würde zu Glück und Harmonie der Menschen beitragen. Dabei dachte sie auch an die Ausstattung der unteren Einkommensschichten mit billigen und schönen keramischen Gegenständen aus Majolika und Steingut. Die Umsetzung ihrer Anregungen blieb nicht ohne Auswirkungen auf die Porzellanherstellung, besonders bei den Entwürfen von Alf Wallander für Rörstrand. Einige seiner Steingutmodelle wurden zu Bestandteilen von Ellen Keys sogenannten „Programmausstellungen" im Stockholmer Arbeiterinstitut im April und September 1899, wo auch mehrere neue Einzelkeramiken von Gustavsberg, Höganäs[8] und P. H. Lundgren[9] gezeigt wurden (siehe Abb. 6).

Auch in dieser Zeit übernahm man Neuheiten aus anderen Teilen Europas, vor allem aus England und Frankreich und später auch aus Österreich und Deutschland. Von grundlegender Bedeutung waren die ästhetischen Bewertungen und sozialästhetischen Programme von John Ruskin und William Morris, die durch William Morris und seinen Kreis und die unterschiedlichen Gruppierungen der Arts-&-Crafts-Bewegung in England in den 1860er Jahren verbreitet worden waren. Schwedische Architekten studierten in diesen Jahren die neue englische Wohnkultur, und Künstler und Kunsthandwerker befassten sich mit Inneneinrichtungen und der kunstindustriellen Produktion. Aus Rörstrand reisten z. B. die Brüder Almström in den 1890er Jahren in die Porzellanfabriken des Kontinents und Englands, ebenso führende Künstler aus Gustavsberg.

Auch auf dem Kontinent gab es Unternehmen, die Anregungen aus England umsetzten, und so die schwedische Entwicklung beeinflussten. In Paris, wo zu dieser Zeit mehrere schwedische Künstler wohnten und studierten, waren die neuen Ideen und Impulse hochaktuell. Man diskutierte unter Schlagworten wie „décoration", „art décoratif" oder „art industriel" über den Einfluss der Künstler auf die Fabriken und deren Produktion. Die Fragen wurden u. a. in der „Union Centrale des Arts Décoratifs" und deren Zeitschrift „L'Art pour tous" aufgegriffen. Man arbeitete in der Vereinigung für die Anpassung der Kunst an die industrielle Produktion und die Verbesserung der Formgebung für Alltagsgegenstände, besonders Möbel und Haushaltsgegenstände, und für deren Verkauf zu günstigen Preisen. In den 1890er Jahren propagierte man moderne und funktionale Formgebung in dieser Zeitschrift, ebenso wie in der unabhängigen „L'Art Décoratif" von 1897. So wurde der Grund für das „Musée des Arts Décoratifs" in Paris gelegt (gegr. 1882). Gleiche Gedanken nahm die weitgereiste und welterfahrene Reformerin Ellen Key in „Skönhet för alla" (vergleiche z. B. den Titel „L'Art pour tous") und in ihren „Programmausstellungen" 1899 auf.

Ähnliche Bestrebungen gab es etwa gleichzeitig in den modernen kunsthandwerklichen Bewegungen in Wien, Darmstadt und München. Mit ihrer strafferen und mehr auf Funktionszusammenhang ausgerichteten Ästhetik, bei der die ornamentaldekorativen Tendenzen den funktionalen Anforderungen nach Form und Material untergeordnet wurden, beeinflussten sie mit einer leichten zeitlichen Verschiebung auch die Entwick

ordinary stoneware models were shown at Ellen Key's 'agenda exhibitions', as they were known, at the Stockholm Workers Institute in April and September 1899, where new ceramics from Gustavsberg, Höganäs[8] and P. H. Lundgren[9] were also shown (see fig. 6).

As was so often the case at that time, new ideas were taken over from other parts of Europe, primarily England and France, and later Austria and Germany. The aesthetic stances and social and aesthetic agendas of John Ruskin and William Morris were of fundamental importance here. The thinking of Morris and his circle was disseminated throughout the various groupings that comprised the English Arts and Crafts movement in the 1860s. During those heady years, Swedish architects studied the new English culture of living, and artists and artisans were preoccupied with interior design and the industrial production of objects used in everyday living to a high aesthetic standard. In the 1890s, the Almström brothers, for instance, travelled for Rörstrand to continental European and British porcelain factories, and leading artists who worked for Gustavsberg did the same.

There were factories in continental Europe that also took up ideas from England and realised them, thus indirectly influencing developments in Sweden. The new ideas and trends were at their height in Paris, where several Swedish artists were living and studying at the time. Discussion revolved around catchwords such as 'decoration', 'art décoratif' and 'art industriel' and the influence artists and artisans might exert on factories and what they produced. Forums for discussion of those issues included the Union centrale des arts décoratifs (UCAD, since 2004 Les Arts Décoratifs) and its journal, L'Art pour tous. UCAD worked for the adaptation of art to mass production concomitantly with improvement in the design of mundane utilitarian objects, especially furnishings and household goods and the sale of such products at reasonable prices. By the 1890s, both the UCAD journal and the independent L'Art Décoratif (1897) advocated modern and functional design. Thus the intellectual cornerstone was laid for the Musée des Arts décoratifs in Paris (founded in 1882). The widely travelled and cosmopolitan reformer Ellen Key espoused the same ideas in Skönhet för alla (cf. the UCAD journal title L'Art pour tous, for instance) and in her 1899 agenda exhibitions.

Similar aspirations surfaced at the same time in the modern applied arts movements in Vienna, Darmstadt and Munich. With their more stringent aesthetic which was strongly targeted at functionality, with decorative tendencies being subordinated to the functional requirements of form and material, the movements in the German-speaking countries also influenced developments in Sweden, albeit with a slight time lag. Victor Adler, director of the Stockholm Technical School (Tekniska skolan) in which the HKS, the Higher Industrial Art School, was a department, reported to the Swedish Association of Applied Arts (Svenska Slöjdföreningen) as early as 1898 on developments in Vienna and Darmstadt and leading architects

Abb. // Fig. 6
Ellen Keys 'Green Room', 1899

Das so genannte „Grüne Zimmer", Ellen Keys zweite Programm-Ausstellung im
Arbeiterinstitut in Stockholm. Die grün lasierten Möbel entwarf der Architekt
Carl Westmann, die Textilien und die Rörstrand-Ziervasen (auf dem Schrank)
wurden von Alf Wallander entworfen.
// Called the 'Green Room', Ellen Key's second agenda exhibition at the Stockholm
Workers Institute. The green varnished furnishings were designed by the
architect Carl Westmann; the textiles and Rörstrand ornamental vases (on the
cupboard) were designed by Alf Wallander.
Varia 1899.

lung in Schweden. Aus Wien und Darmstadt berichtete z. B. der
Rektor der Technischen Hochschule, Victor Adler, bereits 1898
dem Schwedischen Kunstgewerbeverein (Svenska Slöjdföreningen), und einige der führenden Architekten und Künstler leg-
ten umfangreiche Schilderungen ihrer Studienreisen vor. Die
Turiner Ausstellung 1902 wurde u. a. mit Würdigung der Wiener und Glasgower Schulen durch Erik Folcker, Mitglied der
Ausstellungsjury, in den Mitteilungen des Vereins besprochen.
Die Entwicklungen des modernen Stils auf dem Kontinent
waren also in Schweden bekannt.

Diese Tendenzen bestimmten in diesen Jahren auch die Diskussionen im Schwedischen Kunstgewerbeverein, wo Künstler
und Produzenten aufeinander trafen. Es gab viele anregende
Initiativen für die spätere Entwicklung, allen natürlichen
Gegensätzen auf vielen Gebieten zum Trotz. Ein Dauerthema
war auch das „Ersetzen der Kunst durch Handwerk und Industrie", wie es Erik Folcker formulierte. Es ging dabei um neue
Zieldiskussionen, Initiativen für Ausstellungen und Versuche,
auf die Geschmacksbildung der Allgemeinheit und eine neue
Industrieproduktion Einfluss zu nehmen und die Künstler in
die kunstindustriellen Unternehmen zu integrieren. Die Auswirkungen dieser Initiativen zeigten sich nicht nur im Schwedischen Kunstgewerbeverein, in dem der Kunsthistoriker und
Museumsmann Erik Folcker, bis 1912 als Sekretär tätig, einer
der führenden Initiatoren der neuen Entwicklungen in der
Kunstindustrie war. Sie führten auch dazu, dass man sich in
den Unternehmensleitungen die neue Ausrichtung zu eigen
machte und sich erstaunlich eng an die internationalen Trends
anlehnte. Dass mit den neuen Ideen und dem neuen Stil nicht

and practitioners of the arts described their trips abroad for
study in detail. The 1902 Turin Exhibition was written up by
Erik Gustaf Folcker (who was on the exhibition jury and was
the driving force behind the Swedish Association of Applied
Arts) in the annals of the Swedish Association of Applied Arts,
with a special focus on the Viennese and Glasgow schools. Sweden was, therefore, well aware of modern stylistic developments in both Britain and the rest of Europe.

The new trends shaped the debates carried on at the Swedish
Association of Applied Arts, where artisans and industrialists
met. There were numerous exciting ideas that would later come
to fruition despite all obstacles and opposition. A perpetual
favourite for discussion was 'replacing the fine arts with crafts
and industry,' as Erik Folcker put it. What was at stake were
new objectives, proposals for exhibitions and attempts to influence the tastes of the public at large as well as the manufacture
of the new products while integrating artists and artisans in
the businesses that made those products. The results of all
those initiatives were apparent not just in the Swedish Association of Applied Arts, of which the art historian and museum
curator Erik Gustaf Folcker was secretary from 1895, was a
leading light. Folcker continued to play a paramount role in
shaping the new developments in the art industry up to his
resignation in 1912 according to the new debate in the association. Another outcome of the undertakings engaged in by the
Applied Arts Association was that industrialists closely followed international trends, as astonishing as this might seem.
That rethinking on broader lines did not emerge concomitantly
with the new ideas and the new style can be put down to the
prevailing economic and social conditions. Remarkably, when
the new style was harshly criticised in the years shortly before
and after 1910, the arguments advanced against it were virtually the same as those made twenty years previously.

Rörstrand and Gustavsberg – the big factories

Established in 1825 on the island of Värmdö on the eastern
fringes of Stockholm, the Gustavsberg Porcelain Factory grew
into a large business after a turbulent early period. By the close
of the nineteenth century, Gustavsberg was the second largest
porcelain factory in Sweden, employing a workforce of nearly
a thousand and producing a wide range of wares. At that time,
Swedish art ceramics production was led by Rörstrand and
Gustavsberg. Their range included art objects and utilitarian
wares made of hard-paste porcelain and bone china as well as
ordinary stoneware and artist-designed stoneware. The two
leading manufacturers in the field competed with several
smaller Swedish factories and workshops for success at the
large domestic and international artisanal and industrial trade

unmittelbar ein allgemeines Umdenken eintrat, kann ökonomischen und sozialen Ursachen zugeschrieben werden. Es ist bemerkenswert, dass in den Jahren um 1910, als der neue Stil starker Kritik ausgesetzt war, nahezu die gleichen Argumente vorgebracht wurden wie 20 Jahre zuvor.

Rörstrand und Gustavsberg – die großen Fabriken

Die 1825 auf der Insel Värmdö im östlichen Randbereich von Stockholm gegründete Porzellanfabrik Gustavsberg hatte sich nach einer wechselhaften Frühgeschichte zu einem Großbetrieb entwickelt und war gegen Ende des 19. Jahrhunderts mit fast 1.000 Beschäftigten und einem umfassenden Angebot der zweitgrößte Keramikhersteller in Schweden. Die schwedische Kunstkeramik dieser Jahre entstammte hauptsächlich der von Rörstrand und Gustavsberg beherrschten Fabrikproduktion, in der sich neben Kunst- und Gebrauchsartikeln aus Hart- und Knochenporzellan sowie Steingut auch künstlerische Steinzeuge fanden. Die beiden großen Hersteller wetteiferten mit einigen kleineren Fabriken und Werkstätten um den Erfolg auf den großen nationalen und internationalen Kunst- und Industrieausstellungen. Zusammen mit den Kristallglaswerken (Kosta[10] und Reijmyre[11]) und der schwedischen Textilkunst (Handarbetets Vänner und Svensk Konstslöjd = Freunde der Handarbeit und Schwedischer Kunstgewerbe-Verein) konnten sie die Spitzenerzeugnisse des schwedischen Kunstgewerbes in internationalen Ausstellungen präsentieren. Die 1797 gegründete Fabrik Höganäs trat 1897 in Stockholm mit Kunstkeramik im modernen Stil hervor, andere schwedische Fabriken aus Uppsala, Gävle und Göteborg erstmals 1909 in Stockholm und in der 1914 in Malmö veranstalteten Baltischen Ausstellung. Eine kleine Anzahl schwedischer Keramiker, die mit künstlerischem Steinzeug arbeiteten, trat um 1900 hervor. Die künstlerische Keramik konnte sich jedoch erst mit der gesonderten Abteilung für Kunstkeramik des Svenska Slöjdföreningen auf der Stockholmer Ausstellung 1909 dauerhaft etablieren.

Es ist allerdings festzuhalten, dass die künstlerische Keramik dieser Jahre sowohl bei Rörstrand als auch bei Gustavsberg nur von untergeordnetem wirtschaftlichem Interesse war. Sie hatte aber eine große Bedeutung für die Profilierung und die Marktgeltung beider Fabriken. Den größten Teil der Produktion machten nach wie vor das Serviceporzellan und andere Gebrauchsgegenstände aus, bei Rörstrand auch Kachelöfen und Sanitärporzellan sowie technisches Porzellan (insbesondere Isolatoren). Die Kachelofenherstellung wurde nach und nach verringert. Demgegenüber wurde die technische Entwicklung intensiviert, was sich vor allem in Verbesserungen der Herstellungsabläufe, insbesondere aber auch in der Entwicklung neuer Massen und Glasuren äußerte.

fairs. Together with the makers of crystal glass (Kosta[10] and Reijmyre[11]) and the makers of Swedish textiles Handarbetets Vänner (Friends of Crafts) and AB Svensk Konstslöjd Selma Giöbel (Swedish Artistic Crafts Inc.), they presented top-quality Swedish crafts products at the international exhibitions. Höganäs (est. 1797) took part in Stockholm in 1897 with special art ceramics by Helmer Osslund in the modern style. Other Swedish factories in Uppsala, Gävle and Göteborg appeared on the scene in 1909 in Stockholm and the 1914 Baltic Exhibition in Malmö. By 1900 some Swedish art ceramicists had made a name for themselves with fine stoneware. However, it was the 1909 Stockholm Exhibition that put art ceramics on a permanent footing with the special exhibition department.

However, art ceramics were obviously of minor economic importance during those years, both at Rörstrand and Gustavsberg, although the reputation and the market of both firms depended on them. Porcelain services and utilitarian objects still made up most of their output but Rörstrand also manufactured tiled stoves and bathroom fixtures as well as technical porcelain (especially insulators). The manufacture of tiled stoves was gradually scaled back. By contrast, technological research and development were stepped up at Rörstrand: the manufacturing process was improved and new porcelain pastes and glazes were invented.

Fine stoneware had become increasingly popular since the 1890s due to the attention, since the 1889 Paris International Exhibition, that was paid to fine French stoneware, *grès au grand feu*

Abb. // Fig. 7
Große Allgemeine Kunst- und Industrieausstellung in Stockholm // The Great Universal Art and Industry Trade Fair in Stockholm, 1897

Die Rörstrand-Abteilung mit dem neuen Kunstporzellan, gekrönt von Alf Wallanders Schwanenvase; flankiert von der zeitgenössischen Majolika.
// The Rörstrand section featuring the new art porcelain, with Alf Wallander's Swan Vase being the highlight; flanked by contemporary majolica.
Photo: Rörstrand Museum.

Schon seit den 1890er Jahren fand das künstlerische Steinzeug ein wachsendes Interesse, nicht zuletzt auch auf Grund der Aufmerksamkeit, mit der die „Scharffeuerware" aus Frankreich, das „grès au grand feu" der französischen Steinzeugkünstler, seit der Pariser Weltausstellung von 1889 bedacht worden war. Die führenden Künstler bei Rörstrand und Gustavsberg nahmen diese Anregungen ebenso auf wie einige Keramiker und später auch mehrere Tonwarenfabriken. Bei Rörstrand waren es Alf Wallander um 1900 und Nils Lundström nach 1910.

Die beiden Fabrikdirektoren Robert Almström, Rörstrand, und Wilhelm Odelberg, Gustavsberg, engagierten sich persönlich im Schwedischen Gewerbeverein und mit ihren Unternehmen als schwedische Teilnehmer an den großen internationalen Kunst- und Industrieausstellungen. Ihre Söhne und Nachfolger Harald und Knut Almström für Rörstrand und Axel Odelberg für Gustavsberg setzen in den ersten Jahren des 20. Jahrhunderts dieses Engagement fort und gerieten deshalb nach der Ausstellung in Malmö 1914 in das Visier der Kritik. Nichtsdestoweniger gelang es ihnen, die Weichen in Richtung auf die zukünftige Entwicklung zu stellen, indem sie 1917 umfassende Veränderungen vornahmen und neue, junge Künstler einstellten. Die harsche einheimische Kritik an der Ästhetik und Produktion der Jugendstilperiode, u.a. im Schwedischen Gewerbeverein 1914, führte auch in der Keramik zu neuen künstlerischen Ausdrucksformen. Die ersten Ergebnisse einer „schönen Alltagsware" sah man im Herbst 1917 auf der „Heimausstellung" in Liljevalchs Kunsthalle in Stockholm (sie wurde anschließend in Malmö und ein Jahr später in Göteborg gezeigt). Das europäische Kriegsgeschehen und die damit verbundenen sozialen, wirtschaftlichen und technischen Entwicklungen zwangen zu umfassenden Veränderungen auch in der schwedischen Keramikindustrie, und damit änderten sich auch die Bedingungen für die Herstellung von Kunstkeramik. Einige populäre Jugendstil-Formen hielten sich in der großen Rörstrand-Produktion bis 1926, als die Fabrikation nach Göteborg in die dort ausgebaute Filiale verlegt wurde.

Kunstkeramik und „objets d'arts"

Um die Jahrhundertwende zum 20. Jahrhundert erlangte die Kunstkeramik stärkere Wertschätzung, und die keramischen Erzeugnisse wurden nicht selten als einzigartige „objets d'art" betrachtet. Das galt sowohl für die hochgebrannten Werkstattarbeiten mit ihren virtuos gesteuerten Glasuren als auch für die künstlerisch gestalteten Einzelstücke aus den Ateliers der großen Fabriken. Bei Rörstrand gab es neben diesen Unikaten im engeren Sinne auch eine Herstellung in Kleinstserien, bei der die aus Gussformen stammenden Modelle von Hand durch plastische Auflagen ergänzt, bemalt und anschließend signiert wurden. Die so entstandenen Exemplare desselben Modells weisen erhebliche Variationen in Bemalung und Dekor auf, so dass es

[Fr. literally 'high-fired stoneware'], with a fine stoneware body and glazes fired in high-temperature (1,100 to 1,450 °C) kilns used for porcelain. Leading artisans at Rörstrand and Gustavsberg as well as ceramicists working on their own were quick to take up the idea and several pottery factories later did the same. At Rörstrand Alf Wallander started working with high-fired fine stoneware around 1900, followed by Nils Lundström after 1910.

The directors of the two factories, Robert Almström (Rörstrand) and Wilhelm Odelberg (Gustavsberg), were both active in the Swedish Association of Applied Arts and participated in the large international crafts and industrial trade fairs. Their sons and successors Harald and Knut Almström (Rörstrand) and Axel Odelberg (Gustavsberg) carried this commitment on into the early years of the twentieth century and were criticised for doing so after the 1914 Malmö trade fair. Nevertheless, they were the ones who smoothed the way for future developments. In 1917 they hired new young artists. The harsh criticism directed in Sweden, for instance by the Swedish Association of Applied Arts in 1914, at the Jugendstil/Art Nouveau aesthetic and products did not prevent Swedish artisans from developing new forms of artistic expression. The first results of the new trend 'Beautiful everyday wares' showed up in autumn 1917 at the Household Exhibition in Liljevalchs Kunsthalle in Stockholm (it subsequently went to Malmö and a year later to Göteborg).

The First World War and the concomitant social, economic and technical upheavals it wrought forced the Swedish ceramics industry to make comprehensive changes and also altered the conditions for making art ceramics. Some popular Jugendstil/Art Nouveau forms were kept in production on a large scale at Rörstrand until 1926, but ceased when manufacture moved to Göteborg.

Art ceramics and 'objets d'art'

The turn of the century saw art ceramics so highly appreciated that pieces often enjoyed the status of one-of-a-kind 'objets d'art'. This is true both of high-fired workshop pieces notable for the consummate handling of their glazes and one-off designer pieces from factory studios. At Rörstrand, the one-offs were supplemented by limited editions of hand-painted and signed moulded models with hand-sprigged (attached) parts and ornaments. The basic model could thus be considerably varied as far as painting and decoration were concerned. In effect, such pieces were one-offs. They certainly were not inferior in quality to one-of-a-kind pieces and are today equally rare. Heinrich Pudor makes a point of emphasising that all such works [were] *indeed of such exquisite artistry that one [was] tempted to classify them as art rather than as applied art.*[12] However, Rörstrand also mass produced ornamental ordinary stoneware vases decorated with contour-framing and simple

sich hier um Ausführungs-Unikate handelt, die den exzeptionellen Einzelstücken an Qualität keineswegs nachstehen und auch von entsprechender Seltenheit sind. Heinrich Pudor hebt hervor, dass alle diese Arbeiten *in der That von einer künstlerischen Schönheit (sind), daß man versucht ist, sie zur Kunst selbst, nicht zum Kunstgewerbe zu rechnen.*[12] Rörstrand produzierte allerdings auch in großen Serien Ziervasen aus Steingut, die mit Konturdruck und einfacher Bemalung oder einfarbigen Glasuren versehen waren; in einigen Fällen trugen sie den Stempel „Dessin Alf Wallander", um auch hier seinen künstlerischen Anspruch zu dokumentieren.

Die Begriffe Kunstgewerbe, Kunsthandwerk und Kunstindustrie im späten 19. Jahrhundert und um die Jahrhundertwende 1900 können für eine gleitende Skala von einfacher bis hin zu komplizierter Herstellung stehen, vom einzelnen Objekt hin zu einer Serienproduktion in größerem Umfang. Sie waren bisher fast Synonyma. „Industrie" bedeutete Betrieb und sollte nur zum Ausdruck bringen, dass etwas hergestellt wurde und dass damit eine Rohware veredelt und nicht notwendigerweise maschinell in Massenauflage produziert wurde. „Kunst" hingegen betonte, dass sich die Herstellung auf Einrichtungsgegenstände und Zierstücke ausrichtete – und mit dem Begriff „objet d'art" sollte hervorgehoben werden, dass auch kunsthandwerkliche Gegenstände Unikate und ein Stück Kunst seien und deshalb signiert werden mussten.

Die zeitgenössischen keramischen Kunstwerke wurden nach der Qualität des Materials und den Dekorationstechniken, in denen sie ausgeführt waren, kategorisiert. So wurden oft die verschiedenen Kunstprodukte in Gruppen wie Porzellan, Fayence, Steingut, Steinzeug und Irdenware eingeteilt; dazu kamen noch spezielle Massen wie Feldspat- und Knochenporzellan. Ästhetische Qualitäten beurteilte man in Beziehung dazu. *„La porcelaine peut toujours être considérée comme la reine de la céramique; elle demande, quoi qu'on dise, á être toujours traitée avec soin et délicatesse."*[13] So äußerte sich Alexandre Sandier, „directeur des traveaux d'art" in Sèvres, als er über künstlerisches Porzellan auf der Pariser Weltausstellung 1900 schrieb. Heute legt man andere Maßstäbe an die Kunstkeramik und geht von den ästhetischen und künstlerischen Wirkungen aus und erst in zweiter Linie von den chemisch-technischen Aspekten.

Die Kunstauffassung des Historismus im 19. Jahrhundert hatte mit Malerei und Plastik auch die Architektur vor alle anderen Bereiche der „angewandten Kunst" gesetzt. Die Ergebnisse der Kunstindustrie und ihre Form und Dekoration beurteilte man in ihrem Verhältnis zu Vorbildern und nach ihrer technischen Qualität. Wichtig war daher auch, dass das Kunstporzellan in Fabriken hergestellt wurde, die auf ihren hohen technischen Standard verweisen konnte, da Kunstindustrieprodukte wie das Kunstporzellan als angewandte Kunst betrachtet wurden. Man hob gern hervor, wie wohl gelungen z. B. die Wiedergabe von Bouchers Gemälden auf den Prachtvasen der Jahrhundert-

painting or monochrome glazes. Some of these wares bear the stamp 'Dessin [Design] Alf Wallander', documenting a claim to art here as well.

In the late nineteenth century and at the turn of the century, the terms 'applied art', 'crafts' and 'art industry' were applied indiscriminately to any number of processes, ranging from simple to complex, resulting in anything from one-offs to mass-produced wares. Up to 1900, they were used almost synonymously. 'Industry' meant factory-made and was merely intended to express that something had been manufactured, that blanks were finished by means of a particular process, which was not necessarily mechanical or mass production. 'Art', on the other hand, emphasised the making of furnishings and ornamental objects. Finally, the term 'objet d'art', which is still used, was meant to indicate that applied art objects were also one-of-a-kind and indeed, art works, which is why they had to be signed.

Ceramic art works were ranked by the quality of the materials and decoration techniques used to make them. Artisanal products were often classified by material, i.e. porcelain, faience, stoneware and earthenware. In addition, there were special pastes such as feldspar (feldspathic) porcelain and bone china. The aesthetic qualities of a piece were subordinated to the above overarching categories. *'La porcelaine peut toujours être considérée comme la reine de la céramique; elle demande, quoi qu'on dise, á être toujours traitée avec soin et délicatesse.'*[13] ['Porcelain has always been considered the queen of ceramics; it needs, whatever might be said to the contrary, to be treated always with tender care.'] Thus Alexandre Sandier, directeur des traveaux d'art [art director] at Sèvres, writing on the fine porcelain at the 1900 Paris World Exhibition. Today other standards are applied to art ceramics. The most important criterion today is the aesthetic or artistic impact they make; the chemical and technical aspects are of minor importance.

Historicism in the nineteenth century esteemed painting, sculpture and architecture over all fields of applied art. The achievements of the art industry in both form and decoration were evaluated according to their relationship to the works they were modelled after and technical aspects such as the quality of workmanship. It also mattered whether fine porcelain was made at factories that worked to acknowledge high technical standards since the products of the art industry, including fine porcelain, were regarded as belonging to the applied arts. It was the done thing to point out how accurately Boucher paintings were reproduced on *Prunkvasen* [Ger. literally 'magnificent vases for show'] around 1850 and how fine the quality of the porcelain was. Ceramic art objects were not esteemed for their aesthetic value until the decades just before and just after 1900. Not until then – and then only gradually – did artists change their views to accept the fact that ceramics might be a medium in which they could find self-expression.

The basic forms of art ceramics, i.e. vases, urns, jugs, bowls, cups, plates, etc., derived from what were originally forms cre-

mitte war und wie fein die Porzellanqualitäten. Der Eigenwert der keramischen Kunstobjekte wurde erst in den Jahrzehnten um 1900 gewürdigt. Erst dann hatten die Künstler der Zeit nach und nach die Sicht auf die eigenen Ausdrucksmöglichkeiten der Keramik verändert.

Die Grundformen der künstlerischen Keramiken dieser Zeit, also der Vasen, Urnen, Kannen, Schalen, Tassen, Teller usw., gingen auf ursprünglich gedrehte Formen zurück. Sie wurden unterschiedlich gestaltet, dekoriert und glasiert. In der fabrikmäßigen seriellen Produktion wurden sie oft nach einem Originalmodell gegossen und anschließend bearbeitet, so z. B. mit plastischen Auflagen. Die Formen bewahrte man auf, und ihre Vorlagen lassen sich oft in Modellbüchern finden (in Schweden als „Vasenbücher" bezeichnet), die von den Werkmeistern benutzt wurden. Bei einzelnen Keramiken wurde der gedrehte Charakter oft bewusst angestrebt, und jedes Produkt als ein Einzelstück behandelt. Die Spannweite war groß und erlaubte viele Kombinationen und künstlerische Ausdrucksmöglichkeiten. Der Skulpturendekor war ein Zeichen der Zeit, ebenso die Unterglasurbemalung und die wechselnden Glasureffekte.

Dazu kamen andere Kunstobjekte, wie die populären kleinen Tierplastiken, Figurinen u.a.m., außerdem dekorative Wandfliesen. Die Grenzen zwischen Skulptur und traditionell keramischen Formen lockerten sich, und es kam zu fließenden Übergängen. In der Service-Herstellung wurden mehrere Ensembles mit ambitionierter Formgebung im neuen Stil hergestellt, ebenso Kachelöfen und offene Kamine in neuer Gestaltung und mit neuem Dekor.

Die gewollten ästhetischen Effekte verlangten neben speziellen Massen und Glasuren auch technische Voraussetzungen wie eine geeignete Brenntechnik und nicht zuletzt auch ein hohes handwerkliches Können aller Beteiligten.

ated on the potter's wheel and then variously shaped, decorated and glazed. When mass produced in factories, they were often cast from an original model and then worked, for instance, by having separately made parts or ornaments attached to them. The moulds were kept and their models are often encountered in model books (called 'vase books' in Sweden), which were used by master mould-cutters. The hand-thrown character of some pieces was an effect deliberately striven for and each product was treated like a one-off. The range of forms was wide and allowed for numerous combinations and effects expressing artistic individuality. Applied decoration was a sign of the times, as were underglaze painting and variegated effects achieved with glazes.

In addition, there were objets d'art such as the popular little animal sculptures, figurines and the like as well as decorative wall tiles. The boundaries between sculpture and traditional ceramic forms began to blur and transitions were fluid. Tableware services featured sophisticated design and decoration and the same held for tiled stoves and fireplace surrounds.

Creating such deliberate aesthetic effects entailed more than just artistry; apart from special pastes and glazes, technical factors such as using appropriate firing techniques and, not least, consummate workmanship on the part of all concerned had to be taken into consideration.

Die Keramik im Spiegel der großen Ausstellungen
Ceramics Mirrored in the Great Trade Fairs

Hintergrund

Die große Pariser Weltausstellung 1900 war die Krönung einer langen Reihe von Weltausstellungen und internationalen Kunst- und Industrieausstellungen in der zweiten Hälfte des 19. Jahrhunderts. Nach der Anzahl der Aussteller und Besucher war sie die größte, die jemals stattgefunden hat, und ist damit unübertroffen. Die Ausstellungen wurden allerdings im Laufe der Zeit allzu umfassend und unüberschaubar, so dass über eine Begrenzung nachgedacht wurde. Besonders wurde beklagt, dass im Gegensatz zu Bildungsaspekten und dem Studium von Industrie und Kunst der Vergnügungsbetrieb und andere Verlockungen überhandgenommen hätten. Im Pariser Sommer des Jahres 1900 wurde das besonders deutlich; der Effekt verstärkte sich noch dadurch, dass man hier zur gleichen Zeit – nach dem Beginn in Athen vier Jahre zuvor – die erste Olympiade der Neuzeit veranstaltete (siehe Abb. 8, 9).

Diese internationalen Kunst- und Industrieausstellungen waren in erster Linie wichtige nationale Manifestationen. Sie ermöglichten es den Unternehmen, ihre Erzeugnisse, in der weltweiten Marktwirtschaft einer neuen Zeit, international zu präsentieren. Der Anspruch dieser Veranstaltungen war umfassend, und alles, was die Länder vermochten, wurde gezeigt und dokumentiert: Bildung und Kultur, Technik, Industrie- und Konsumwaren, Kunst und Kunstindustrie. Im damals noch Vereinigten Königreich Schweden-Norwegen hatten beide Länder eigene Pavillons. Die bedeutenden Unternehmen und Fabriken nahmen zudem in den großen Industriehallen mit Ständen oder zuweilen auch mit eigenen Pavillons teil. Auch das zu Russland gehörende Großfürstentum Finnland hatte eigene Pavillons in der Absicht, seine nationale Eigenart gegenüber dem Zarenreich zu dokumentieren.

Die ersten nationalen Ausstellungen von Technik- und Industrieprodukten waren schon seit der zweiten Hälfte des 18. Jahrhunderts durchgeführt worden – u. a. in London, Hamburg, Prag und Paris. Ihnen folgten mit der Industrialisierung einige

Background

The great 1900 Paris World Exposition marked the zenith of a long series of universal exhibitions and international art and industrial trade fairs in the latter half of the nineteenth century. To judge by exhibitor and visitor numbers, it was the largest of its kind ever to have taken place and in this respect has never been surpassed. The exhibitions, however, became with time all too comprehensive and bewilderingly vast so that ideas for limiting their scope were mooted. It was particularly deplored that the entertainment industry and other attractions were overshadowing the educational aspects and the serious study of industry and art. That was particularly apparent in Paris in the summer of 1900; the effect was enhanced because the first Olympic Games of modern times – after they had been held in

Abb. // Fig. 9
L'Exposition Universelle Paris, 1900

Die schwedische Abteilung am Invalidenplatz, mit Rörstrand, Gustavsberg, Kosta und „Freunde der Handarbeit" (links) und „Schwedische Kunstgewerbeausstellung S. Giöbel". Die Vitrinen der Porzellanfabriken gestalteten Alf Wallander bzw. Gunnar Wennerberg.
// The Swedish section at Place des Invalides, with Rörstrand, Gustavsberg, Kosta and 'Friends of Crafts' (left) and 'The Swedish Applied Arts Exhibition S. Giöbel'. The display cases for the porcelain factories were designed by Alf Wallander and Gunnar Wennerberg.
Le Figaro Illustré, special issue *La Suède à l'Exposition*, 1900.

nationale und internationale Veranstaltungen. Die Weltausstellungen wurden mit „The Great Exhibition of the Works of Industry of all Nations" im Crystal Palace in London 1851 eingeleitet. Sie gab den Ton an, zum einen architektonisch durch die epochale Konstruktion des Hauptpavillons aus Eisen und Glas, und nicht zuletzt auch durch die Menge an Gegenständen, die technische Neuerungen in einer industrialisierten Produktion vorwiesen. Diese Entwicklung setzte sich bis zum Ersten Weltkrieg fort, und etwa alle fünf Jahre gab es in den führenden Industrieländern wichtige Weltausstellungen, im Wechsel mit Internationalen Kunst- und Industrieausstellungen. Rörstrand und Gustavsberg nahmen seit den 1850er Jahren an den meisten von ihnen teil, so u. a. in Paris 1889 und 1900, in Chicago 1893, in St. Petersburg 1901 und 1908, in Turin 1902, in St. Louis 1904, in Liège 1905, in Brüssel 1896 und 1910, in Gent 1912 und in San Francisco 1915.

In Schweden waren Gewerbe- und Industrieausstellungen schon in den 1820er Jahren veranstaltet worden – vorwiegend in Stockholm. Seit Anfang 1866 jedoch gab es auch gemeinsame skandinavische Veranstaltungen. Die Stockholmer Ausstellung dieses Jahres war die erste in Schweden mit internationalem Format. Ihr folgten nordische Ausstellungen in Kopenhagen 1872 und 1888 und in Göteborg 1891 und 1896. Sie fanden, bis zu ihrem Abschluss 1914 in Malmö, in der „Allgemeinen Kunst- und Industrieausstellung" in Stockholm 1897, die auch Russland mit einbezogen hatte, ihren Höhepunkt. Auch bei einer Anzahl inländischer Industrieausstellungen präsentierten Rörstrand, Gustavsberg und Höganäs ihre Produkte. Die wichtigeren unter ihnen waren die Ausstellungen in Gävle

Athens four years previously – had taken place in Paris at the same time (see fig. 8, 9).

Those international art and industrial exhibitions were primarily important manifestations of national grandeur. They enabled firms to present their products internationally in the global market economy of a new era. The claims made by those events were comprehensive; everything the countries concerned were capable of was flaunted and documented: education and culture, technology, industrial and consumer wares, art and the art industry. In what was then still the United Kingdoms of Sweden and Norway, the two countries each had a pavilion. Major companies and manufactories also took part with stalls in the large industrial halls or even occasionally with pavilions of their own. The Grand Duchy of Finland, which belonged to Russia, maintained pavilions with the intention of documenting its national individuality within the tsarist empire.

The earliest national trade fairs exhibiting the products of technology and industry had been held since the latter half of the eighteenth century – at venues such as London, Hamburg, Prague and Paris. In the course of industrialisation, the early trade fairs were followed by national and international events. The Great Exhibition of the Works of Industry of all Nations held at the Crystal Palace in London in 1851 initiated the international trade fairs. It was a trendsetter, on the one hand, in architecture with its ground-breaking main pavilion constructed of cast iron and glass, and, on the other, due to the vast number of objects signalling technical innovation in industrialised production. That development continued until the First World War and at intervals of roughly five years there were important international exhibitions alternating with global art and industrial trade fairs in the leading industrial countries. Rörstrand and Gustavsberg participated from the 1850s in most of them, at the turn of the century in Paris in 1889 and 1900, Chicago in 1893, St Petersburg in 1901 and 1908, Turin in 1902, St. Louis in 1904, Liège in 1905, Brussels in 1896 and 1910, Ghent in 1912 and San Francisco in 1915.

Trade and industry fairs had been mounted in Sweden since the 1820s – mainly in Stockholm. Since 1866, however, there had also been pan-Scandinavian events of this kind. The Stockholm trade fair that year was the first to be held in Sweden in an international format. It was followed by Nordic trade fairs in Copenhagen in 1872 and 1888 and in Göteborg in 1891 and 1896. In Stockholm in 1897 these Scandinavian fairs attained its zenith with the *General Art and Industrial exposition*, also included Russia, and finally in Malmö with the Baltic Exhibition. Rörstrand, Gustavsberg and Höganäs also presented their products at a number of Scandinavian domestic industrial trade fairs, of which the most important were the exhibitions in Gävle (1901), Helsingborg (1903) and Norrköping (1906). 'Objets d'art' were first shown in Göteborg in 1896. Art ceramics were displayed in the Stockholm Art Hall in 1897. The

1901, Helsingborg 1903 und Norrköping 1906. „Objets d'arts" wurden zum ersten Mal 1896 in Göteborg gezeigt. In der Stockholmer Kunsthalle gab es 1897 Kunstkeramik zu sehen. Das Malmö Museum arrangierte 1904 eine Ausstellung von modernem schwedischem und dänischem Porzellan. In Norrköping zeigte man 1906 eine kleinere Abteilung künstlerischer Tonwaren. Auf der „Allgemeinen Schwedischen Ausstellung von Kunsthandwerk und Kunstindustrie" in Stockholm jedoch gab es zum ersten Mal eine gesonderte Abteilung für künstlerische Keramik. In Malmö 1914 zeigte der Gewerbeverein modernes Kunsthandwerk, auch Keramik, in einem eigenen Pavillon.

Es gab auch eine Reihe von Ausstellungen, in denen vor allem Rörstrand, speziell mit Alf Wallanders Arbeiten, aber auch mit denen anderer führender Künstler, hervortrat. Rörstrand konzentrierte sich bewusst auf die Einführung des neuen Kunstporzellans auf dem Markt und forcierte seit 1896 seine Teilnahme in Göteborg und Malmö, Paris, Berlin und Brüssel. Die Ausstellung im neuen Kopenhagener Kunstindustrie-Museum im Dezember 1897 ist besonders interessant, da dort das moderne Kunstporzellan von Rörstrand gemeinsam mit modernen englischen Papiertapeten und Werken des finnischen Bildhauers Ville Vallgren (1855–1940) gezeigt wurde. Der neue Kopenhagener Museumsdirektor Prof. Pietro Krohn (1840–1905), zuvor Chef von Bing & Grøndahl, zeichnete für diese Kombination verantwortlich.

Die keramischen Erzeugnisse der großen Fabriken nahmen eine Sonderstellung ein: sie repräsentierten eine gelungene Verbindung zwischen technischem Können und neuer künstlerischer Formgebung. Die großen Kunstausstellungen waren damit ein wichtiges Forum. Sie dienten einerseits als wichtige Inspirationsquellen, boten aber andererseits auch die Möglichkeit, neue Entwicklungen wirkungsvoll zu präsentieren und unter den vielen Besuchern Interesse dafür zu wecken, wobei man über die umfassende Berichterstattung der Presse auch eine größere Allgemeinheit erreichen konnte. Für Rörstrand und Gustavsberg brachten die Erfahrungen aus der Teilnahme

Abb. // Fig. 10
Nach der L'Exposition Universelle Paris, 1900, ordnete man bei Rörstrand auf dieser „Medaillentafel" alle gewonnenen *Grands Prix*, Ehrenpreise und weitere Medaillen der letzten 50 Jahre an.
// After the 1900 Paris L'Exposition Universelle, all Grands Prix, honourable mentions and other medals awarded to Rörstrand over the past fifty years were arrayed on this 'medals board'.
Rörstrand Museum.

Malmö Museum arranged an exhibition of modern Swedish and Danish porcelain in 1904. In Norrköping a small section was devoted to art ceramics in 1906. The General Swedish Exhibition of Applied Art in Stockholm, on the other hand, was the first of these trade fairs to have a separate section for art ceramics. The Swedish Association of Applied Arts showed modern applied arts, including ceramics, in a pavilion of its own in Malmö in 1914.

There was also a number of exhibitions at which Rörstrand stood out, primarily because of Alf Wallander's work but also that of other leading artists. Rörstrand concentrated intentionally on introducing the new art porcelain to the market and from 1896 pushed participation in the Göteborg and Malmö, Paris, Berlin and Brussels trade fairs. The exhibition at the new Danish Museum of Decorative Art in Copenhagen in December 1897 is particularly interesting because the modern Rörstrand art porcelain was shown there together with contemporary English wallpapers and works by the Finnish sculptor Ville Vallgren (1855–1940). The director of the new Copenhagen museum, Professor Pietro Krohn (1840–1905), formerly head of Bing & Grøndahl, was responsible for that combination of exhibits.

The ceramic pieces produced by the large manufactories were special as art industry as something between crafts and mere industrial products. They represent a successful union of technical skill and new artistic design. The large art shows were an important forum for them. On the one hand, they served artists as major sources of inspiration yet, on the other, they also provided an effective launch pad for new developments and for keeping the many visitors to the exhibitions interested, with comprehensive press coverage ensuring that a broader public was reached. The experience gained from participating in those events benefited production at Rörstrand und Gustavsberg and represented at the same time constant new challenges that were met by hiring new artists and realising new ideas. This development continued from the 1890s so that innovations in art ceramics are chronicled, as it were, in the presentations.

Prizes awarded at the major exhibitions had enormous significance. Early in the history of the trade fairs Grands Prix as well as gold, silver and bronze medals and certificates were awarded for special artistic achievement and technological innovation. They were much coveted by manufacturers, as can be seen from the Rörstrand and Gustavsberg catalogues with the lists of prizes won proudly printed on their front covers (see fig. 10, 11, 12).

Firms often competed with large special splendid pieces of vases and urns executed to an excellent technical standard with fine quality porcelain and artistic decoration. Art and technique were to be united. Exhibition design, often consisting of large, stepped pyramids, was intended to impress, with a wealth of exhibits, many of which were very large indeed. Display cases were surmounted by the best pieces; services tended to be

Abb. // Fig. 11, 12
Auszeichnungen // Awards

Rörstrand erhielt den „Grands Prix" der L'Exposition Universelle Paris, 1900. Auch einzelne Künstler der Fabrik erhielten Gold-, Silber- und Bronzemedaillen. Hier einige Diplome für den Künstler Karl Lindström (Bronzemedaille in Paris 1900 und Silbermedaille in Liège 1905). Rörstrands Tochterfirma Arabia erhielt ebenfalls Goldmedaillen.
// Rörstrand got a 'Grands Prix' from the 1900 Paris L'Exposition Universelle. Individual Rörstrand artists were also awarded gold, silver and bronze medals. Here some certificates awarded to the artist Karl Lindström (bronze medal in Paris 1900 and silver medal at Liège 1905). Arabia, the Rörstrand subsidiary, also won gold medals.
Rörstrand Museum.

an diesen Veranstaltungen einen Gewinn für die Produktion und wurden zugleich zu einer immer neuen Herausforderung, der man durch das Engagement neuer Künstler und die Verwirklichung neuer Ideen zu entsprechen versuchte. Diese Entwicklung setzte sich ab den 1890er Jahren fort, so dass sich die Neuerungen in der Kunstkeramik in den Präsentationen wie in einer Chronik verfolgen lassen.

Die Preisvergabe bei den großen Ausstellungen hatte große Bedeutung. Schon früh wurden der „Grand Prix" sowie Gold-, Silber- und Bronzemedaillen und Diplome für besondere künstlerische Leistungen und technische Errungenschaften verliehen. Sie waren bei den Herstellern sehr begehrt, was man nicht zuletzt auch aus Rörstrand und Gustavsberg Katalogen und Preisverzeichnissen ersehen kann, auf deren Vorderseiten sie stolz abgedruckt wurden (siehe Abb. 10, 11, 12).

Oft konkurrierte man mit großen Prunkvasen und Urnen in hervorragender technischer Qualität der Ausführung und feiner Porzellanqualität mit künstlerischen Dekoren. Kunst und Technik sollten eine Verbindung eingehen. Die Ausstellungsgestaltung, oft große Pyramiden mit treppenartigen Absätzen, zielten darauf, mit der dargebotenen Fülle und der Größe der Ausstellungsstücke zu imponieren. Die Vitrinen wurden von den Prachtexemplaren gekrönt, die Service wurden mehr auf den unteren Etagen gezeigt. Diese Art der Präsentation findet sich im ganzen 19. Jahrhundert, ohne dass sich das Bild merklich änderte. Der Stil der Prunkstücke änderte sich erst 1897 in Stockholm. In Paris dominierte dann „L'Art Nouveau".

Rörstrand und Gustavsberg nahmen mit eigenen Abteilungen und im Rahmen des schwedischen Beitrags an den internationalen Ausstellungen teil; diese hatten einen „spin-off"-Effekt. Auf Chicago 1893 folgten mehrere Ausstellungen in verschie-

shown on the lower levels. This type of presentation occurred throughout the nineteenth century with little perceptible change. The showpieces did not change in style until the 1897 Stockholm exhibition where the majolica vases were changed to Art Nouveau. In Paris 1900 the Art Nouveau dominated. Rörstrand and Gustavsberg were allocated both with their own sections and in the Swedish displays at the international exhibitions; such company placement had a 'spin-off' effect. The 1893 Chicago World's Fair was followed by several trade fair exhibitions in American cities, including San Francisco in 1894 and later also in big Swedish cities. Such activities, for instance the 1904 St. Louis World's Fair (The Louisiana Purchase Exposition), created major export markets. Equally important were the trade fairs in St Petersburg in 1901 and 1908, which opened up the Russian market for Rörstrand (and its subsidiary Arabia).

Paris and the 1900 L'Exposition Universelle

The 1897 General Arts and Industrial Exhibition in Stockholm represented a breakthrough for the new art ceramics from Rörstrand and Gustavsberg; Rörstrand presented its modern range (some twenty objects by Wallander) but also traditional services and ornamental majolica pieces of the kind still highly prized in Sweden at that time (see fig. 13).
The big exhibition of that era – for Rörstrand too – was the 1900 Paris World Exposition. At that time Paris was the world's capital of industrial engineering and art. In summer 1900 'tout le monde' met at the greatest trade show on earth. Swedish

denen amerikanischen Städten, darunter in San Francisco 1894 und danach auch in schwedischen Großstädten. Durch diese Aktivitäten, so u.a. die Ausstellung in St. Louis 1904, ergaben sich größere Exportmöglichkeiten. Gleiche Bedeutung kam den Ausstellungen in St. Petersburg 1901 und 1908 zu, wo sich der russische Markt für Rörstrand (und seine Tochterfirma Arabia) öffnete.

Paris und L'Exposition Universelle 1900

1897 erreichte die neue Kunstkeramik von Rörstrand und Gustavsberg auf der Allgemeinen Kunst- und Industrieausstellung in Stockholm ihren Durchbruch; Rörstrand präsentierte sein modernes Programm (etwa 20 Objekte von Wallander), aber auch traditionelle Service und Zierstücke aus Majolika, wie sie in Schweden immer noch geschätzt wurden (siehe Abb. 13).

Die große Ausstellung der Epoche – auch für Rörstrand – war die Weltausstellung in Paris 1900. Paris war die Hauptstadt der Technik und der Kunst. Im Sommer 1900 traf sich hier „tout le monde" auf der gigantischsten aller Weltausstellungen. Angereiste Schweden waren begeistert: *„Die gegenwärtige Ausstellung in Paris dürfte ohne Zweifel nicht nur als die vollständigste und umfassendste aller bisherigen Ausstellungen angesehen werden, sondern auch als eine der am besten organisierten, elegantesten, geschmackvollsten und leuchtendsten"[14]* schrieb der schwedische Journalist Herman Ring in seiner Veröffentlichung über diese Ausstellung. Auf einer Fläche von 120 Hektar im Stadtgebiet und zusätzlich 110 Hektar in Vincennes waren 83.047 Aussteller aus 40 Ländern und 21 französischen Kolonien vertreten. Nahezu 51 Millionen offiziell gezählte Besucher überfluteten die Ausstellung und die Stadt mit ihren 3 Millionen Einwohnern in einer Zeit, in der das allgemeine Transportmittel die Eisenbahn war.

Die Weltausstellung war eine Huldigung an das vergangene Jahrhundert und dessen menschliche und technische Entwicklung, dessen Erfindungen und Entdeckungen. Gleichzeitig sollte sie für das kommende Jahrhundert ein Auftakt sein – um wieder Herman Ring zu zitieren: *„Die Pariser Ausstellung von 1900, eröffnet als Liebeserklärung an das Jahrhundert der menschlichen Wunderwerke, ist in sich selbst ein Wunderwerk, so großartig, so voller Hoffnung auf alles, was das Jahrhundert der Dampfkraft und der Elektrizität geprägt hat."*

„Schaut man von den Champs Elysées über die prächtige neue Alexanderbrücke hinüber auf die vergoldete Kuppel des Invalidenhotels, erblickt man sie eingefasst von weißen glänzenden Palais wie die Steine auf einem Spielbrett [...]" schrieb im Mai der Korrespondent der Zeitung „Dagens Nyheter". Die Schau beanspruchte ein enormes Areal: 100 Hektar im Stadtzentrum

Abb. // Fig. 13
Allgemeine Kunst- und Industrieausstellung // The Universal Art and Industry Trade Fair in Stockholm, 1897

Eingang mit Industriehalle. Rörstrand, Gustavsberg und Höganäs zeigten ihre Kollektionen im neuen Stil, und auch das neue dänische Kunstporzellan wurde präsentiert. In der Kunsthalle konnte man außerdem das moderne französische Steinzeug und die Keramik von Agnès de Frumerie und Herman Neujd sehen; Alf Wallander hatte eine eigene Abteilung mit Kunstkeramik.
// The entrance with the industrial hall. Rörstrand, Gustavsberg and Höganäs showed their collections in the new style and the new Danish art porcelain was also presented. In addition, modern French fine stoneware and ceramics by Agnès de Frumerie and Herman Neujd were displayed to the public; Alf Wallander had a section of his own devoted to art ceramics.
Photo: The Nordic Museum.

visitors to the Paris Exposition raved about it: '*The present exhibition in Paris must undoubtedly be viewed not only as the most complete and comprehensive of all trade fairs to date but also as one of the best organised, most elegant, smartest and most brilliant'[14]* wrote the Swedish journalist Herman Ring in a publication on the Paris show. Covering a surface area of 120 hectares within the city limits and an additional 110 hectares in Vincennes, the Paris Exposition hosted 83,047 exhibitors from forty countries and twenty-one French colonies. According to the official statistics, the exposition and the city with its population of 3,000,000 were overwhelmed by a tide of nearly 51,000,000 visitors, and this at a time when rail represented the universal means of transportation.

The Paris Exposition amounted to homage paid to the century past and its human and technological development, its inventions and discoveries. At the same time it was intended as a prelude to the coming century – to quote Herman Ring again: '*The 1900 Paris Exposition, inaugurated as a declaration of love to a century of marvels of human ingenuity, is in itself a marvel, so magnificent, so full of hope was it in everything a century of steam power and electricity had shaped.*'

'*When one looks from the Champs Elysées across the splendid new Pont Alexandre to the gilded dome of the Hôtel des Invalides, one sees it framed by gleaming white palaces like the stones on a playing board [...]*' wrote the correspondent of the Swedish

Abb. // Fig. 14
Das „Schwedische Landhaus" auf der L'Exposition Universelle Paris, 1900. Entworfen vom Architekten Ferdinand Boberg.
// The 'Swedish Country House' at the 1900 Paris L'Exposition Universelle. Designed by the architect Ferdinand Boberg.
Le Figaro Illustré, special issue. La Suède à l'Exposition, Paris 1900.

mit Pavillons auf dem Marsfeld und rings um den Eiffelturm und das Trocadero, von der Esplanade des Invalides bis hinauf zu den Champs Elysées und der Place de la Concorde, wo das palastähnliche Eingangszentrum Porte Binet lag. Die großen Ausstellungsgebäude für die unterschiedlichen Industrieabteilungen, darunter die der schwedischen Porzellan- und Glaswerke, befanden sich an der Esplanade des Invalides. Entlang des Seine-Ufers, zwischen den großen Ausstellungsfeldern, standen die nationalen Pavillons an der Rue des Nations, darunter auch der schwedische. Die neuen Kommunikationsmöglichkeiten und die Elektrizität würdigte man mit dem Elektrizitätspalast als Zentrum. Alle Gebäude der Schau wurden nachts elektrisch beleuchtet. Innerhalb der Exposition konnte man einen elektrisch betriebenen Zug oder die rollenden Trottoirs zur Fortbewegung benutzen. Im Juli wurde auch die erste Metro eröffnet, und man konnte Hector Guimards Metro-Stationen im neuen Stil bewundern. Gleichzeitig drehte sich alles um die Manifestation der französischen Kultur, die bei Kunst und Skulptur im Grand Palais und bei der Kunstindustrie im Petit Palais und an der Esplanade des Invalides die Darstellung beherrschte, u.a. mit französischer Keramik aus unterschiedlichen Epochen. Siegfried Bing war ein eigener Pavillon „L'Art Nouveau" mit den neuesten Ergebnissen aus seinen Ateliers und der von ihm vertretenen Künstler und Hersteller zugesprochen worden.

newspaper *Dagens Nyheter* in May. The exhibition took up an enormous surface area: 100 hectares in the heart of the city, with pavilions on the Champs de Mars and surrounding the Eiffel Tower and the Trocadero, from the Esplanade des Invalides on up to the Champs Elysées and Place de la Concorde, where Porte Binet, the palatial entrance to the fairgrounds was located. The large exhibition buildings for the various industrial sections, including the Swedish porcelain and glass factories, were on the Esplanade des Invalides. The national pavilions, including the Swedish one, were on the Avenue des Nations along the bank of the Seine. The new communication technologies and electricity were duly honoured with a Palace of Electricity as the hub of the fair. Electric light illuminated all buildings at the exposition by night. Visitors were conveyed about the fairgrounds by an electrically powered train or moving walkways. The first Métro was also opened in July and the public could admire Hector Guimard's Métro stations in the new style. At the same time everything revolved around displaying French culture, which dominated the scene with art and sculpture in the Grand Palais and industrial art in the Petit Palais and on the Esplanade des Invalides, including French ceramics from various periods. Siegfried Bing had been allocated a pavilion of his own for 'Art Nouveau' with the most recent products from his studios and the artists and manufacturers he represented.

Sweden and Rörstrand at the 1900 Paris World Exposition

Sweden's pavilion, the 'Swedish Country House', was on Avenue des Nations. It was designed by the architect Ferdinand Boberg, who succeeded in creating something really remarkable with this building. The pavilion, shaped like pagoda with an observation platform – like the bridge of a battleship – was roofed with shingle, which the French public interpreted as fish scales. The finale was a bell tower twenty-five metres high, from which banners fluttered. The pavilion was highly controversial; depending on the critic's viewpoint, it was deemed bizarre, repugnant or innovative (see fig. 14). Some non-Swedish critics regarded it as the architecture of the future as displayed in several of the structures built for the exposition, including the exciting architecture of the Finnish pavilion. One journalist wrote: '*The best building of the whole complex is the representative house of Sweden. Here is no hollow pomp, no shallow imitation. The straightforward style in wood is impressive in its simplicity and dignity. Everything develops harmoniously and logically from the character of the material. The Swedes and the Finns appear to be the pioneers of a young and triumphant beauty.*'[15]

The Swedish pavilion was an advertisement for the country. It housed several exhibitions that were national in theme, notably

Schweden und Rörstrand auf der Weltausstellung Paris 1900

Schwedens Pavillon, das „Schwedische Landhaus", lag an der Rue des Nations. Architekt war Ferdinand Boberg, dem mit diesem Bauwerk etwas wirklich Bemerkenswertes gelungen war. Der Pavillon, geformt wie ein Baumkuchenschloss mit Kommandobrücke – ähnlich eines Schlachtschiffs – war mit Schindeln gedeckt, die die französische Öffentlichkeit als Fischschuppen interpretierte. Die Krönung war ein 25 Meter hoher Glockenturm mit wehenden Fahnen. Der Pavillon bot Anlass zu Diskussionen und wurde je nach Standpunkt als bizarr, abschreckend oder innovativ beurteilt (siehe Abb. 14). Jedenfalls erweckte er Aufmerksamkeit, was beabsichtigt war. Einige ausländische Kritiker betrachteten die Bauweise als die Architektur der Zukunft, wie sie in mehreren neu errichteten Ausstellungsgebäuden, so auch in Finnlands architektonisch reizvollem Pavillon, vorgeführt wurde. Ein Journalist schrieb: *„The best building of the whole complex is the representative house of Sweden. Here is no hollow pomp, no shallow imitation. The straightforward style in wood is impressive in its simplicity and dignity. Everything developes harmoniously and logically from the charakter of the material. The Swedes and the Finns appear to be the pioneers of a young and triumphant beauty."*[15]

Der Pavillon war ein Aushängeschild für Schweden. Er enthielt verschiedene Ausstellungen zu nationalen Themen, vor allem das so genannte Königszimmer, vorgesehen für das Stockholmer Schloss – gestaltet als ein elegantes Vorgemach für Oskar II. mit vergoldeten Möbeln von Boberg und Prinz Eugéns Gemälden des Stockholmer Schlosses, flankiert von vier textilen Wandbehängen der Malerin Anna Boberg mit Darstellungen von Landschaften in unterschiedlichen Jahreszeiten. Weitere Themen waren Tourismus und traditionelle Kultur. Zu beiden Seiten und in der Mittelhalle arbeiteten in kleinen Räumen Gewerbetreibende, Handwerker und Weberinnen in Volkstracht. Einige Beispiele für Kunstkeramik von Rörstrand und Gustavsberg zeigte man im Königszimmer.

Nach dem Konzept der französischen Organisatoren sollten die nationalen Pavillons nationale Themen aufgreifen, während die Industrieprodukte in gesonderten Pavillons zur Ausstellung gelangten. Neben dem eigenen Ausstellungsgebäude nahm Schweden in 15 der unterschiedlichen „Klassen" oder „Abteilungen" teil. Entsprechend gab es einzelne Pavillons u. a. für Zentrifugen und Isolatoren, für spezielle schwedische Erzeugnisse der Metallverarbeitung mit nationalen Besonderheiten, u. a. aus den mechanischen Werkstätten Bolinder, der Waffenfabrik Huskvarna und dem Eisenwerk Fagersta. Mehrere andere Sachgebiete fand man in den Pavillons auf dem Marsfeld und am Invalidenplatz. Rörstrand, Gustavsberg und die Vereinigten Glaswerke (Kosta und Reijmyre) waren in der Abteilung XII: „Dekoration, Einrichtung und Möblierung von Gebäuden", einer

Abb. // Fig. 15
Die Rörstrand-Abteilungen in Paris // The Rörstrand sections in Paris, 1900

Anna Bobergs große Pfauenvase ist auf dem Stand zentral positioniert.
// Anna Boberg's large Peacock Vase occupies a central position on the stand.
Le Figaro Illustré, special edition *La Suède à l'Exposition*, Paris 1900.

one in what was known as the King's Room, which was intended for the Stockholm palace – designed as an elegant antechamber for King Oscar II with gilded furniture by Boberg and Prince Eugén's paintings of the Stockholm palace, flanked by four tapestries by the painter Anna Boberg featuring landscapes representing the seasons of the year. Other themes were tourism and traditional culture. On both sides of the central hall and in it tradesmen, craftsmen and women weaving were at work dressed in Swedish national costumes. Examples of art ceramics from Rörstrand and Gustavsberg were shown in the King's Room.

The French organisers wanted the national pavilions to address national themes whereas the industrial products were displayed in separate pavilions. In addition to the Swedish exhibition building Sweden placed products in fifteen of the various 'classes' or 'sections'. For this purpose there were specific pavilions, for instance for centrifuges and electrical insulators, devoted to the speciality metal products used in manufacturing for which Sweden was renowned, including selections from Bolinder, the engineering workshop, Huskvarna, the small arms and household appliances manufacturer and the Fagersta iron and steel works. Several other industries in which Sweden excelled were represented in pavilions on the Champs de Mars and at Place des Invalides. Rörstrand, Gustavsberg and the United Glassworks (Kosta and Reijmyre) were in Section XII: 'Decoration, furnishings and architectural appointments', a Swedish universal show. Furniture and textiles were also shown there, including products from contemporary Swedish applied arts businesses such as Friends of Crafts (weaving, etc), the Swedish Artistic Crafts Exhibition Inc. S. Giöbel (furnishings, textiles, etc), the K. A. Almgren silk mill and furniture workshops such as Max Sachs, Bodafors and A. L. Matsson.

The location of the Swedish section elicited harsh criticism from Swedish journalists. The exhibition was in a side gallery of the large exhibition hall along with industrial art from around the world. The complaint voiced was that the surface area was not large enough. Norway had been allocated twice as

gemeinsamen schwedischen Schau. Dort zeigte man auch Möbel und Textilien, u. a. von zeitgenössischen schwedischen Kunsthandwerks-Unternehmen wie den „Freunden der Handarbeit" (Webarbeiten u. a.), der „Schwedischen Kunstgewerbeausstellung S. Giöbel" (Möbel, Textilien u. a.), K. A. Almgrens Seidenweberei, von einigen Möbelwerkstätten wie Max Sachs, Bodafors und A. L. Matsson. Die Platzierung der schwedischen Abteilung rief scharfe Kritik der schwedischen Journalisten hervor. Die Ausstellung befand sich in einer der Seitengalerien in der großen Ausstellungshalle mit internationaler Kunstindustrie am Invalidenplatz. Man fand, die Fläche sei zu gering. Norwegen konnte über doppelt so viel verfügen und war ebenso wie Dänemark in der Zentralhalle hervorragend platziert. Auch befanden die schwedischen Rezensenten übereinstimmend, diese beiden Länder wären künstlerisch von den Schweden weitaus übertroffen worden.

Schweden war mit ca. 400 Unternehmen und über 100 Künstlern vertreten. Insgesamt 28 Große Preise, 81 Gold-, 65 Silber- und 48 Bronzemedaillen und 36 lobende Erwähnungen gingen an die beteiligten Unternehmen und Künstler. Ein Grand Prix ging an Rörstrand, Goldmedaillen an Gustavsberg und Kosta (ebenso an Arabia), und deren führende Künstler erhielten verschiedene Medaillen und Anerkennungen. Alf Wallander z. B. konnte eine Goldmedaille entgegennehmen.

Weltausstellung Paris 1900 – und die Keramik

Die Keramik nahm auf der Weltausstellung großen Raum ein. Man konnte z.B. im Musée Centennal in einer umfassenden Retrospektive die Entwicklung des Porzellans aus Sèvres und anderer französischer Hersteller sehen.

Die moderne Kunstkeramik einer Reihe von hervorragenden europäischen Fabriken wurde in der Industriehalle und den unterschiedlichen Pavillons der Nationen gezeigt. Keramik gehörte zu den höchstgeschätzten Erzeugnissen. Frankreichs Beteiligung war überwältigend und imposant. Sèvres nahm großen Raum ein und hatte einen eigenen Pavillon. Das neue Profil der Fabrik, besonders auf dem Gebiet der Kunstkeramik und bei dekorativen keramischen Arbeiten mit Kacheln und Fliesen, fand große Beachtung. Auch die zahlreichen Porzellan-Hersteller aus Limoges und andere französische Werke machten auf sich aufmerksam. Das neue Sèvres-Porzellan mit Flambé- und Kristall-Glasuren, das damals in Mode gekommen war, und andere Neuheiten traten in Konkurrenz zu den Erzeugnissen aus Kopenhagen und Berlin. Spezielle Beachtung galt dem modernen französischen Steinzeug mit vielen Variationen in Grau und Braun und erdfarbenen Glasuren nach japanischem Vorbild. Alle führenden französischen Keramiker waren vertreten, und eine besondere Aufmerksamkeit galt dem französischen Steinzeug.

much exhibition space and, like Denmark, was superlatively positioned. The Swedish reviewers were also unanimous in the opinion that Sweden was far superior to those two countries from the artistical point of view.

Sweden was represented by about four hundred businesses and more than one hundred artisans. A total of 28 Grands Prix, 81 gold, 65 silver, 48 bronze medals and 36 honourable mentions were awarded to exhibiting Swedish firms and artisans. One Grand Prix went to Rörstrand, gold medals were awarded to Gustavsberg and Kosta (as well as Arabia) and their leading artists were also the recipients of medals and honourable mentions. Alf Wallander was a gold medal winner.

The 1900 Paris World Exposition – and ceramics

Ceramics played a major role at the 1900 Paris Exposition. The Musée Centennal, built expressly for the exposition, showed a comprehensive retrospective tracing the development of Sèvres and other French porcelain.

Modern art ceramics from a number of outstanding European manufactories was shown in the Industrial Hall and at the various national pavilions. Ceramic products were among the most highly appreciated of all those shown. The French display was impressive, in fact stunning. Sèvres took up so much space that it filled a pavilion of its own. The new ranges at Sèvres, particularly in art ceramics and decorative ceramic appointments with stove and fireplace tiles met with an overwhelmingly favourable response. The many porcelain manufacturers from Limoges and elsewhere also attracted attention. The new Sèvres porcelain with flambé (reduced copper) and crystal glazes that had become fashionable at the time and other novelties competed against products from Copenhagen and Berlin. Japanese-inspired modern French fine stoneware with glazes in numerous gradations of earthy greys and browns imitating Japanese pottery was particularly admired. All the leading French ceramicists were represented and French stoneware attracted a great deal of attention. A commemorative retrospective was organized for the French sculptor and ceramicist Jean Carriès (1855–1894), who had died six years before. Along with Sèvres porcelain, fine stoneware attested to the dominance of French ceramics.

Of the other countries represented, the Danish firms Bing & Grøndahl, featuring art works by J. F. Willumsen,[16] and the Royal Copenhagen Porcelain Manufactory as well as the porcelain factories in Berlin, Meißen, Nymphenburg, Rosenthal, The Hague, St Petersburg and Vienna as well as the Rookwood Pottery Company of Cincinnati in Ohio, also met with a positive response. The United States of America sent a comprehensive stock of exhibits, of which Tiffany glass attracted the most

Für den sechs Jahre zuvor verstorbenen französischen Bildhauer und Keramiker Jean Carriès (1855–1894) arrangierte man eine Gedenkausstellung. Neben dem Porzellan aus Sèvres dokumentierte insbesondere das künstlerische Steinzeug die führende Position der französischen Keramik. Von den anderen Nationen fanden speziell die beiden dänischen Unternehmen Bing & Grøndahl mit den künstlerischen Arbeiten von J. F. Willumsen[16] und die Königliche Porzellanfabrik, aber auch die Porzellanmanufakturen von Berlin, Meißen, Nymphenburg, Rosenthal, Den Haag, St. Petersburg und Wien und ebenso die amerikanische Fabrik Rookwood Pottery in Cincinnati große Beachtung. In dem umfangreichen Beitrag der Vereinigten Staaten von Amerika zog besonders das Tiffany-Glas die Aufmerksamkeit auf sich, aber auch die deutschen Fabriken mit einigen ihrer bedeutenden Keramiker, die auch auf Rörstrand und Gustavsberg Einfluss hatten, wurden in den Berichten aus Paris lobend hervorgehoben.

Die neuen stilistischen Tendenzen bestimmten in besonderer Weise das Erscheinungsbild der künstlerischen Keramik. „L'Art Nouveau" war ein neuer Stil, der zu einer Veränderung der Formen, der Techniken und auch der Glasuren führte. Die

Abb. // Fig. 16
Gunnar Wennerberg, Knut Almström und Alf Wallander auf dem Weg zur L'Exposition Universelle Paris, Mai 1900
// Gunnar Wennerberg, Knut Almström and Alf Wallander on their way to the Paris L'Exposition Universelle in May 1900

Das Bild entstand vermutlich in Atelierkulisse bei einem Zugwechsel in Deutschland.
// The picture was presumably shot against a studio backdrop when the Rörstrand artists were changing trains in Germany.
From Alf Wallander's photo album. The Nordic Museum.

attention. The German factories with some of their leading ceramicists, who also exerted an influence on Rörstrand and Gustavsberg, were singled out for praise in the reports dispatched from Paris.

The art of ceramics was in the front line of the new stylistic trends. Art Nouveau was a new style that led to changes in form, techniques and even glazing. Japanese and Chinese inspiration was still perceptible although the distinctive forms of expression were already apparent in the new style. Japanese art and applied arts, which were shown in a separate exhibition building, on the other hand, attracted attention and interest, notably the exquisite Japanese lacquerwork and, of course, ceramics.

By 1896 Rörstrand had begun to launch its new art ceramics on the market. The 1897 exhibition in Stockholm revealed considerable advances. Even before that date, Rörstrand was striving to attract attention abroad. Since 1896 Rörstrand had shown work in Göteborg and Malmö, Berlin and Paris. Art porcelain from Rörstrand was also featured at Siegfried Bing's Paris gallery 'L'Art Nouveau' and the Hamburg and Cologne branches from 1897. In autumn 1897 Rörstrand took part in a special exhibition mounted by the Copenhagen Industrial Art Museum and in 1898 in the 'Moderne Keramik' exhibition at the Berlin Applied Arts Museum. That same year Rörstrand was also present at the winter exhibition at the Austrian Applied Arts Museum in Vienna. It was the 1900 Paris World Exposition that brought Rörstrand international recognition and acclaim.

The Rörstrand art ceramics, stylistically very much under the sway of Alf Wallander and Algot Eriksson were very well received. This is equally true of objets d'art signed by Nils Lundström, Karl Lindström and Anna Boberg as well as Waldemar Lindström's animal figurines. An up to that point unknown type of art porcelain now became a Rörstrand speciality: sophisticated feldspar porcelain[17] with sprigged, often pierced, decoration painted in subtly nuanced underglaze colours.[18] What was known as 'Rörstrand noir' also caused a stir, featuring mainly floral decoration on a black ground in underglaze painting. There were also pieces in *pâte-sur-pâte*,[19] with lustre glaze,[20] crystal glaze[21] and other special glazes such as *rouge chinois*.[22] Faience[23] was also shown as were services by Wallander and Eriksson.

The growing interest in ceramics at the 1900 Paris World Exposition, attested to not only in extensive international press coverage but also in the numerous acquisitions made by the large museums and many private collectors, had been anticipated by the commitment shown by those involved with preparations for the trade fair. For the Swedish contingent, the managing directors of the large factories and their leading artisans had travelled to France before the exposition was inaugurated; hence Knut Almström, accompanied by Alf Wallander and Gunnar Wennerberg[24] had come to Paris with the intention of checking the exhibition arrangement in the industrial hall and preparing for the presentation (see fig. 16). Later the Rörstrand

japanischen und chinesischen Anregungen ließen sich noch erkennen, aber der neue Stil hatte seine charakteristischen Ausdrucksformen gefunden. Die in einem eigenen Ausstellungsgebäude gezeigte japanische Kunst und das Kunsthandwerk zogen ihrerseits Aufmerksamkeit und Interesse auf sich, besonders die kunstvollen Lackarbeiten, aber vor allem die Keramik. Rörstrand hatte schon 1896 damit begonnen, seine neue Kunstkeramik auf den Markt zu bringen. Die Ausstellung 1897 in Stockholm ließ bereits bedeutende Fortschritte erkennen. Schon vorher waren die Bemühungen der Fabrik darauf gerichtet, auch im Ausland Aufmerksamkeit zu erlangen. Seit 1896 beteiligte man sich in Göteborg und Malmö, Berlin und Paris. Künstlerische Porzellane von Rörstrand wurden seit 1897 auch in Siegfried Bings Pariser Galerie „L'Art Nouveau" und deren Filialen in Hamburg und Köln angeboten. Im Herbst 1897 nahm Rörstrand an einer Spezialausstellung im Kopenhagener Kunstindustrie-Museum teil, 1898 an der Ausstellung „Moderne Keramik" im Kunstgewerbemuseum Berlin, und im selben Jahr war man auch auf der Winterausstellung des Österreichischen Museums für Angewandte Kunst in Wien vertreten. Doch erst mit der Weltausstellung in Paris erlangte man internationale Aufmerksamkeit und Anerkennung. Rörstrands Kunstkeramik, deren Erscheinungsbild insbesondere von Alf Wallander und Algot Eriksson bestimmt wurde, zog große Beachtung auf sich. Dies galt auch für die künstlerischen Objekte von Nils Lundström, Karl Lindström und Anna Boberg, desgleichen für die Tierfiguren von Waldemar Lindström. Es war eine bislang unbekannte Art künstlerischer Porzellangestaltung, die jetzt zur Besonderheit der Fabrik wurde: hochentwickelte Feldspatporzellane[17] mit skulpturalen, teilweise durchbrochenen Dekoren und mit Bemalung in fein abgestuften Unterglasurfarben[18]. Große Aufmerksamkeit erregte auch das so genannte „Rörstrand Noir" mit vorwiegend floralen Dekoren auf schwarzem Grund in Unterglasurbemalung. Es gab auch Stücke in „Pâte sur pâte"[19], mit Lüsterglasur[20], Kristallglasur[21] und anderen Spezialglasuren wie „rouge chinois"[22]. Daneben wurden auch Fayencen[23] ausgestellt und ebenso Service von Wallander und Eriksson.

Das gesteigerte Interesse, das die Keramik auf dieser Weltausstellung fand und das sich nicht nur in den ausführlichen Berichten der internationalen Presse, sondern auch in den zahlreichen Einkäufen der großen Museen und vieler Privatsammler zeigte, hatte sich bereits in dem Engagement der Beteiligten während der Vorbereitungen angekündigt. Von schwedischer Seite waren die Leiter der großen Fabriken und ebenso deren führende Künstler vor der Eröffnung nach Frankreich gereist; so waren Knut Almström gemeinsam mit Alf Wallander und Gunnar Wennerberg[24] eigens mit der Absicht nach Paris gekommen, die Ausstellungsanordnung in der Industriehalle zu überprüfen und die Präsentation vorzubereiten (siehe Abb. 16). Aus Rörstrand reiste später auch der Werkmeister Axel Lindström mit seinem Sohn Waldemar an. Auch andere Künstler und Keramiker besuchten diese wichtige Ausstellung.

Abb. // Fig. 17
Esposizione Internationale de Arte Decorativa Moderna, Turin 1902

Rörstrand- und Gustavsberg-Objekte in der schwedischen Abteilung. Rörstrands Kunstporzellan erregte große Aufmerksamkeit.
// Rörstrand and Gustavsberg objects in the Swedish section. The Rörstrand art porcelain caused quite a stir.
The Nordic Museum.

foreman, Axel Lindström, joined them there with his son Waldemar. Other Swedish artists and ceramicists also visited this important exhibition.

Follow-up and realignment in Turin 1902

The big 1901 St Petersburg exhibition was a recreation of the 1900 Paris Exposition. The 1902 Turin Exposition, the *Esposizione internazionale di arte decorativa moderna,* on the other hand, was a very interesting follow-up event and also represented a major milestone for the applied arts. It was the first show to be orientated towards modern and contemporary decorative art – Historicism was banished from the premises. Hence Turin, even more clearly than Paris two years previously, was perceived as a manifestation of the new style (see fig. 17).

Some fifteen European countries, including Sweden, Norway and Denmark, as well as the United States of America and Japan, exhibited at Turin. The exhibition revolved around architecture, interior decoration and furnishings. The ceramic arts were essentially represented by the artisans and firms that had showed in Paris in 1900.

Sinuous Art Nouveau with its boldly undulating, dynamic play of line enjoyed – one might say – a second heyday, especially in furnishings and wall decorations and to a certain extent in ceramics as well. The new style noticeably shaped the look of the French, Belgian and German sections. The breakthrough to more stringent form and decoration, however, came with some forward-looking works from Vienna and Glasgow.

England earned an Honourable Mention for objects placed by the Arts and Crafts Exhibition Society. The Scottish division,

Nachfolge und Neuorientierung in Turin 1902

Die große Ausstellung in St. Petersburg 1901 war eine Neuauflage der Pariser Ausstellung von 1900. Dagegen war die Ausstellung in Turin 1902, die „Esposizione internazionale di arte decorativa moderna", eine sehr interessante Nachfolge-Veranstaltung aber auch ein wichtiger Meilenstein für die dekorative Kunst. Es war die erste Schau, deren Ausrichtung auf die moderne und aktuelle dekorative Kunst gerichtet war – aller Historismus war untersagt. Auf diese Weise wurde sie im Vergleich zu Paris zwei Jahre zuvor noch deutlicher als Manifestation des neuen Stils empfunden (siehe Abb. 17).

Etwa 15 europäische Länder, darunter auch Schweden, Norwegen und Dänemark, sowie die Vereinigten Staaten und Japan beteiligten sich. Im Mittelpunkt standen Architektur, Innendekoration und Mobiliar. Die Keramik war im Wesentlichen durch dieselben Künstler und Firmen vertreten wie in Paris 1900.

Der schwingende Jugendstil mit seinem betont wellenförmigen, dynamischen Linienspiel erlebte hier – so kann man sagen – noch einmal einen Höhepunkt, insbesondere bei den Möbeln und Wanddekorationen, aber teilweise auch in der Keramik. Er bestimmte vor allem das Erscheinungsbild der französischen, belgischen und deutschen Abteilungen. Zukunftweisend war jedoch der Durchbruch einer strafferen Form- und Dekorgestaltung in einigen Arbeiten aus Wien und Glasgow.

England errang einen Ehrenplatz mit den Objekten der Arts and Crafts Exhibition Society. Die größte Aufmerksamkeit erreichte allerdings die Schottische Abteilung mit der Schule von Glasgow, daneben auch Österreich und Deutschland. Die schwedische Abteilung befand sich zwischen Deutschland und den Vereinigten Staaten in einem Saal, den wiederum der Architekt Ferdinand Boberg gestaltet hatte. Die schwedischen Teilnehmer waren dieselben wie in Paris 1900, d.h. Keramik aus Rörstrand und Gustavsberg, Glas aus den Vereinigten Glaswerken, dazu die „Freunde der Handarbeit" usw. Obwohl es aus schwedischer Sicht nicht so viele Neuheiten gab, fand die schwedische Abteilung mehr Aufmerksamkeit und mehr Medienbeachtung als in Paris. In zahlreichen Berichten der internationalen Presse wurden sowohl die Gestaltung der Exponate als auch ihre betont moderne Präsentation hervorgehoben.

In den anschließenden internationalen Ausstellungen, an denen Rörstrand und Gustavsberg beteiligt waren, setzte sich ein stärker an der Funktion orientierter Einrichtungsstil durch. In der rückblickenden Betrachtung hatte der Jugendstil in den Jahren um die Turin-Ausstellung 1902 seinen ästhetischen Höhepunkt erreicht. Die Forderung nach mehr funktionaler Formgebung und Anpassung an die Erfordernisse des Alltags führte einige Jahre später dann auch zu neuen ästhetischen Zielen. Der Auftritt der beiden schwedischen Fabriken in Stock-

Abb. // Fig. 18
Rörstrand-Abteilung auf der Allgemeinen Schwedischen Ausstellung für Kunsthandwerk und Kunstindustrie
// The Rörstrand section at the Universal Swedish Trade Fair for the Applied Arts and Industrial Art, Stockholm 1909.
The Nordic Museum.

notably the Glasgow School, made the biggest splash, followed by Austria and Germany. The Swedish section was between Germany and the United States of America in a hall that had been designed by the Swedish architect Ferdinand Boberg. The Swedish contingent was made up of the exhibitors who had shown wares at the 1900 Paris Exposition, i.e. Rörstrand and Gustavsberg with ceramics, the United Glassworks with their glass and the Friends of Crafts, etc. Although there was not so much that was new from the Swedish side, the Swedish section attracted more attention from the public and acclaim from the press than it had at the Paris Exposition. Both the design of the Swedish exhibits and the boldly modern presentation were remarked on in numerous international press reports.

A more functional style in furnishings and interiors predominated at subsequent international trade fairs where Rörstrand and Gustavsberg were exhibitors. Viewed in retrospect, Jugendstil/Art Nouveau attained its aesthetic zenith in the years immediately before and just after the 1902 Turin exhibition. The demand for more functional design and adaptation to the needs of everyday living again led a few years later to new aesthetic aims. The trend showed up clearly at the exhibitions mounted by the two Swedish porcelain factories in Stockholm in 1909 and Malmö in 1914. The era of Jugendstil/Art Nouveau art ceramics was a thing of the past.

At Rörstrand experiments in developing new forms of artistic expression in ceramics continued synchronously with efforts to develop further the established Rörstrand style by incorporating new ideas. By the close of the first decade of the twentieth century, however, unmistakable signs of stagnation had set in. Even renewed experiments with glaze effects and streamlined Art Nouveau decoration failed to score more than a modest success. At Gustavsberg the focus was on fine stoneware decorated with the special Gustavsberg sgraffito technique.[25]

holm 1909 und Malmö 1914 machte diese Tendenz deutlich. Die Zeit der künstlerischen Jugendstil-Keramik war vorbei. Bei Rörstrand setzte man die Versuche zur Entwicklung neuer künstlerischer Ausdrucksformen in der Keramik fort und war gleichzeitig um eine Weiterentwicklung des etablierten Stils durch die Einbeziehung neuer Ideen bemüht. Gegen Ende des ersten Jahrzehnts des 20. Jahrhunderts gab es jedoch deutliche Anzeichen einer Stagnation, und auch erneute Versuche mit Glasureffekten und einer gestrafften Jugendstilornamentik waren nicht besonders erfolgreich. Das Schwergewicht von Gustavsbergs Kunstkeramik lag auf Steinzeug mit ihrer speziellen Sgraffito-Technik.[25]

Die Ausstellungen Stockholm 1909 und Malmö 1914

In Stockholm 1909 waren die beiden großen Fabriken mit eigenen Abteilungen vertreten. Rörstrand und Gustavsberg traten hier vorwiegend mit neuen zukunftsweisenden Spezialitäten auf. Das Interesse an Kunstglasuren war sehr groß. Die Ausstellungsbeiträge vermittelten jedoch den Eindruck, als ob die nun arrivierten Künstler in ihren jeweiligen Ausdrucksformen festgefahren wären: die Jugendstilkeramik à la Rörstrand und Gustavsberg hatte ihren Zenit überschritten. Der Schwedische Gewerbeverband hatte zum ersten Mal eine Sonderabteilung für kunstkeramische Arbeiten mit einem halben Dutzend jüngerer freischaffender Mitarbeiter der großen Fabriken eingerichtet. Aber auch die dort gezeigten Versuche, die französische Steinzeugkeramik der 1890er Jahre für Schweden zu übernehmen, brachten keine überzeugenden Ergebnisse.

1914 präsentierten sich nicht nur Rörstrand, Gustavsberg und Höganäs in Malmö mit eigenen Abteilungen, sondern auch die Göteborg-, die Lidköping- und die Gävle-Porslinsfabrik, die vereinigten Betriebe von Upsala-Ekeby mit der St. Eriks Lervarufabrik und Bobergs Fajansfabrik. Daneben gab es einen Pavillon des Gewerbeverbands mit einer großen Kunstkeramik-Abteilung. Rörstrand und Gustavsberg erhielten schlechte Kritiken, die sich vor allem auf ihren Mangel an künstlerischer Innovation und die unzureichende Funktionalität ihrer Tafelservice richtete. Unter der Scharffeuerware fanden sich jedoch viele interessante Objekte. Obwohl der Jugendstil vorbei war, konnte er sich in der breiteren Fabrikproduktion noch für etwa ein Jahrzehnt halten.

The exhibitions at Stockholm in 1909 and Malmö in 1914

In 1909 both Rörstrand and Gustavsberg were represented with sections of their own in Stockholm. The two largest Swedish manufactories went public there primarily with new, forward-looking speciality wares. There was a great deal of interest in art glazes. However, the pieces shown conveyed the impression the artists had stuck fast in the forms of expression in which they had long since established their reputations: Art Nouveau ceramics in the Rörstrand and Gustavsberg manner were past their prime. For the first time, the Swedish Association of Applied Arts had organised a special section for art ceramics produced for the large factories by half a dozen young freelancers. Even the manifest attempts made there by Sweden to emulate the French fine stoneware of the 1890s brought no satisfactory results.

In 1914 Rörstrand, Gustavsberg and Höganäs were among the Swedish ceramic firms with allocated sections of their own at the Malmö show, along with the Göteborg, Lidköping and the Gävle Porcelain Manufactory, Upsala-Ekeby, St. Eriks Lervarufabrik and the Boberg Faience Factory. There was also a special pavilion of the Swedish Association of Applied Arts with a large art ceramics section. Rörstrand and Gustavsberg earned unfavourable reviews deprecating their lack of aesthetic innovation and the insufficient functionality of their tableware services. Nonetheless there were many interesting objects among the high-fired wares. Although the Jugendstil/Art Nouveau period was over, a watered-down version of the style would persist for about a decade in fairly broad-based production.

Abb. // Fig. 19
Rörstrand-Abteilung auf der Baltischen Ausstellung
// The Rörstrand section at the Baltic Exhibition in Malmö, 1914
Photo: The Nordic Museum.

Die Fabrik, die Produktion und die Kunst-Keramik
The Factory, its Products and Art Ceramics

Leitung und Herstellung

In der zweiten Hälfte des 19. Jahrhunderts hatte sich Rörstrand zu einem großindustriellen Unternehmen mit Millionen-Umsatz entwickelt. Das Fabrikgelände war ausgebaut und durch viele neue Anlagen erweitert worden, darunter mehrere Dampfmaschinen, Werkstätten, Mahlwerke und Öfen. 1890 war die Anzahl der Brennöfen auf 36 angestiegen. In den Jahren nach 1850 hatte es hier noch einige Hundert Beschäftigte gegeben; um die Jahrhundertwende zum 20. Jahrhundert waren es etwa 1.100. Rörstrand gehörte nach dem Umfang seines Umsatzes zu den zehn größten Unternehmen in Schweden (siehe Abb. 1).

Nördlich von Helsinki, im damaligen Großfürstentum Finnland, hatte 1874 die Aktiengesellschaft Arabia, eine Tochterfirma von Rörstrand, ihre Produktion aufgenommen. Zur Mitarbeit bei Arabia wurden kontinuierlich verschiedene Werkmeister und Porzellanarbeiter von Rörstrand abgestellt. Ein großer Teil des Produktsortiments waren Modelle und Muster aus Rörstrand, u. a. die Standardmodelle von gegossenen Vasen für die Majolikaproduktion, für Lüster- und Kristallglasuren und für die Unterglasurbemalung. Einige Formen und Dekore gingen auf Hugo Hörlin und Alf Wallander zurück. Parallel dazu übernahm Arabia jedoch auch Anregungen von den Fabriken des Kontinents und versuchte, sich von Rörstrand zu emanzipieren.

Im Laufe des 19. Jahrhunderts war die Produktion von Haushaltsgeschirr, Kachelöfen und technischem Porzellan kontinuierlich angestiegen; gleichzeitig nahm auch der Anteil zier- und kunstkeramischer Gegenstände zu. Neue Materialien und neue technische Verfahren, aber auch ein stark verbesserter Produktionsapparat trugen zu Rörstrands schneller Entwicklung bei und ermöglichten die Herstellung von Ware in unterschiedlicher Qualität für unterschiedliche Kundenkreise. Die Objekte, Formen und Dekore entsprachen den verschiedenen internationalen Modetrends der Zeit, wobei man sich auch von den englischen und den großen kontinentalen Fabriken inspirieren ließ.

Management and production

During the latter half of the nineteenth century, Rörstrand grew into a large industrial enterprise with turnover amounting to millions. The factory premises were extended and enlarged by the addition of many new facilities, including several pieces of steam-driven machinery, mills and kilns. By 1890 the number of kilns had grown to thirty-six. After 1850 it employed a workforce of several hundred; by the turn to the twentieth century the workforce numbered about 1100. Measured by turnover Rörstrand was one of the top ten Swedish businesses (see fig. 1).

In 1874, Arabia, a Rörstrand subsidiary, began production north of Helsinki, in the then Grand Duchy of Finland. Foremen and porcelain workers were constantly sent from Rörstrand to work at Arabia. Most of the Arabia product range consisted of models and patterns from Rörstrand, including the standard models of cast majolica vases, the formulas for crystal glazes and patterns for underglaze painting. Some forms and decoration schemes were the work of Hugo Hörlin and Alf Wallander. In parallel, however, Arabia also assimilated inspiration from continental porcelain factories and attempted to emancipate itself from Rörstrand.

Over the course of the nineteenth century, the output of household tableware, tiled stoves and technical ceramics had steadily risen at Rörstrand, accompanied by growth in the share of decorative ceramics and objets d'art. New materials and new technologies as well as considerable improvements in production processes contributed to rapid development at Rörstrand and facilitated the manufacture of wares of varying quality levels targeting several market segments. The objects themselves, both in form and decoration, matched the international fashion trends of the day, notably inspired by the English and the large continental producers.

As already noted, two young, talented and energetic enthusiasts were behind the expansion at Rörstrand. At the age of twenty-

Wie bereits erwähnt, standen hinter dieser Expansion zwei junge, begabte und energische Enthusiasten. Der 27-jährige Holdo Stråle (1826–1896) hatte seinen Vater als Fabrikdirektor 1853 abgelöst. Stråle, aber vor allem Robert Almström (1834–1911), der nach seinen Studien in England schon 1855 die Verantwortung für die technische Entwicklung übernommen hatte, trieben die Arbeit voran. Almström wurde technischer Disponent, übernahm 1893 allein die Leitung und wurde zum gleichen Zeitpunkt Haupteigentümer von Rörstrand (siehe Abb. 2). Holdo Stråle war schon frühzeitig im Schwedischen Gewerbeverein tätig gewesen; seine Rolle in den Organisationskomitees zur Vorbereitung der Teilnahme an den Industrieausstellungen wurde gegen Ende des 19. Jahrhunderts von Almström übernommen. Stråle verfasste mehrere Bücher, u.a. über die frühe Geschichte der Manufakturen Rörstrand (1879) und Marieberg (1880). Robert Almström seinerseits schrieb eine Reihe längerer Beiträge zur Geschichte der Keramik mit dem Schwerpunkt auf technischen Aspekten. Beide kümmerten sich auch um den Aufbau einer umfangreichen Bibliothek und die Zusammenstellung einer großen musealen Sammlung, die den Künstlern der Fabrik als Studiensammlung dienen sollten; diese Sammlung war auch der Öffentlichkeit zugänglich.

Die internationalen Kontakte wurden auf unterschiedliche Weise gepflegt. Robert Almström sandte seine Söhne Harald (1871–1944) und Knut (1873–1955) und die künstlerischen Mitarbeiter Alf Wallander und Algot Eriksson auf Studienreisen in die großen Betriebe auf dem Kontinent und besonders auch nach England. Knut Almströms Reisetagebuch vom Sommer und Herbst 1895 ist ein anschaulicher Beleg dafür, dass ein Teil der dabei gesammelten Erfahrungen in der Einführung technischer Neuheiten bei Rörstrand wirksam wurde. Studienreisen zu den großen internationalen Ausstellungen waren eine Selbstverständlichkeit. Auch der alternde Robert Almström stand den Strömungen der Zeit offen gegenüber und setzte unter dem Eindruck des Erfolges, den die beiden Kopenhagener Manufakturen mit Arnold Krog und Pietro Krohn erzielt hatten, vor der Ausstellung von 1897 auf eine Handvoll junger Künstler. Seine beiden Söhne unterstützten ihn dabei, die für die neue Kunstkeramik und mit den neuen Glasuren enthusiastisch arbeiteten. Aus einem Brief Robert Almströms an Pietro Krohn über den Beitrag von Rörstrand für die Ausstellung im Kunstindustriemuseum Kopenhagen im Dezember 1897 geht das deutlich hervor: „[...] einesteils bin ich zu altmodisch, um etwas einschätzen zu können, aber Wallander und meine Söhne wollen mitmachen." Dagegen kommt in einem Brief an Krohn vom Februar 1898 Harald Almströms Enthusiasmus klar zum Ausdruck: „[...] und es ist ein Vergnügen, mit neuen Dingen arbeiten zu dürfen [...]".[26]

Schon seit dem 18. Jahrhundert hatte Rörstrand eigene Verkaufsgeschäfte in der Innenstadt von Stockholm unterhalten. Eine repräsentative Einrichtung entstand 1890 mit dem Umzug an den Stureplan (siehe Abb. 20). Ein großes Schild oberhalb

Abb. // Fig. 20
1884 eröffnete Rörstrand ein Ladenlokal im neuen Geschäftszentrum am Stureplan in Stockholm. Die Geschäftsführung übernahm J. O. Lundqvist.
// In 1884 Rörstrand opened an outlet in the new business centre am Stureplan in Stockholm. J. O. Lundqvist became managing director. Stockholm City Museum.

seven, Holdo Stråle (1826–1896) had succeeded his father as managing director in 1853. Stråle, and especially Robert Almström (1834–1911), who after training in England had assumed responsibility for technical development by 1855, were the powerhouses behind growth at Rörstrand. Almström became technical expediter and in 1893 sole director of Rörstrand as well as majority shareholder (see fig. 2). Holdo Stråle had worked for the Swedish Association of Applied Arts at an early date; in the late nineteenth century Almström took over Stråle's role on the committee responsible for organising participation in industrial trade fairs. Stråle was the author of several books, including two on the early history of the Rörstrand (1879) and Marieberg (1880) factories. Robert Almström wrote a number of quite long essays on the history of ceramics with a focus on the technical aspects of production. Both Stråle and Almström were committed to building up a library and amassing a large museum collection to be used as a study collection by artisans working at Rörstrand. The collection was also made accessible to the public at large.

Forging ties abroad was handled in various ways. Robert Almström sent his sons, Harald (1871–1944) and Knut (1873–1955), as well as the leading artists employed at Rörstrand Alf Wallander and Algot Eriksson, on study tours to the Continent and England. Knut Almström's travel diary covering summer and autumn 1895 provides ample confirmation that some of the experience thus gained was effectively put into practice at Rörstrand through the implementation of new technologies. Study tours to the large industrial trade fairs were a regular feature. Remaining receptive to current trends as he grew older, Robert Almström was so impressed by the success the two Copenhagen porcelain factories had had with Arnold Krog and Pietro Krohn that he opted for trusting in the abilities of a handful of young artisans before the 1897 Copenhagen exhibition. Almström's two sons supported him by putting their support enthusiastically behind the new art ceramics and the new

Abb. // Fig. 21, 22
Harald Almström (1870–1944) und // and Knut Almström (1873–1955)

Beide arbeiteten in Rörstrand seit Mitte der 1890er Jahre und
übernahmen 1909 die Fabrikleitung.
// Both worked at Rörstrand from the mid-1890s and became
co-directors in 1909.
Photo: National Library Stockholm.

des Geschäftes warb für „Rörstrands Ausstellung von Porzellan
& Kachelöfen". Ab 1898 befand sich das Geschäft in einem
Neubau in der Innenstadt an der Biblioteksgatan. Hier gab es
auch eine große Abteilung mit Ziervasen, Tierfiguren und anderen Kunstgegenständen. Geschäft und Ausstellung wurden
bereits seit 1884 in enger Zusammenarbeit mit J. O. Lundqvists
Einrichtungsgeschäft, dem vornehmsten der Stadt, betrieben.
Zu dieser Zeit verfügte Rörstrand auch über ein gut entwickel-
tes Vertriebssystem mit Wiederverkäufern im ganzen Land,
insbesondere den Einrichtungshäusern und den neu entstandenen Warenhäusern in größeren Städten wie Stockholm,
Göteborg und Malmö. Eine Anzahl von Reisevertretern pflegte
die Kontakte zu den Wiederverkäufern und suchte gleichzeitig
nach neuen Kunden.

Auch im Ausland, und zwar sowohl in den skandinavischen
Ländern als auch in Berlin, Paris, London und mehreren anderen Städten, gab es Depots, in denen die Produkte von Rörstrand ausgestellt und verkauft wurden. In Paris wurden schon
ab 1896 in Siegfried Bings[27] berühmter Galerie „L'Art Nouveau
Bing" einige Kunstporzellane von Rörstrand angeboten. Seit
1910 war J. H. Vernon, Inc. in New York Generalagent für die
Vereinigten Staaten und Kanada.

Robert Almströms Söhne Harald und Knut, ausgebildet an der
KTH (Königliche Technische Hochschule), arbeiteten in der
Fabrik, übernahmen 1909 deren Gesamtleitung und behielten
sie bis Anfang der 1920er Jahre. Der Architekt Hugo Tryggelin
(1846–1924), als „Chefdessinateur" seit 1873 angestellt, war bis
1909 tätig; unter seiner Leitung hatte sich ein Stamm von
Werkmeistern gebildet, denen die Verantwortung für bestimmte
Teilbereiche oblag, u. a. für die Glasuren, die Ausführung der
Dekore und die Durchführung der Brennvorgänge, aber auch
für die gesamte Kachelofenherstellung. Der mit dem Ausschei-

glazes. That is clearly attested in a letter written by Robert Almström to Pietro Krohn on the Rörstrand share of the exhibition
at the Copenhagen Industrial Art Museum in December 1897:
'[...] *on the one hand, I am too old-fashioned to be able to judge
anything of that kind but Wallander and my sons want to be in
on it.*' In a letter written to Krohn in February 1898 by Harald
Almström, the younger Almström's enthusiasm is patently
obvious: '[...] *and it is a pleasure indeed to be able to work with
new things [...]*'.[26]

Since the eighteenth century Rörstrand had maintained retail
outlets in the Stockholm city centre. A suitably grand empo-
rium was established in 1890, when Rörstrand moved to the
Stureplan (see fig. 20). A long sign above the entrance adver-
tised 'Rörstrand Display of Porcelain & Tiled Stoves'. From 1898
the shop was in a new building on Biblioteksgatan in the city.
It also devoted a large section to a display of ornamental vases,
animal figurines and other objets d'art. The shop and the exhibition had been in operation since 1884 in close collaboration
with J. O. Lundqvist Furnishings, the most exclusive shop of its
kind in Stockholm. Even then Rörstrand also had a well-devel-
oped marketing and distributing network with retailers
throughout Sweden, notably at furniture shops and the department stores that were opening in larger cities such as Stockholm, Göteborg and Malmö. Several travelling salesmen maintained Rörstrand's ties with retailers while keeping an eye out
for a new clientele.

Outside Sweden, both in the Scandinavian countries as well as
Berlin, Paris, London and several other European cities, there
were outlets where Rörstrand products were displayed and
sold. As early as 1896 some pieces of Rörstrand art porcelain
were sold at Siegfried Bing's[27] celebrated Gallery L'Art Nouveau
Bing in Paris. From 1910 J. H. Vernon, Inc. in New York were
the general agents for the United States and Canada.

Robert Almström's sons Harald and Knut, who had trained at
the KTH (Royal Technical Institute), worked at Rörstrand,
becoming co-directors in 1909, which they remained until the
early 1920s. The architect Hugo Tryggelin (1846–1924), hired
as *chefdessinateur* [head designer] in 1873, remained active at
Rörstrand until 1909; under his supervision a team of foreman
had been trained on the job for specialising in the various divisions, including glazing, decorating and firing as well as manufacturing tiled stoves from start to finish. Hugo Tryggelin's
retirement and the concomitant handover to the next generation also led to fundamental changes in Rörstrand's own
weighting of the individual areas of production within the company; a revision that affected not only their utilitarian household wares but even more so the Rörstrand art ceramics (see
fig. 21, 22).

Since several years of searching for a suitable new location near
Stockholm had proved fruitless, Rörstrand bought the Göteborg Porcelain Manufactory in 1914 and after the 1918 merger,
out of which grew Rörstrand Factories, some areas of produc-

den von Hugo Tryggelin verbundene Generationswechsel führte auch zu einer grundlegenden Veränderung in der fabrikinternen Bewertung der einzelnen Produktionsbereiche, die sich nicht nur auf die Erzeugnisse für den täglichen Bedarf, sondern auch und vor allem auf die künstlerische Keramik auswirkte (siehe Abb. 21, 22).

Da die mehrjährige Suche nach einem passenden Ort für eine Neugründung in der Nähe von Stockholm ergebnislos geblieben war, kaufte man 1914 „Göteborgs Porzellanfabrik" und überführte im Anschluss an die 1918 erfolgte Konzernbildung zu „Rörstrands Fabriken" nach und nach Teile der Produktion in das Werk auf der Insel Hisingen in Göteborg. Göteborgs Porzellanfabrik hatte an den Ausstellungen in Stockholm 1909 und Malmö 1914 teilgenommen – in Malmö mit „Luxusartikeln", u. a. Vasen in „Fayence" mit Unterglasurbemalung von „ansprechenden Motiven" mit Adlern und Mohnblumen. Während des Ersten Weltkriegs litt die gesamte Wirtschaft, und auch in den Nachkriegsjahren setzte die Erholung nur zögernd ein. Die Anlagen in Stockholm wurden in dem bestehenden Zustand noch bis zum 200. Jahrestag weitergeführt. Im Oktober 1926 fand der letzte Brennvorgang statt; danach wurde der Betrieb eingestellt und Rörstrand in Göteborg etabliert.

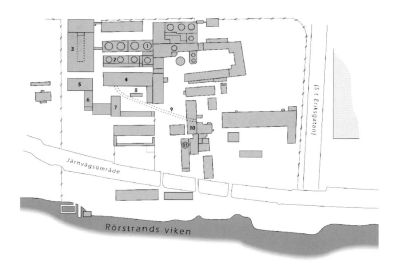

Abb. // Fig. 23
Rörstrands Fabrikgelände, Plan von 1897 // The Rörstrand factory premises, plan from 1897

Die Verwaltung zog 1890 in ein großes Bürogebäude im Anschluss an das Magazinhaus (Nr. 3) um. Ein neues hohes Werkstattgebäude überragte den Platz (Nr. 4). Ein unterirdischer Tunnel (Nr. 9) erleichterte die Transporte u.a. von Tonerden zum Werkstatthaus.
// In 1890 the administration moved into a large office building connected to the storehouse (No. 3). A high new workshop building towered over the square (No. 4). A subterranean passage (No. 9) facilitated the transport of clay, etc, to the workshop building.
Reconstruction, drawn by Bertil Anderberg in Rörstrand in Stockholm, 2007.

Die fabrikmäßig hergestellte Kunst-Keramik

Die Herstellung von Kunst-Keramik – Unikate, Serienproduktion in Porzellan und Steingut u. v. m. – in den beiden großen Fabriken am Rande von Stockholm in den 1890er Jahren und um die Jahrhundertwende vollzog sich im Wesentlichen nach gleichen Produktionslinien. Rörstrand und Gustavsberg hatten ihre Kenntnisse und Verfahrensweisen in erster Linie aus England bezogen. Die schwedischen Fabriken importierten auch den größten Teil der benötigten Rohstoffe von dort, besonders die wichtigste Zutat, das Kaolin[28] aus Cornwall. Die folgenden Angaben über die Produktion bei Rörstrand fußen auf einigen gedruckten Berichten von Robert Almström und Gunnar Ekerot und einer Dokumentation sowie Interviews und Fotos im Zusammenhang mit der Auflösung von 1926.

Das Fabrikgelände von Rörstrand lag am nordwestlichen Stadtrand von Stockholm im Anschluss an den Rörstrandssee und den Karlbergskanal. Bei der Anlage des ersten Rörstrandwerkes 1726 wurden Teile der Schlossanlage benutzt. Das Hauptgebäude blieb Wohnhaus, während die Flügelgebäude für die Produktion genutzt wurden. Nach und nach dehnte sich die Fabrik westlich des Schlosses zum Wasser hin aus. Die einschneidendsten Veränderungen geschahen in der zweiten Hälfte des 19. Jahrhunderts. Die Fabrik wurde modernisiert und zur großindustriellen Anlage, hauptsächlich für die Massenproduktion von Servicen und Haushaltswaren, Kachelöfen

tion were gradually transferred to the island of Hisingen in Göteborg. The Göteborg Porcelain Factory had successfully exhibited products at the 1909 trade fair in Stockholm and at Malmö in 1914 – at Malmö 'luxury articles', including vases in 'faience' decorated in underglaze painting featuring 'pleasing motifs' such as eagles and poppies. The Swedish economy as a whole suffered during the First World War, and even in the post-war years recovery was slow. The old Rörstrand facilities in Stockholm were maintained without further renovation until the manufactory's bicentenary. The kilns were fired up for the last time in Stockholm in October 1926; production then shut down and Rörstrand moved to Göteborg.

Factory-made art ceramics

The manufacture of art ceramics – one-offs, serially produced models in porcelain and lead-glazed earthenware, and so on – followed essentially the same production guidelines at both large factories on the outskirts of Stockholm in the 1890s and at the turn of the century. Rörstrand and Gustavsberg had drawn their knowledge of processes and techniques primarily from England. The Swedish manufactories also imported most of the raw materials needed from England, notably the most impor-

und technischem Porzellan. Gegen Ende des 19. Jahrhunderts war die Fabrik ein umfangreicher Industriekomplex rings um das ursprüngliche Schloss. 1889 gab es hier zehn Dampfmaschinen, gleichzeitig wurde die Elektrizität eingeführt. In den 1880er Jahren hatte man 12 Brennöfen gebaut, einige ältere Gebäude zu Werkstatträumen umgebaut und ein neues Kachellager errichtet. 1882 wurden Mahlwerk- und Schlämmereigebäude eingerichtet. Knapp 10 Jahre später, 1890, gab es an die 100 Drehscheiben, 15 Drehbänke, 265 Formscheiben, 18 Druckpressen und nicht weniger als 36 verschiedene Öfen. Ständig wurde gebaut, um die Anlagen der technischen Entwicklung und den neuen Bedürfnissen der Produktion anzupassen. In den 1890er Jahren errichtete man weitere Neubauten, darunter ein neues Bürogebäude. Dieses neue Verwaltungs- und Magazingebäude schloss auch Ausstellungsräume und Laboratorien, eine Bibliothek, die Porzellansammlung (das „Museum") und den Zeichensaal mit ein. Außerdem kamen noch weitere Brennöfen dazu; 1899 hatte die Fabrik 22 Öfen für Schrüh- und Glattbrand und 18 Muffelöfen.

Die technischen Vorgänge beschrieb Robert Almström in einem umfassenden Artikel „Tonware und ihre Herstellung" im „Buch der Erfindungen", VII, 1903[29], mit einer Darstellung der Geschichte der Keramik und sehr ausführlicher Beschreibung unterschiedlicher keramischer Massen[30], ihre Herstellung und Dekorierung. Der Artikel wurde 1904 in Buchform veröffentlicht und zeigt in imponierender Breite die umfassenden Kenntnisse des Autors. Robert Almström beschreibt zwar den Herstellungsprozess im Allgemeinen; man kann aber davon ausgehen, dass er auf der Produktion in seiner eigenen Fabrik durch die 1890er Jahre aufbaut, da mehrere Illustrationen die Herstellungsvorgänge bei Rörstrand zeigen. Im Übrigen stimmen seine Schilderungen auch mit dem mehr journalistischen Bericht in der Veröffentlichung „Schwedische Industriewerke und -anlagen" überein, der 1899 von deren Redakteur Gunnar Ekerot verfasst wurde.

Bei der Auflösung von Rörstrand in Stockholm 1926 erstellten das Technische Museum und das Nordische Museum eine Dokumentation, die sowohl Werkstattgebäude und Produktionstechnik als auch das Material einheitlich nach Form, Zweck, Fotos und Beschreibung im ersten eigentlichen Dokumentarfilm der schwedischen Museumswelt festhielt.

Die Rörstrand-Produktion in den 1890ern basierte zum großen Teil noch auf Handwerkstechnik, wenngleich Maschinen die schwereren Arbeitsvorgänge oder die stärker standardisierten Produktionsabschnitte wie die Herstellung der Massen ständig vereinfachten. Der Grund für den großen Anteil an Handarbeit liegt in den vielen handwerklichen Einzelschritten im Prozess der Herstellung und in der Aufteilung der Produktionsvorgänge in zahlreiche spezialisierte Schritte. Viele Beschäftigte, Männer, Frauen und Kinder, waren mit der Herstellung der verschiedenen Massen, dem Formen, Gießen, Drehen und Drechseln in unterschiedlichen Werkstätten, mit dem Model-

tant ingredient, kaolin, white china clay,[28] from Cornwall. The following data related to production at Rörstrand are based on a few printed reports written by Robert Almström and Gunnar Ekerot and the documentation in interviews and photos carried out just before the closing down of the old factory in 1926.

The Rörstrand factory premises were located on the northwestern fringes of Stockholm with access to Lake Rörstrand and the Karlberg Canal. When the first Rörstrand works were built in 1726, parts of it were housed in the castle. The main building continued to be used as housing while production went on in the wings. Gradually the factory spread westward from the castle to the water. The most radical changes took place in the latter half of the nineteenth century, when the factory was modernised and turned into an industrial facility on a large scale, primarily for mass producing table services and household wares, tiled stoves and technical ceramics. By the end of the nineteenth century, the factory was an extensive industrial complex surrounding the original castle. In 1889, when electricity was installed, there were ten steam-driven machines. In the 1880s twelve kilns for firing pottery had been constructed, some older buildings had been converted for use as workshops and a new storage facility for tiles had been built. In 1882 mills and a facility for preparing clay and slip were established. Just ten years later, in 1892, there were about a hundred potters' wheels, fifteen lathes, two hundred and sixty-five turntables, eighteen presses and no fewer than thirty-six different kilns. Building went on continuously to keep the facilities up to the latest technological standards and meet new production needs. In the 1890s more buildings were erected, including a new office building. It housed administrative offices and storage facilities as well as exhibition rooms and laboratories, a library, the porcelain collection (the 'Museum') and a draughting room. In addition, more kilns were installed; by 1899 the factory had set up twenty-two kilns for bisque and glost firing and eighteen muffle furnaces.

Robert Almström himself has described the technology in an extensive article on 'Lervarorna och deras tillverkning',[29] along with an outline of the history of ceramics and a very detailed description of the various pastes used in ceramics,[30] how they were made, and ceramic decoration. Published in book form in 1904, the article is an impressive testimonial to its author's broad-ranging knowledge. Robert Almström generalises on the production process but it is safe to assume that he was drawing on production at his own factory during the 1890s since several illustrations show work going on at Rörstrand. Incidentally, his descriptions also tally with the more journalistic approach chosen by Gunnar Ekerot, in his article 'Rörstrands Porslinsfabrik' in Svenska Industriella Verk och Anläggningar (Industrial works in Sweden, 1899).

With the closure of the Rörstrand facility in Stockholm in 1926, the Technical Museum and The Nordic Museum together maintained a documentation in interviews, descriptions, photos and

lieren, verschiedenen Malarbeiten, dem Musterdruck und anderen Dekorationsverfahren und schließlich mit dem Glasieren und dem Brennen in den verschiedenen Öfen beschäftigt. Nach und nach verbesserte man die Ausstattung und modernisierte die Produktionsabläufe; auch die Elektrifizierung führte zu besseren Arbeitsbedingungen als Voraussetzung für eine fortschrittlichere Produktion.

Bei Rörstrand dominierte die Herstellung von Haushalts- und Serviceware. Auch die Produktion von Kacheln und Kachelöfen nahm in der zweiten Hälfte des 19. Jahrhunderts kontinuierlich zu. Die Kunstkeramik hatte zu dieser Zeit im Rahmen der Gesamtproduktion nur den Rang einer exklusiven Spielerei, war aber nichtsdestoweniger auch in wirtschaftlicher Hinsicht von Bedeutung, da sie der Fabrik zu internationaler Beachtung und Anerkennung und damit auch zu besseren Absatzmöglichkeiten für ihr gesamtes Programm verhalf. Daher ist es verständlich, dass die Vertrautheit mit den Produktionsabläufen und eine umfassende Kenntnis der unterschiedlichen keramischen Massen, Techniken und Dekorarten auch für die jungen Künstler als unabdingbare Voraussetzungen galten, um neue Kunstwerke für Rörstrand zu schaffen.

Die *Herstellung von Kunstkeramik* umfasst, vereinfacht gesagt, die Schritte, die auch für die Fabrikproduktion insgesamt galten. Die jeweilige Masse in plastischer Konsistenz konnte durch Modellieren, Eindrehen[31], Gießen oder Pressen in Formen gestaltet werden. Flüssige Massen wurden für die Serienproduktion in Gussformen, üblicherweise aus Gips, ausgeformt. Die Bearbeitung von gedrehten Stücken vollzog sich gewöhnlich nach dem Abdrehen. Die halbtrockenen oder trockenen Gegenstände konnten durch Stempeln, Anguss, Modellierung, Bemalung, Ritztechnik, oder Schlickermalerei[32] verziert werden. Nach dem Trocknen erfolgte ein Schrühbrand bei ca. 800–1.000 °C; bei der Dekorierung der gebrannten Rohware wurden Bemalung, Spritz- oder Stempeldekor, Umdruck usw. eingesetzt; die abschließende Glasierung erfolgte durch Tauchen, Spritzen oder mit dem Pinsel. Der Glasurbrand von einfacher Irdenware vollzog sich gewöhnlich bei 950–1.000 °C, von Steinzeug bei 1.200–1.300 °C, von Porzellan bei 1.250–1.400 °C. Danach konnte ein weiterer Dekorvorgang erfolgen, z.B. durch Bemalen, Bespritzen, Stempeln, Druck usw. mit Email- oder Lüsterfarben[33] gefolgt von einem weiteren Brennvorgang bei 700–800 °C.

Keramik ist der Oberbegriff für Erzeugnisse aus einer Reihe nichtmetallischer anorganischer Stoffe, die im Brand gehärtet werden. Es gab eine Reihe von unterschiedlichen Zusammensetzungen, und in den Fabriken nutzte man verschiedenartige Massen für mehr oder minder hochqualifizierte Gebrauchs- und Kunstgegenstände.

Das *Material* für die Porzellanherstellung kam gewöhnlich per Schiff direkt in die Fabrik an der Rörstrandsbucht. Ein großer Teil des benötigten Rohmaterials, vor allem Kaolin, wurde aus England importiert; weitere Importe kamen aus Frankreich

a documentary film, which recorded the workshop building, production techniques as well as objects and the first ever dedicated documentary produced by Swedish museums.

In the 1890s production at Rörstrand was still largely based on craftsmanship although machinery facilitated difficult processes or more standardised production phases such as the making of pastes. The reason so much work was done by hand was that there were many individual steps in the manufacturing process that could only be dealt with in that way and each of the many phases of production was in turn highly specialised. A large workforce, men, women and children, were employed to make the moulds, cast pieces, throw other pieces on the wheel and turn some at lathes in various workshops as well as make models, do the kinds of painting and decorating needed and finally glaze and fire the pieces in the various kilns. Plant and machinery were gradually improved and production was rationalised; in addition, electrification ameliorated working conditions and enabled more advanced manufacturing.

Household wares and table services were the most important range of goods made at Rörstrand. During the latter half of the nineteenth century, the output of tiles and tiled stoves steadily increased. At that time art ceramics figured merely as a marginal line in luxury goods yet, economically speaking, was nonetheless important for that since it brought Rörstrand international recognition and acclaim, hence a broader market for the Rörstrand range as a whole. Understandably, therefore, familiarity with production stages and a broad knowledge of ceramic pastes, techniques and types of decoration were regarded as indispensable qualifications for artists, especially the younger generation, employed to create new art works for Rörstrand.

Making art ceramics entails, put simply, the same steps as any other factory production. The paste chosen had to be of a ductile consistency for being modelled, moulded,[31] slip-cast or pressed into moulds. Fluid pastes were used for casting, usually in plaster casts, in serial production. Pieces were thrown on the wheel and were usually worked over after they had been removed from the lathe. Objects that were nearly dry or leather hard might be decorated by stamping, coating with slip, modelling, painting, incising or trailing (*pastillage*).[32] After drying, pieces were subjected to biscuit firing at approx. 800 – 1,000 °C; fired unglazed pieces were painted, given splashed, stamped, or transfer-print decoration; glazes were applied by dipping, splashing or painting with a brush. Glost firing of simple earthenware usually took place at temperatures of 950 – 1,000 °C, fine stoneware at 1,200 – 1,300 °C and porcelain at 1,250 – 1,400 °C. It might be followed by a second process of decoration, applied, for instance, by painting, splashing, stamping, imprinting, etc., with enamel or lustre colours,[33] followed by a third firing at 700 – 800 °C.

Ceramics is the generic term for products made of a number of non-metallic inorganic materials which are hardened by firing. There were quite a few different paste compositions and

und Deutschland. Rörstrand hatte allerdings auch eigene bedeutende Feldspat- und Quarzgruben bei Ytterby an der Insel Resarö, nördlich von Stockholm.

Die Herstellung. *„Die moderne Bereitung von Porzellanmasse gleicht einem großen Brauhaus, wo alle Ingredienzen kontrolliert, ausgemessen und gemischt werden müssen, damit die ebenmäßigsten und unvergleichlichsten Produkte gewonnen werden können."*[34] Die Herstellung ging in mehreren Werkstattgebäuden in Rörstrand vor sich, das größte von ihnen war die so genannte Große Werkstatt. Einige technische Anordnungen unterstützten die Produktion und verbesserten die Arbeitsabläufe. Es gab große Trockenschränke mit besonderen Belüftungs- und Absauganlagen und große Entlüfter im Dach für ein gutes Raumklima. Zur Bindung von Tonstaub wurde regelmäßig Wasser über den Fußboden gespritzt. Diese Bedingungen konnten in der Zeit als ausreichend gelten, blieben aber von modernen Standards noch weit entfernt.

Im ersten Stock des Großen Werkstatthauses gab es Platz für die Dreher und Drechsler, die maschinelle Formung von größeren Stücken, z. B. Becken und Kannen, und den Guss von verschiedenen Teilen; hier entstanden auch Kunstobjekte. Im zweiten Geschoss war der Herstellung von Kaffeetassen, Untertassen und Tellern und im dritten Stockwerk die Fertigung von Knochenporzellan. Eine Sonderabteilung im obersten Stockwerk war die Gusswerkstatt für größere Stücke, meist „Luxusartikel" sowie Säulenpodeste und größere Vasen. Daneben gab es auch eine Werkstatt für die „Handmodellausformung" von größeren Stücken, wie Sanitärporzellan. Im Dachgeschoss war das große Lager für Gipsformen untergebracht. Die Herstellung des Steingutprogramms erfolgte in einem in der Nähe der See gelegenen Werk mit eigenen Werkstätten und Öfen.

Erden, Formen und Modelle. Wie schon erwähnt, wurden Ende des 19. Jahrhunderts viele unterschiedliche keramische Massen hergestellt. Für Tafelgeschirr benutzte man einfacheres Steingut, das unter der Handelsbezeichnung „gewöhnliche Fayence" oder „gewöhnliches Porzellan" angeboten wurde. Die Qualität des echten Porzellans fand sich nicht nur bei dem Feldspat- und dem Knochenporzellan, sondern auch bei den Erzeugnissen aus einer besonders aufbereiteten Feinsteingutmasse, mit der Bezeichnung „Ironstone". Die hervorragenden Eigenschaften dieser Massen waren vor allem den jeweils unterschiedlichen Mischungen von Feldspat, Quarz und Kaolin zu verdanken; dem Knochenporzellan wurde noch ein großer Prozentsatz von Knochenasche zugefügt. Anfangs waren diese Qualitäten nur für Ziergegenstände und kostbarere Sonderbestellungen von Tafelgeschirr vorgesehen.

Durch die weitere Bearbeitung erhielt die Masse eine von Luftblasen freie, leicht formbare oder fein fließende Konsistenz. Die Stücke wurden durch Drehen oder Ausformen in Gipsformen und durch Hinzufügen von plastischen Details nachbearbeitet. Die Drehscheiben wurden gewöhnlich mit Riemen und mit Dampfkraft betrieben. Mit der Einführung der Dampfkraft ent-

Abb. // Fig. 24
Dreher bei der Arbeit // A turner at work, ca 1900

at factories different pastes were used depending on the quality desired, utilitarian wares or objets d'art.

The *raw material* for making porcelain paste was usually shipped directly to the Rörstrand factory, which was situated on the waterfront. Much of the raw material needed, notably kaolin was imported from England; other imports came from France and Germany. Rörstrand did, however, have a major feldspar and quartz pit at Ytterby on the island of Resarö north of Stockholm.

Manufacture. '*Modern preparation of porcelain paste is reminiscent of what goes on at a large brewery, where all ingredients have to be inspected, measured and mixed to a consistent standard to ensure that the smoothest possible and most perfect products can be made.*'[34] Manufacture at Rörstrand took place in several workshop buildings, the largest of which was the so-called Great Workshop. Technical guidelines supported production and streamlined the process. There were large drying cupboards with special ventilation and exhaust abstraction systems as well as large ventilators in the roof to ensure air quality. Floors were regularly sprayed with water to lay clay dust. Working conditions were regarded as more than adequate in those days but were still far from modern standards.

The first floor of the Great Workshop building housed the operators of the potter's wheels and lathes, mechanical shaping of quite large pieces such as basins and jugs and the casting of parts; here objets d'art were also made. On the second floor coffee cups, saucers and plates were made and on the third floor bone china (true porcelain). A special division on the top floor housed the casting workshop for large pieces, usually 'luxury articles', as well as columnar pedestals and large vases. Next to it was a workshop for 'shaping models by hand' of larger pieces, including sanitary ceramics. A large storage facility for plaster moulds was housed in the loft. Lead-glazed earthenware was made in a facility with workshops and kilns of its own near the water.

wickelte man in den 1880er Jahren eine Anzahl Maschinen zur Herstellung von Tafelgeschirr, darunter solche zur Ausformung von Tassen und Tellern. Die (halb-)maschinelle Herstellung basierte auf der älteren Technik und vollzog sich in zwei Stufen. Das „Blatt", das aus Tonmasse von entsprechender Größe abgeschnitten oder mit Hilfe einer Blattzeichenmaschine ausgedrückt worden war, wurde auf einem rotierenden „Amboss" aus Gips befestigt. Anschließend erfolgte die Formung mit Hilfe einer Metallschablone, die mit Handkraft über den Tonklumpen gedrückt wurde. Es gab auch Maschinen für größere runde Gegenstände, wie Kannen, Krüge, Vasen usw. und Pressen für die Ausformung von Kacheln und Fliesen. Die Oberflächen der getrockneten Stücke wurden von Nähten und eventuellen Verunreinigungen befreit; dann kamen die Gegenstände in so genannte Kapseln und anschließend in den Schrühbrand.

Das „Modellbuch" oder „Vasenbuch" (ein Loseblattsystem) enthält Umrisszeichnungen der verschiedenen Grundmodelle für Ziervasen, die in diesen Jahren in der Produktion benutzt wurden (siehe Abb. 26). Wahrscheinlich begann man 1872 mit dem Anlegen solcher „Vasenbücher". Es gibt noch weitere Exemplare von kopierten, handgezeichneten „Vasenbüchern", die in der Fabrik vermutlich als Vorlagen genutzt wurden. Das Verzeichnis enthält mehrere 100 Modelle. Es wurde bis etwa 1920 fortgeführt. Die Mehrzahl der dort vorhandenen Formen ist in den mit Abbildungen versehenen Preislisten zu finden, oft mit unterschiedlichen Glasuren und Dekoren. Dort finden sich im Rahmen der „Standardproduktion" auch Hinweise auf die mehr

Earths, moulds and models. As mentioned above, many different ceramic pastes were being made by the close of the nineteenth century. Tableware was made of quite simple lead-glazed earthenware that was marketed as 'common faience' or 'common china'. The quality standard for obtaining genuine porcelain applied not only to feldspar porcelain and bone china but also to products made of a specially prepared stone-china paste known as 'ironstone'. The properties specific to those pastes were primarily due to the varying of the amounts of feldspar, quartz and kaolin in their composition; a larger percentage of bone ash was added to make bone china. Initially quality standards only applied to ornamental objects and expensive bespoke tableware.

Further processing gave paste a ductile or slightly fluid consistency free of air bubbles. Pieces were afterwards worked on the lathe or moulded in plaster moulds and sprigged details might be added. The potter's wheels were usually driven by belts and steam power. Along with steam power, a number of machines for making tableware, including some for moulding cups and plates, were introduced in the 1880s. (Semi-) mechanical manufacture was based on older techniques and was accomplished in two phases. A 'sheet' cut out of a ball of paste of a desired size or extruded from a press was fastened to a rotating 'anvil' of plaster. Then it was shaped with the aid of a metal template that was pressed over the lump of clay by hand. There were also machines for making quite large cylindrical objects such as jugs, tankards, vases, etc., and presses for shaping stove and

Abb. // Fig. 25
Eine der Gießerei-Werkstätten im Großen Werkstattgebäude, späte 1890er Jahre.
// One of the casting workshops in the large workshop building, late 1890s.
Photo: RM.

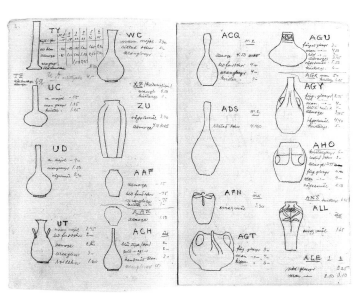

Abb. // Fig. 26
Rörstrand führte ein großes „Modellbuch", in dem alle Gießmodelle von den Werkmeistern verzeichnet wurden. Hier ein Buch von ca. 1890–1910; rechts unten einige Modelle von Alf Wallander aus den 1890er Jahren.
// Rörstrand kept a large 'models ledger', in which all models for casting were entered. Here a book dating from ca 1890–1910; bottom right, some models by Alf Wallander from the 1890s.
The Nordic Museum.

Abb. // Fig. 27
Trockenöfen // Drying kiln, 1890er Jahre // 1890s

Einsetzen der Kapseln in einen Ofen. Das Brenngut wird zum ersten Mal in einem Rohwarenofen in aufeinandergestapelten Kapseln gebrannt. Die Öfen waren bis zu 7 m hoch und hatten einen Durchmesser von ca. 6 m. Ein Brennvorgang konnte bis zu 55 Stunden dauern.
// Putting saggers into a kiln. Unfired pieces receive the first firing in a kiln in stacked saggers. The kilns were up to 7 m high and approx 6 m in diameter. Firing could take up to 55 hours.
Photo: Technical Museum.

Abb. // Fig. 28
Signe Andersson, Porzellanmalerin // porcelain painter
Photo: Private collection (ES).

skulptural geformten Modelle von der Hand Rörstrander Künstler dieser Jahre sowie Tiere und andere figürliche Arbeiten; mitunter sind auch Signaturen und Datierungen vorhanden.

Das Brennen. Vor der endgültigen Fertigstellung durchlief ein Stück für gewöhnlich zwei, mitunter aber auch drei bis vier Brennvorgänge. Zunächst erfolgte ein Schrühbrand in so genannten Kapseln, damit Schäden durch Feuer- oder Raucheinwirkung vermieden oder doch wenigstens vermindert wurden. Unterschiedliche Porzellanqualitäten schrühte man bei unterschiedlichen Temperaturen. Auch bei den verschiedenen Glasurmischungen musste in Abhängigkeit von den Farben, deren chemischer Zusammensetzung und der Zusammensetzung des Scherbens auf diese Temperaturunterschiede geachtet werden. Nach dem Schrühbrand durchliefen die Stücke die einzelnen Werkstätten zum Dekorieren und Glasieren; danach wurden sie ein zweites Mal gebrannt. Dieser so genannte Glattbrand erfolgte in denselben Öfen und auch hier wieder in Kapseln. Ein dritter Brennvorgang war notwendig für die als „Emailbemalung" bezeichnete Bemalung auf der Glasur. Email- und majolikabemalte Stücke wurden bei verschiedenen Temperaturen in so genannten Muffelöfen gebrannt. Gewisse Farben und Glasuren, u. a. das „Rouge flambé" und Metallfarben, erforderten einen besonderen Brand, die so genannte Scharffeuer-Reduktion, die eine spezielle Brandführung und sehr hohe Temperaturen erforderte.

Das Dekorieren. Bei Rörstrand gab es für die unterschiedlichen Dekorationsverfahren mehrere Malsäle und eine separate Druckwerkstatt. Für die Bemalung standen sechs größere Räume zur Verfügung. Hier waren etwa 200 Personen beschäftigt. Nach dem ersten Brand und vor dem Glasurbrand wurden die Farben direkt auf den geschrühten Scherben aufgebracht.

floor tiles. Once the pieces dried, the surfaces were 'repaired', freed of seams and other possible blemishes; then the pieces were put into what are called chambers for the biscuit firing. The 'model book' or 'vase book' (a loose-leaf system) contains outline drawings of the various basic models used for the ornamental vases that were in production during those years (see fig. 26). The vase books were probably begun in 1872. There are even more examples of copied vase books with drawings done by hand that were probably used as guidelines at the factory. Several hundred models are listed. The list was continued until about 1920. Most of the forms listed there recur in the price lists alongside pictures of the models, many of them with choices of glazes and decoration. There are also references within the 'standard range' to more sculpted, handmade models by the Rörstrand artists of those years as well as animals and other figurines; signatures and dates also occur on occasion.

Firing. Before it was finished, a piece underwent usually two, sometimes three or even four firings. First came a biscuit firing, with the pieces contained in what is called a chamber to avoid or at least lessen damage from fire or smoke. The temperature of the biscuit firing varied according to the quality of the porcelain paste. The temperature also had to be adjusted to suit the composition of the glazes, which depended on the colours desired, the chemical composition needed to produce them and the composition of the clay body of the pieces being fired. After the biscuit firing, the pieces were dispatched to specific workshops for decorating and the application of glazes; then they were fired a second time. Called the glost firing, this second firing took place in the same kiln and again chambers were used. A third firing was needed for the type of overglaze painting executed in what are known as 'enamel colours'. Pieces

Abb. // Fig. 29
Die Glasierer-Werkstatt war eine der gefährlichsten Arbeitsplätze in der Fabrik. Schon früh baute man Ventilatoren ein, aber viele Arbeiter starben an Bleivergiftung.
// The glazing workshop was one of the most dangerous places to work at the factory. Ventilators were built in at an early date but many workmen died of lead poisoning.
From *Arbetets söner* (Sons of Work), 1906.

Abb. // Fig. 30
Druckdekor. Muster wurden auf verschiedene Stücke aufgedruckt, rechts Drucker mit Druckwalzen.
// Printed decoration. Patterns were printed on various pieces; right: printers with printing rollers.
Photo 1896. Almström 1903.

Die leicht fließenden Schmelz- oder Emailfarben, die mit Öl oder Terpentin angerührt waren, wurden auf die bereits glasierten Stücke aufgetragen. Die Farben für die Rohware enthielten gewöhnlich die gleichen Metalloxide, die auch bei der Färbung der Masse und der Glasuren verwendet wurden, und waren mit einem Zusatz von Verdünnungs- und Flussmitteln versehen, z. B. fein gemahlener Porzellanmasse. Almström gibt ein Beispiel für die Verwendung mehrerer Farbzusammenstellungen. Üblich waren mit dem Pinsel gemalte oder aufgedruckte Dekore. In einzelnen Fällen fanden auch Schwämmchen oder Stempel aus Kork oder Holz Verwendung. Die malerischen Dekore wurden mit der freien Hand aufgetragen; bei standardisierten Vorlagen wurden die Konturen des Musters mit Schablonen übertragen, um eventuelle Details ergänzt und farbig ausgefüllt. Eine einheitliche Grundfarbe erreichte man durch das Eintauchen in ein Glasurbad. Wie Almström angab, hatte man in den letzten Jahren auch damit begonnen, die Fondgründe aufzusprühen, was sich u. a. an einigen von Astrid Ewerlöfs kleinen Kunstvasen beobachten lässt. Hinzu kamen verschiedene Spezialtechniken wie Vergoldung oder Versilberung und die Lüstrierung unter Verwendung unterschiedlich schimmernder Metallfarben.

Auch der Musterdruck war üblich, entweder von ganzen Mustersätzen oder aus verschiedenen Einzelteilen zusammen gesetzten Mustern. Diese Vorgehensweise war verbreitet bei Tafelgeschirr, kam aber auch bei künstlerischen Stücken vor, u. a. bei einigen der wallanderschen Serienprodukte und bei Stücken in Standardproduktion mit unterschiedlichen Lüsterdekoren, die durch Freihandmalerei ergänzt wurden. Es gab bei Rörstrand drei Abteilungen für den Unterglasurdruck auf Rohware und den Aufglasurdruck; dort waren etwa 100 Personen

painted in enamel colours and majolica painted with overglaze lead colours were fired in muffle chambers at varying temperatures. Certain colours and glazes, including *rouge flambé* and metallic colours had to be high fired, i.e. at very high temperatures, and in a reducing atmosphere, rich in carbon monoxide rather than oxygen.

Decorating. At Rörstrand there were several painting rooms for the various types of decoration as well as a separate workshop for transfer printing. Six quite large rooms were available for painting. A workforce of some 200 was employed for this purpose. After the first firing and before the glost firing, the colours were applied directly on to the biscuit body. The fluid glaze or enamel colours, which were mixed with oil or turpentine, were applied to pieces that were already glazed. The colours for the blanks usually contained the same metallic oxides that were used to colour the paste and the glazes and were mixed with thinners and fluxes, which might consist of finely ground porcelain paste. Almström gives an example of the use of several colour compositions.

Most decoration was either applied with brushes or transferprinted. In some cases small sponges or stamps of cork or wood were used. Painterly decoration was executed freehand; the contours of standardised patterns were transferred with stencils and details might be added and filled in with colour. A uniform ground colour was achieved by dipping a piece in a glazing bath. As Almström noted, in more recent years the practice of spraying on the ground colour was adopted, which can be seen, for instance, on some of Astrid Ewerlöf's small art vases. Then there were various specialist techniques such as gilding or silvering and creating metallic lustre through the use of various iridescent metallic colours.

Transfer printing was also commonly used, either with sets of entire patterns or patterns composed of separate parts. This process was widely used for tableware although it also occurred on art pieces, such as some of Wallander's serial products and others that were in standard production with various types of lustre decoration that were supplemented by freehand painting. At Rörstrand there were three divisions for underglaze transfer printing on undecorated ware as well as overglaze transfer printing; a workforce of about 100 was employed for transfer printing. Transfer printing entailed transferring decoration to thin paper from engraved copperplates made in a special engraving workshop. The paper with the printed decoration was firmly pressed on to the ware, which was then dipped in water, causing the paper to dissolve. After the piece dried, it was simply fired to remove remains of the paper, oil and varnish so that the piece could then be glazed and glost fired. That was a convenient way of quickly and simply decorating ornamental earthenware pieces.

Glazing. The 'recipe book' mentioned above that Almström began in 1893 describes mixing the various glazes, applying them, and methods of decorating and firing pieces (see fig. 31). New recipes continued to be added for several years. The notes contain most of the glazes used in the 1890s and the first decade of the twentieth century, including all experiments conducted at Rörstrand under the sway of the then pervasive Japonism and revived interest in Chinese art. The glazes discussed include *rouge chinois* for feldspar porcelain, various aventurine[35] and crystal glazes,[36] aventurine and *rouge flambé*

beschäftigt. Im Umdruckverfahren wurden die Dekore in einer Druckpresse von gravierten Kupferplatten, die in einer speziellen Gravurwerkstatt hergestellt worden waren, auf dünne Papiere übertragen. Nachdem diese auf der Wandung festgerieben worden waren, wurde das Stück in Wasser getaucht, so dass sich das Papier ablöste. Nach dem Trocknen erfolgte ein einfaches Brennen zur Entfernung der Papierreste, Öl und Firnis; danach konnte glasiert und glatt gebrannt werden. Auf diese Weise wurden viele Zierstücke in Steingut schnell mit einfachen Dekoren versehen.

Glasieren. Das vorher erwähnte „Rezeptbuch", das Almström ab 1893 begonnen hatte, beschreibt die verschiedenen Glasurmischungen, ihre Aufbringung auf den Stücken, verschiedene Dekormöglichkeiten und Brennverfahren (siehe Abb. 31). Mehrere Jahre lang waren neue Rezepte hinzugefügt worden. Hier sind die meisten der Glasuren aus den 1890ern und den ersten Jahrzehnten des 20. Jahrhunderts enthalten, z. B. alle Versuche unter japanischem und chinesischem Einfluss. Man findet z. B. Rouge chinois für Feldspatporzellan, verschiedene Aventurin-[35] und Kristall-Glasuren[36], Aventurin und Rouge flambé ineinander gemalt, unterschiedliche Metall- und Lüsterglasuren wie Kupfer- und Silberlüster sowie Uranglasuren[37], wie sie bei der neuen Kunstkeramik zur Anwendung gekommen waren. Hier finden sich auch Anweisungen für die Unterglasurbemalung, die Aufbringung unterschiedlicher Glasuren, Pfirsich- und Pflaumenfarbigkeit, die dunkelgrüne Schwalbenserie, die Indisch-Blau-Serie und eine neue blaugrüne Variante sowie für verschiedenfarbige Flussmittel, desgleichen eine Anleitung für Druckdekore. Das Ganze gibt einen interessanten Einblick in die systematische und „wissenschaftliche" Arbeitsweise bei der Entwicklung von neuen Dekoren und Glasuren.

Die Kunstkeramik. Im großen Werkstattgebäude von Rörstrand gab es eine Abteilung, die der Herstellung künstlerischer

Abb. // Fig. 33
Alf Wallander in seinem Atelier
bei Rörstrand // in his studio at
Rörstrand, ca 1900

Aus Wallanders Sammlung von
Zeitungsausschnitten // From
Wallander's press-cuttings book.
NMA.

Abb. // Fig. 34
Hilma Persson, Waldemar Lindström und // and Mela Anderberg (stehend
// standing) im Atelier bei Rörstrand // in a studio at Rörstrand.
Photo: Dated 21 November 1900.

Keramik vorbehalten war. Man arbeitete dort hauptsächlich in Feldspatporzellan, dessen besondere Porzellanqualität Rörstrand entwickelt hatte und mit dem man auf den großen Ausstellungen so erfolgreich gewesen war. Die Bemalung erfolgte mit Unter- und Aufglasurfarben. Kontinuierlich wurden künstlerische Objekte gefertigt, und immer gab es einen Absatzmarkt für exklusivere Ware. Mit besonderer Intensität entstanden die Objekte für die großen Ausstellungen, da dort die Präsentation künstlerischer Neuentwicklungen erwartet wurde – und das fast jedes Jahr. In den 1890ern überwogen bei Ausstellungen noch die traditionellen Modelle. Erst kurz vor der Jahrhundertwende erfolgte die Umstellung auf modernere Formen und Dekore. Auf der Ausstellung 1897 stand die neue Freihandmodellierung für die Presse und das Publikum im Mittelpunkt des Interesses.

Gunnar Ekerot gab 1898 einen aufschlussreichen Einblick in die Herstellung künstlerischer Keramik: „[...] *Sobald ein Gegenstand durch Drehen und Drechseln seine Grundform erhalten hat, wird er der Bearbeitung per Hand mittels Ausschaben und Auflagen aus gleicher Masse unterworfen. Dadurch wird das Stück mit Ornamenten, Blumen, Figuren u. ä. vollendet. Wenn es fertig modelliert und getrocknet ist, wird es bei niedriger Temperatur gebrannt, danach mit Metalloxydfarben – entweder Metallsalzlösungen oder Metalloxyden – versetzt mit passenden Flussmitteln, dekoriert. Danach wird es wieder einem Brand bei niedrigeren Temperaturen unterworfen, glasiert und wiederum bei 1.500–1.600 °C gebrannt. Das Stück kann nun als fertig gelten oder oberhalb der Glasur mit Metalloxydfarben bemalt und aufs Neue einem scharfen Brand bei über 1.500 °C ausgesetzt werden. Alle diese Operationen müssen mit äußerster Genauigkeit ausgeführt werden. In Sonderheit führen die erforderlichen hohen Temperaturen in vielerlei Hinsicht Risiken für das Misslingen mit sich. Besonders schwierig in der Herstellung sind die in den letz-*

combined and all sorts of metallic and lustre glazes, such as copper and silver lustre as well as uranium glazes[37] of the kind used on the new art ceramics. Here there are also instructions for underglaze painting, applying different types of glazes, producing the colours called peach and plum, painting the dark green swallow series, the East India-Blue series and a new blue-green variant as well as for making fluxes in different colours and instructions for transfer-printing decoration. Taken as a whole, the notes provide an interesting glimpse of the systematic and 'scientific' approach to developing new decoration schemes and glazes.

Art ceramics. A section of the large Rörstrand workshop building was reserved for the making of art ceramics. Work done there was mainly in feldspar porcelain, a type of porcelain developed at Rörstrand to a particularly high quality standard and very successful indeed at the large trade fairs. It featured both underglaze and overglaze painting. Objets d'art were always in production and there was invariably a market for more exclusive wares. Particular care was lavished on the objects made to be exhibited at the large trade fairs since new artistic developments were expected to be presented there – and this nearly every year. In the 1890s the traditional models still represented the bulk of exhibits at trade fairs. The switch to more modern forms and decoration schemes did not take place until just before the turn of the century. At the 1897 exhibition, the new freehand modelling was the focal point for the press and the public.

In 1898 Gunnar Ekerot provided some instructive insights into the making of art ceramics: '[...] *As soon as an object has been given its basic form through being thrown on the wheel and turned on the lathe, it is subjected to being handworked, scraped out and decorated with sprigging made from the same paste. Thus a piece is finished with decoration, flowers, figures, and so*

Abb. // Fig. 35, 36
Tierfiguren, gegossen und bemalt in modernen Unterglasurfarben, waren eine
von Rörstrands Spezialitäten. Der beste Tierplastiker war Waldemar Lindström;
von ihm stammen etwa 160 Arbeiten. Den abgebildeten „Seetaucher" entwarf
Alf Wallander. Die Produktion ging bis 1926.
// Animal figurines, cast and painted in modern underglaze colours, were a
Rörstrand speciality. The best animal modeller was Waldemar Lindström; about
160 works are known from his hand. The 'Loon' was made by Alf Wallander.
Animal figurines were in production until 1926.
Rörstrand Museum.

ten Jahren eingeführten neuen Fabrikate mit „Rouge flambé"
oder Kristallglasuren, deren Herstellung äußerste Sorgfalt bei
Dekoration und Brand erfordert".

In die Künstlerateliers für Kunstkeramik brachte man die Halb-
fabrikate, Kruken, Vasen u. a. als Ausgangsmaterial für die neue
Freihandmodellierung der Modelle von Alf Wallander, aber
auch der zahlreichen eigenen Modelle und plastischen Dekore,
die durch Algot Eriksson sowie Nils und Waldemar Lindström
gestaltet worden waren. Im Anschluss an eine Ausstellung in
Gävle im Oktober 1897 berichtete Alf Wallander darüber, wie
es war, als *das Kunstwerk geschaffen wurde*: „*Wallander machte
erst die Zeichnung für die Form, dann führte er diese aus, nahm
sie so feucht und weich, wie sie war, nebst einem Klumpen Porzellanmasse an sich. Er modellierte nun nach eigener Vorstellung
die gewünschten Figuren. Alles zusammen musste dann ordentlich trocknen, gebrannt und hinterher bemalt werden, dann noch-
mal gebrannt und glasiert werden. War nun alles gut gegangen,
so dass kein zusätzliches Bemalen oder Brennen vonnöten zu
sein schien, war das Kunstwerk fertig*".[38]

In diesen Ateliers entstanden auch die verschiedenen gegossenen Tierfiguren, vorwiegend nach Waldemar Lindströms
Modellen. Die Dekore variieren, von kräftigen Majolikafarben,
wie sie u.a. Wallander anfangs benutzt hatte, bis zu zart abgestuften Unter- und Aufglasurfarben und unterschiedlichen
Resultaten von Experimenten.

In einem Interview anlässlich seiner Pensionierung bei Rörstrand 1935 berichtete Waldemar Lindström darüber, wie viele
Tierfiguren hergestellt wurden. Er hatte insgesamt zwischen
300 und 400 Modelle entworfen; das größte war eine Eule in

*on. After it has been completely shaped and dried, it is fired at
a low temperature, then decorated with metallic oxide colours
– either solutions of metallic salts or metallic oxides – mixed
with the appropriate fluxes. It is subsequently subjected again
to firing at low temperatures, glazed and once again fired, at
1 500–1 600° [C]. Now the piece can be regarded as finished or
overglaze painting with metallic oxide colours can be applied
before the piece is exposed once again to high firing above
1 500°. All these operations must be executed with the utmost
precision. The necessary high firing temperatures in particular
were risky in several respects. The new wares with "rouge flambé"
or crystal glazes are especially difficult to make because they
require the utmost care with decoration and firing.'*

Half-finished tankards, vases, etc., were taken to the studios for
art ceramics to be worked freehand as the Alf Wallander models along with numerous other Rörstrand models and sprigged
decoration, which had been designed by Algot Eriksson as well
as Nils and Waldemar Lindström. After an exhibition in Gävle
in October 1897, Alf Wallander reported on how it was when
'*a work of art was created*': '*First Wallander did the drawing for
the mould, then he executed the mould, taking it, as moist and
soft as it was, along with a clump of porcelain paste. Then he
would model the figurines desired according to his own idea.
Everything then had to dry properly, be fired and subsequently
painted, then fired again and glazed. If everything had gone well,
so that no additional painting or firing seemed to be needed, the
objet d'art was finished.*'[38]

The various cast animal figurines were also created in those
studios, most of them from models by Waldemar Lindström.
Decoration schemes ranged from vibrant majolica colours of
the kind Wallander had initially used to subtly nuanced underglaze and overglaze colours and the varying results of experi-
mentation.

In an interview Waldemar Lindström gave on entering retirement from Rörstrand in 1935, he reported on how many animal
figurines were made. He had personally designed between
three hundred and four hundred models, of which the largest
was a life-sized owl. He described the phases of the process
from design to execution. First he designed a clay model; it
would then be divided into several parts. After that he would
make a plaster mould of each part. The porcelain paste was
poured into those moulds, the individual pieces reunited and
the whole piece worked over before it was subjected to the first
firing. '*Then comes painting – and that is by no means the easi-
est of processes. The various colours are sprayed on and then
outlined with goose-feather brushes. After that the figurine is
dipped in glaze and fired harder than before – then it's done.
The above mentioned owl, for instance, was so difficult to make
that we only succeeded in producing two nearly flawless examples [...] Even when figurines came from the same mould, they
were never completely identical. Repairing, retouching and especially painting were what made each piece different to the one*

natürlicher Größe. Er schilderte die Abläufe vom Entwurf bis zur Ausführung. Zuerst gestaltete er ein Tonmodell; dieses wurde anschließend in mehrere Teile zerlegt. Dann fertigte er für jedes Teil eine Gipsform. In diese Formen goss man dann die Porzellanmasse, setzte die Einzelteile zusammen und überarbeitete das ganze Stück, bevor es in den ersten Brennvorgang kam. *„Dann kommt die Bemalung – und das ist beileibe nicht die leichteste Prozedur. Die verschiedenen Farben werden aufgespritzt und dann mit Pinseln aus Gänsefedern nachgezeichnet. Anschließend wird die Figur in die Glasur getaucht und härter als vorher gebrannt – dann ist sie fertig. Die erwähnte Eule z. B. war so schwierig herzustellen, dass uns nur zwei fast fehlerfreie Exemplare geglückt sind [...] Auch wenn die Figuren aus derselben Form stammten, so glichen sie niemals einander. Nachbehandlung, Retusche und besonders die Bemalung bewirkten, dass jedes Stück anders als das vorige geriet“.* Die Fertigung der Tiermodelle endete, als die Fabrik ihre Produktion nach Göteborg überführte, wo man *„nicht ausreichend hart brennen konnte“.*[39]

DIE LINDSTRÖMS – WERKMEISTER UND KÜNSTLER IN DREI GENERATIONEN

Es gab Familien, deren Mitglieder mehrere Generationen lang bei Rörstrand gearbeitet haben. Die Lindströms gehörten dazu. Sie dienten als Porzellanarbeiter und Porzellanmaler, als Künstler, Vorarbeiter und Werkmeister, schließlich als Vertreter („Reisende“). Sie formten das, was man den „Rörstrand-Geist“ nennt, das Engagement aller für die Fabrik.

Erik Olsson, der sich später Lindström nannte (1808–1867) war als Landwirt und Pächter in Spånga und Täby nördlich von Stockholm tätig und zog 1848 mit seiner Familie nach Rörstrand. Zum Zeitpunkt des Einzuges hatte er sechs Kinder, vier Söhne und zwei Töchter. Später wurden zwei weitere Söhne geboren. Alle sollten bei Rörstrand Arbeit finden. Die ältesten Söhne, Erik (1837–1891), Gustaf (1840–1897), Petter (1842–1888) und Axel (1850–1917) wurden alle „Porzellanmacher“, Vorarbeiter und Werkmeister in der Fabrik. Der fünfte Sohn, Clæs Oscar (1855–1932) avancierte zum Vorarbeiter und Werkmeister bei Arabia. Erik, Gustaf und Axel engagierten sich ab 1871 im Lutherischen Missionsverband und halfen mit beim Aufbau eines eigenen Versammlungskreises bei Rörstrand. Anfangs erhielten sie Beistand des „Disponenten“ in dem Bemühen, an den Sonntagnachmittagen das Neue Schulhaus anzumieten, um dort Treffen veranstalten und Sonntagsschule halten zu können. Es ist unklar, ob Stråle oder Almström diese Unterstützung gewährten. Aber Almström zeigte bei mehreren Gelegenheiten patriarchalisches und wohlwollendes Interesse an der geistigen Entwicklung und Bildung der Arbeiter und an deren Krankheitsfürsorge, Rentenkasse usw. 1877 begann man damit, Laienpredigten abzuhalten, und die Schar der Gläubigen wuchs. 1882 wurde

before it.' Moving production to Göteborg put an end to the modelling of animal figurines, because there *'it was not possible to fire them hard enough.'*[39]

THE LINDSTRÖMS – THREE GENERATIONS OF FOREMEN AND ARTISTS

There were some families who worked at Rörstrand for several generations. The Lindströms were one of those families. They worked both as porcelain makers and porcelain painters, as artisans, assistant foremen and foremen and ultimately also as representatives ('travelling salesmen'). They shaped what is known as the 'Rörstrand spirit', universal employee commitment to the factory.

Erik Olsson, who later changed his name to Lindström (1808–1867), was a smallholder and tenant farmer in Spånga and Täby north of Stockholm. In 1848 he moved with his family to Rörstrand. At the time he moved he had six children, four sons and two daughters. Two more sons were born after the move. All of them would work at Rörstrand. His older sons, Erik (1837–1891), Gustaf (1840–1897), Petter (1842–1888) and Axel (1850–1917), were all 'porcelain makers', assistant foremen and foremen at the Rörstrand factory. The fifth son, Clæs Oscar (1855–1932), was promoted to assistant foreman and foreman at Arabia. Erik, Gustaf and Axel were committed members of the Lutheran Mission Society from 1871 and helped to build up a local congregation in Rörstrand. At first they were supported by the 'financial manager' in their efforts to rent the new schoolhouse on Sunday afternoons for holding meetings and Sunday school. It is not known whether Stråle or Almström supported this endeavour. Almström did, however, on several occasions demonstrate a benign patriarchal interest in the development and education of the workmen as well as health care, old-age pensions, etc. In 1877 lay preachers became active and the community of worshippers grew. Established in 1882 with sixteen members, the 'Rörstrand Circle' would exist for sixty-one years. In 1884 the small congregation purchased a piece of property in the street Karlbergsallee nearby the factory, where donations from richer members and credits made it possible to acquire a block of flats and an assembly building with two halls seating 350 and 500 in a wing facing a courtyard. In 1914 the congregation built the Emmaus church, also in Karlbergsallee. The brothers Erik, Gustaf and Axel succeeded one another as mayor. Peter is said to have been in poor health due to the insalubrious atmosphere in the factory. He died young, as did his brother Erik.

In the third generation, Karl Lindström (1865–1935), one of Erik's three children, became a porcelain painter and was one of the most outstanding turn-of-the-century artisans. Several of Gustaf's nine children became workmen and porcelain

Abb. // Fig. 37
Der Chef Axel Lindström mit Familie // Foreman Axel Lindström with his family,
ca 1885

Von links Lydia, beschäftigt im Büro, Ingrid, Ehefrau Maria und Werkmeister
Axel Lindström an der Kopfseite des Tisches, daneben der „Reisende" (Vertreter)
Ruben und der Künstler Waldemar Lindström.
// From the left: Lydia, office worker, Ingrid, Lindström's wife Maria, and foreman
Axel Lindström at the head of the table, next to him Ruben, the 'travelling
salesman' (representative) and the artist Waldemar Lindström.
Photo: Private collection.

der „Rörstrandskreis" aus 16 Mitgliedern gebildet, der 61
Jahre lang bestehen sollte. 1884 kaufte die kleine Gemeinde
ein Grundstück an der Karlbergsallee (in der Nähe der Fabrik), wo es mit Hilfe von Spenden reicherer Gemeindemitglie-
der und Krediten gelang, ein Mietshaus und ein Versamm-
lungshaus mit zwei Sälen für 350 bzw. 500 Besucher in einem
Flügel zum Hof hin zu errichten. 1914 baute die Gemeinde
die neue Emauskirche, auch diese an der Karlbergsallee. Die
Brüder Erik, Gustaf und Axel lösten einander als Gemeinde-
vorsteher ab. Petter soll kränklich gewesen sein, verursacht
durch das ungesunde Klima in der Fabrik. Er starb frühzeitig, wie auch sein Bruder Erik.

In der dritten Generation wurde Karl Lindström (1865–1935),
eines von Eriks drei Kindern, Porzellanmaler und einer der
hervorragendsten Künstler um die Jahrhundertwende. Mehrere von Gustafs neun Kindern wurden Fabrikarbeiter und
Porzellanmaler. Von Axels fünf Kindern wurde Waldemar
(1875–1941), auch er einer der besten Künstler, 1917 Werkmeister und 1926 Werkstattleiter in Göteborg. Der zweite
Sohn Ruben (1878–1942) verkaufte als Agent Rörstrands
Ware, und Lydia (1886–1983) arbeitete als Kassiererin im
Werk. Ein Verwandter, Albin Lindström, arbeitete und
wohnte im Rörstrandwerk.

Ein weiterer „Lindström", bei dem es sich nicht um einen
Verwandten handelt, bezeugt, wie fähige Porzellanarbeiter
zwischen den Fabriken hin- und herzogen: Bernhard Lind-
ström (geb. 1837) und seine Schwester, die Porzellanmalerin
Augusta Lindström, verheiratet mit dem Modelleur Frans
Oscar Hallin, wechselte 1869 in die Porzellanfabrik Aluminia

painters at the factory. Of Axel's five children, Waldemar
(1875–1941), also one of the best artists, became factory foreman in 1917 and head of the Göteborg workshop in 1926.
Axel's second son, Ruben (1878–1942), was an agent for marketing Rörstrand wares and Lydia (1886–1983) worked as the
factory paying teller. A relative, Albin Lindström, worked
and lived at the Rörstrand factory.

Another 'Lindström', who was not related, shows how capable porcelain workers tended to transfer from manufactory
to manufactory: Bernhard Lindström (b. 1837) and his sister,
Augusta Lindström, a porcelain painter married to the modeller Frans Oscar Hallin, transferred to the Aluminia porcelain factory in Copenhagen in 1869. Bernhard became 'head
modeller' at Aluminia. Frans August Hallin (1865–1947), son
of Oscar and Augusta, started collaborating very closely with
Arnold Krog in 1885 and had a share in developing the new
underglaze painting at the Royal Copenhagen Porcelain
Manufactory. He later transferred to Bing & Grøndahl, where
he rose to the position of production manager.

REMEMBRANCE OF AN OLD PORCELAIN PAINTER

*'Mother and Father were employed at the factory. Mother first
when she was a young girl, then as a married woman and, after
Father became ill, upstairs in the painting room. And so it went
without saying that I would start there, too. I left school at the
age of ten because I had to take care of my little brother when
both Mother and Father were at the factory. When I was twelve
years old, I was overjoyed at being allowed to work with my
mother upstairs in the painting room. We had neither courses
nor classes at a vocational school. All we had to do was to
watch closely and imitate what the others were doing. The
foreman in the room showed us beginners some things and we
did our best. When I recollect that time, it seems remarkable
what used to be expected of a child. We were supposed to
practise painting the patterns that were so popular then, five
narrow parallel bands with gold rims on the inside. It sometimes happened when our little fingers had managed four borders with infinite care that the fifth was irregular and then
everything had to be redone along with it.*

*The working day began at 8 o'clock in the morning and we
didn't stop working at the factory until 8 o'clock in the evening,
except for Saturday: then work stopped at 6 in the evening.
The lunch break was from 12 noon until 2 and there was a sort
of coffee break about 4 in the afternoon. That was exhausting
indeed for us little girls but there was nothing we could do
about it. We did everything to learn, everything to be able to
earn our first wages. It took us a long time to be good enough
to take home "grown-up" monthly wages of 3–4 Kroner. Child
labour was not properly appreciated. When I grew older and
was supposed to earn decent wages, the hourly wages were not*

nach Kopenhagen. Bernhard wurde „Obermodelleur" bei Aluminia. Oscars und Augustas Sohn Frans August Hallin (1865–1947) wurde 1885 zu einem der engsten Mitarbeiter von Arnold Krog und beteiligt an der neuen Unterglasurmalerei in der Königlichen Porzellanfabrik in Kopenhagen. Später wechselte er zu Bing & Grøndahl, wo er zum Produktionschef aufstieg.

DIE ALTE PORZELLANMALERIN ERZÄHLT.

„Vater und Mutter waren in der Fabrik angestellt. Mutter anfangs als junges Mädchen, dann als verheiratete Frau, als Vater krank geworden war, oben im Malsaal. Und dann wurde es so selbstverständlich, dass ich dort auch anfing. Die Schule beendete ich mit zehn Jahren, denn ich sollte ja auf meinen kleinen Bruder aufpassen, wenn beide, Vater und Mutter, in der Fabrik waren. Als ich zwölf war, war ich überglücklich, weil ich dann oben im Saal bei meiner Mutter arbeiten durfte. Wir hatten weder Kurse noch Unterricht in der Berufsschule. Es galt nur aufzunehmen und nachzumachen, was die anderen taten. Der Werkmeister im Saal zeigte uns Anfängern einiges, und wir taten unser Bestes. Wenn ich an die Zeit zurück denke, dann klingt das merkwürdig, wie viel man damals von einem Kind gefordert hat. Wir sollten uns üben mit dem Malen der damals so beliebten Muster, fünf schmalen parallelen blauen Rändern mit Goldrand nach innen. Wenn die kleinen Finger mit unendlicher Beschwernis vier Ränder zusammengebracht hatten, konnte es geschehen, dass die fünfte ungleichmäßig wurde, und dann musste alles zusammen noch einmal gemacht werden.
Der Tag begann um 8 Uhr morgens, und erst um 8 Uhr abends war Schluss mit der Arbeit in der Fabrik, nur am Sonnabend, da war schon um 6 Uhr Feierabend. Von 12 bis 2 war Mittagspause, und eine Art Kaffeepause gab es gegen 4 Uhr. Das war anstrengend genug für uns Winzlinge, aber wir kannten es ja nicht anders. Wir taten alles, um zu lernen, alles, um unseren ersten Lohn zu verdienen. Es dauerte lange, bis man es so gut konnte, dass man einen so ‚großen' Lohn von 3–4 Kronen im Monat bekam. Kinderarbeit wurde nicht hoch eingeschätzt. Als ich älter geworden war und ordentlich Lohn kriegen sollte, war der Stundenlohn nicht so groß. In dem Jahr der großen Ausstellung in Stockholm, hatte ich 25 Öre Stundenlohn [...] Wir hatten einen herrlichen Malsaal mit 24 Fenstern und Aussicht über den See. Es war eine gute Atmosphäre und die Stimmung im Allgemeinen war gut dort in den Malsälen. Aber ich habe mich immer darüber gewundert, dass unsere Augen das aushielten. Sogar zu Weihnachten hatten wir nur Petroleumlampen, eine für jeden von uns."
Interview mit Frau Vilhelmina Pettersson, in Nya Dagligt Allehanda
11/2 1927

all that good. The year of the big Stockholm exhibition I earned hourly wages of 25 Öre. [...] We had a wonderful painting hall with twenty-four windows and a view out over the lake. The work climate was good and the mood in general was cheerful in the painting rooms. But I was always amazed that our eyes could stand the strain. Even at Christmas we had only one paraffin lamp apiece, one for each of us."
Interview with Ms Vilhelmina Pettersson, in Nya Dagligt Allehanda
11 Feb. 1927

Die Kunst-Keramik
The Art Ceramics

Abb. // Fig. 38
Hugo Hörlin (1851–1894), künstlerischer
Berater u.a. in Rörstrand von // art consultant
for Rörstrand and other firms, 1888–1894.
Neue Illustrierte Zeitung 1894.

Rörstrand und die Künstler

Die künstlerischen Vorbilder für Rörstrand waren oft französische und englische Porzellanfabriken: Formen und Motive wurden häufig auf direktem Wege bei der Konkurrenz durch Studien auf verschiedenen Ausstellungen oder auch aus Musterbüchern übernommen. Bei Rörstrand gab es aber ausgebildete Former, Graveure und Maler, die in diesem Geist Kunstwerke schufen. Seit den 1870er Jahren wuchsen bei einer Reihe von bedeutenden Unternehmen auf dem Kontinent die künstlerischen Ambitionen. In Frankreich und England begannen die größeren Keramikwerke in wachsendem Maße künstlerische Kräfte für die Formgebung, speziell von „Luxus-" und Zierstücken, in Anspruch zu nehmen. Das spiegelte sich auch in den Kollektionen für die verschiedenen Industrieausstellungen wider. Rörstrand folgte hier der internationalen Entwicklung. Schon vor der Jahrhundertwende hatte man qualifizierte Maler für einzelne Spezialaufträge und zur Vorbereitung der großen Ausstellungen herangezogen. Dazu gehören der Dekorationsmaler und Bildhauer Henrik Nerpin in den 1860er und 1870er Jahren sowie in der Zeit vor der Ausstellung von 1897, der Dekorationsmaler Adolph Neumann 1878–1888 und der Porzellanmaler Josef Anton Vogel 1883 und noch einmal in den 1880ern und 1890er Jahren. Ab 1857 beschäftigte die Fabrik auch meh-

Rörstrand and the artists

Rörstrand tended to draw on French and English porcelain manufactories for ideas: forms and motifs were often directly copied from competitors, either through study at trade fairs or from their pattern books. At Rörstrand there were, however, trained repairers, engravers and painters who created art works in the inimitable Rörstrand manner. Since the 1870s the major continental porcelain factories had grown increasingly ambitious. In France and England the larger ceramics works had begun to hire artists to design their products, especially 'luxury' and ornamental pieces. That trend was also reflected in the collections launched at the various trade fairs. Rörstrand followed international developments in this respect.

Even before the turn of the century, qualified porcelain painters had been hired for special commissions and for preparing to show Rörstrand products at the large exhibitions. Among them in the 1860s and 1870s was Henrik Nerpin, a decoration painter and sculptor. In the era before the 1897 exhibition, the decoration painter Adolph Neumann was at Rörstrand from 1878 to 1888 and Josef Anton Vogel, a porcelain painter, was hired in 1883 and again in the 1880s and 1890s. From 1857 Rörstrand employed several architects, who submitted the design drawings for tiled stoves. Alfons Eugène Bourennery, a porcelain painter, is another noteworthy artist recorded as working for Rörstrand since 1870.

In 1872 the young architect Hugo Tryggelin (1846–1925) was hired. Passionately devoted to Rörstrand, he became *chefdessinateur* [head designer] and, in that position, was the first art consultant at the manufactory. Together with management, Tryggelin determined the course of pattern development in tableware and designed numerous splendid exhibitions objects as well as quite a number of tiled stoves, some trade-fair display cases and most of the new workshop buildings and employee housing on the factory premises. He shaped the Rörstrand aesthetic more than any other artist employed by the factory.

After the 1888 Copenhagen exhibition, Hugo Hörlin (1851–1894), another architect, was hired as an art consultant responsible for the development of art ceramics and tableware (see fig. 38). He, too, was an upper secondary school instructor at the Technical School and founded the Higher Industrial Art School (HKS) in 1879. He was also active in the Swedish Asso-

rere Architekten, die Entwurfszeichnungen für Kachelöfen lieferten. Eine besondere Erwähnung verdient auch der seit 1870 nachweisbare Porzellanmaler Alfons Eugène Bourennery.

1872 verpflichtete man den jungen Architekten Hugo Tryggelin (1846–1925). Er hing mit ganzer Seele an der Fabrik, wurde ihr „Chefdessinateur" und damit der erste künstlerische Ratgeber. Zusammen mit der Fabrikdirektion bestimmte er die Musterentwicklung im Tafelgeschirr, entwarf viele Prunkvasen und eine große Zahl von Kachelöfen, einige Ausstellungsvitrinen und Preisverzeichnisse und die Mehrzahl der neuen Werkstatt- und auch Wohngebäude. Mehr als jeder andere prägte er um die Jahrhundertwende das künstlerische Erscheinungsbild von Rörstrand.

Nach der Kopenhagener Ausstellung von 1888 wurde der Architekt Hugo Hörlin (1851–1894) als künstlerischer Berater für die Entwicklung von Kunstkeramik und Tafelgeschirr eingestellt (siehe Abb. 38). Auch er war Oberlehrer an der Technischen Schule und hatte 1879 die Höhere Kunstindustrieschule (HKS) begründet. Er war auch im Gewerbeverein tätig und entwarf u. a. dessen Abteilungen für die Ausstellungen in Kopenhagen 1888 und Chicago 1893; auch für die Rörstrandabteilung in Göteborg 1891 hatte er sich engagiert. Hörlin schuf mehrere Dekor- und Servicemuster sowie Modelle und Muster zur Ausführung in Majolika, die durch Glas- und Keramik-Arbeiten der italienisch-venezianischen Renaissance inspiriert waren. Er war es auch, der zusammen mit dem jungen und bei Rörstrand aufgewachsenen Algot Eriksson die Unterglasurbemalung nach dänischem Vorbild einführte.

Die Göteborger Ausstellung 1891 war noch von Majolika in zahlreichen Variationen beherrscht, doch konnte man bereits den Einfluss einiger neuer Künstler bemerken. In seiner Zeitschrift „Svensk Konstslöjd" (Schwedisches Kunstgewerbe) hob Hörlin mehrere von ihnen lobend hervor, und einige traten auf der Ausstellung in Chicago 1893 mit neuen Arbeiten in Erscheinung. Außer Algot Eriksson seien in diesem Zusammenhang Erik Hugo Tryggelin, der Modellmeister Axel Öberg, die Maler Anselm Pettersson und C.J. Johansson sowie die jugendlichen Karl Lindström und Mela Anderberg genannt. Die berühmte „maurische Fontäne", der Höhepunkt der Ausstellung in Göteborg, war von Hugo Tryggelin gezeichnet, von Axel Öberg modelliert und von Hugo Hörlin in Farbe gesetzt worden. Nach Hörlins Tod wurde der Maler Alf Wallander, Hörlins Schüler an der HKS, als sein Nachfolger eingestellt. Daneben wurden vor der Stockholmer Ausstellung 1897 noch eine Reihe anderer junger Keramiker verpflichtet.

In Rörstrand gab es um die Jahrhundertwende neben dem leitenden Künstler Alf Wallander eine beeindruckende Anzahl von schöpferisch tätigen Künstlern und Keramikern. Das gilt in gewissem Maße auch für den Konkurrenten Gustavsberg, wo Gunnar Wennerberg als künstlerischer Leiter wirkte. Alf Wallander und Gunnar Wennerberg fanden dabei Unterstützung durch die starken Persönlichkeiten an der Spitze der

Abb. // Fig. 39
Hugo Hörlin: Vasen-Experiment
// experimental vase, ca 1890
Private collection. Photo: Bengt Nyström.

ciation of Applied Arts and his designs for that body included sections for the 1888 Copenhagen exhibition and the 1893 Chicago World's Fair; he also demonstrated his commitment to Rörstrand by designing their exhibition section at the 1891 Göteborg trade fair. Hörlin created several patterns for decoration and tableware services as well as models and patterns to be executed in majolica, inspired by Italian and Venetian Renaissance glass and ceramics. Hörlin also collaborated with the young Algot Eriksson, who had grown up at Rörstrand, on introducing the Danish process for underglaze painting.

The predominant ware at the 1891 Göteborg exhibition was still majolica of various kinds yet the influence of a handful of young artists was already evident. In his journal, *Svensk Konstslöjd* [Swedish Applied Art], Hörlin singled out several of them for praise and some of them appeared at the 1893 Chicago World's Fair with new work. Apart from Algot Eriksson, other noteworthy artists who worked at Rörstrand then were Erik Hugo Tryggelin, Axel Öberg, a master modeller, Anselm Pettersson and C. J. Johansson, both of them painters, as well as the young Karl Lindström and Mela Anderberg. The drawing for the celebrated *Moorish Fountain*, the highlight of the Göteborg exhibition, was by Hugo Tryggelin, the model was by Axel Öberg and the piece was painted by Hugo Hörlin. After Hörlin died, Alf Wallander, a pupil of his at the HKS, was hired to replace him as a painter. In addition, several young ceramicists were hired before the 1897 Stockholm exhibition.

At the turn of the century, Rörstrand employed an impressive number of creative artists and ceramicists besides Alf Wallander, by then the leading artist at the factory. The same held to a certain extent for Gustavsberg, Rörstrand's chief competitor, where Gunnar Wennerberg was the leading artist. Alf Wallander and Gunnar Wennerberg were both supported by strong personalities at the head of their firms: Robert Almström and

Abb. // Fig. 40
Hugo Tryggelin, ca 1900
Svenskt Porträttgalleri vol. XX,
1901.

Unternehmen: Robert Almström und Wilhelm Odelberg standen selbst mitten in der Produktion und bestimmten deren Einrichtung und Ausrichtung. Bei Rörstrand war außerdem, wie erwähnt, Hugo Tryggelin in hervorgehobener Position für neue Servicemodelle und -dekore und die Formgebung von Kachelöfen zuständig. Den führenden Künstlern und den Unternehmensleitern stand eine große Anzahl von kompetenten „Porzellanmalern" und „Formern" zur Seite, die bei der Herstellung von Serviceporzellan und in der Arbeit mit der seriellen Kunstkeramik eine große Rolle spielten.

Hugo Tryggelin verblieb als „Chefdessinateur" bis 1909 (siehe Abb. 40). Mittlerweile mehr mit Aufgaben im Bauwesen betraut, gestaltete er als Architekt die neuen Werkstatt- und Wohngebäude der Anlage in Rörstrand. Schon vorher hatte sich ein Kreis von kompetenten Werkmeistern und Vorarbeitern gebildet, die für die verschiedenen Werkstattbereiche, die Dekoration, die Glasuren, die Brennerei und die Kachelofenherstellung verantwortlich waren. Der leitende Künstler Alf Wallander, den eine enge Freundschaft mit den Söhnen Almström verband, hatte die größte Bedeutung für das ästhetische Profil vom Ende der 1890er Jahre bis zu der Zeit um 1910. Er bestimmte auch die Art und Weise, in der sich Rörstrand auf den größeren Ausstellungen dieser Jahre präsentierte.

Die bedeutendsten Beispiele der Kunstkeramik dieser Zeit sind als „Objets d´art", von dem allgemeinen Angebot abgehobene künstlerische Einzelarbeiten, zu betrachten. Daneben gab es eine größere Zahl von populären Modellen, die gegossen und nachbearbeitet, mit einfacher Bemalung oder einfarbiger Glasur versehen und in größeren Serien produziert wurden. Alf Wallanders Vase mit zwei Nixen von 1896, die in vielen Glasurvariationen auftaucht und in den Preisverzeichnissen bis 1926 vorkommt, kann als Beispiel dafür dienen, ebenso eine große Zahl von Waldemar Lindströms kleinen Tierfiguren. Viele der serienmäßig hergestellten Kunstobjekte und auch ein ganzer Teil der Produktion von einfach plastisch dekorierten Stücken tragen den Charakter von „Standard Rörstrand".

In dieser Zeit, als die Beachtung von Urheberrechten im heutigen Sinn noch nicht durchgesetzt war, kam das Erscheinungs-

Wilhelm Odelberg were personally involved in production and were the ones to decide what was produced. As mentioned above, Hugo Tryggelin was in charge of the artistic profile, from designing new models for services and decoration as well as tiled stoves. The leading Rörstrand artists and management could draw on a large number of competent porcelain painters and repairers, who played an important role in the making of porcelain services and serially produced art ceramics.

Hugo Tryggelin remained at Rörstrand as *chefdessinateur* until 1909 (see fig. 40). By then more involved in building, he was the architect who designed the new workshop building and housing on the Rörstrand premises. Even earlier, a group of competent foremen and assistant foremen had been formed to oversee the various workshop areas, decoration, glazing, firing and the manufacture of tiled stoves. Alf Wallander, the head artist, who had forged close ties of friendship with Robert Almström's sons, was of the utmost importance for shaping the Rörstrand aesthetic from the late 1890s to about 1910. He also determined how Rörstrand was presented at the major trade fairs of those years.

The most important examples of art ceramics in those days should be viewed as objets d'art, artistic one-offs that stood out in the general product range. There were also quite a number of popular models that, cast and worked over, simply painted and given a coat of monochrome glaze, were serially produced in rather large quantities. Their work is exemplified by the 1896 Alf Wallander vase featuring two mermaids which occurs in many glaze variations and is in the Rörstrand price lists until 1926, and numerous small Waldemar Lindström animal figurines. Many of the serially produced objets d'art and also much of the output of simple pieces decorated with sprigging are representative of the 'standard Rörstrand' look.

At that time, when copyright legislation in the modern sense was not yet in force, the appearance of numerous art objects might resemble original Japanese and Chinese pieces, French fine stoneware or products by numerous continental and other European competitors very loosely indeed. The Swedish factories had no qualms about seeking inspiration from Sèvres, Berlin, Nymphenburg, Copenhagen or Staffordshire. Foreign ideas and forms were borrowed, glazes imitated and decoration emulated.

Vessel and sculpture

In the years just before and after the turn of the century, art ceramics became discernibly more sculptural in design and a growing interest in the use of new materials and effects was evident; consequently transitions, combinations and eclectic forms were very much evident on a sliding scale ranging from vases and dishes with sprigged decoration to ceramic sculpture in the true meaning of the word. Sculptural objects were

bild einer großen Zahl künstlerischer Objekte den Originalen aus der japanischen und chinesischen Keramik, der französischen Steinzeugkunst oder den vielen konkurrierenden zeitgenössischen keramischen Fabriken des Kontinents sehr nahe. Die schwedischen Fabriken ließen sich gern von Sèvres, Berlin, Nymphenburg, Kopenhagen oder Staffordshire inspirieren. Man orientierte sich an fremden Ideen, entlehnte Formen, imitierte Glasuren und ließ sich von Dekoren anregen.

Gefäß und Skulptur

In den Jahren um die Jahrhundertwende lässt sich auch in der künstlerischen Keramik eine stärkere Hinwendung zur plastischen Gestaltung und ein wachsendes Interesse an dem Einsatz neuer Materialien und Effekte feststellen, so dass es zu Über-

painted, glazed and fired like vessel forms. In this connection, the most interesting objets d'art are the works Alf Wallander produced in 1895/96, which are undoubtedly sculptural ceramics noticeably inspired by Paul Gauguin and Thorwald Bindesbøll. Several pieces of his exemplify such eclectic forms, including the large dragon vases, the piece known as the Owl Dish and other works with emphatically sculptural decoration. The large Peacock Vase, made by Anna Boberg a year later also belongs to this context.

Figurines and animal figurines were also moulded at both Rörstrand and Gustavsberg in porcelain of quite fine quality. Wallander, who also worked in this field, made a name for himself with several small sculptures, such as Naiads in the waves and animal figurines. Rörstrand already had a large range of china animals when Waldemar Lindström authorised another one hundred and sixty animal figurines for serial production,

Abb. // Fig. 42, 43
Aufnahmen von Vasen und Tieren // Photos of vases and animal figurines, ca 1900/1910

Diese Fotos sind in mehreren Serien mit mehreren hundert abgebildeten Objekten erhalten geblieben, häufig mit Preisangaben versehen. Die Fotos wurden vermutlich bei Vertreter-Besuchen verwendet.
// Several series of these photos depicting hundreds of vases have survived, often with prices noted. The photos were presumably used when representatives visited wholesalers and retailers.

gängen, Kombinationen und Mischformen auf Vasen und Schalen mit plastischem Dekor bis zu keramischen Skulpturen im eigentlichen Sinne kam. Die plastischen Objekte wurden wie die Gefäßformen bemalt, glasiert und gebrannt. Am interessantesten ist in diesem Zusammenhang Alf Wallanders Produktion der Jahre 1895/96, mit der er zweifellos eine Skulpturkeramik entwickelte, die Anregungen von Paul Gauguin und Thorwald Bindesbøll aufnahm. Es gibt mehrere Beispiele für diese Mischformen, darunter die großen Drachenvasen, die so genannte Eulenschale und andere Stücke mit stark plastischem Dekor. In diesen Zusammenhang gehört auch die große Pfauenvase, die Anna Boberg im darauf folgenden Jahr zeigte.

Auch Figurinen und Tierfiguren wurden bei Rörstrand und auch bei Gustavsberg in feinerer Porzellanqualität ausgeformt. Wallander, der auch auf diesem Gebiet tätig war, wurde für mehrere kleine Skulpturen mit Najaden in Meereswogen und mehrere Tierplastiken berühmt. Rörstrand hatte bereits ein großes Angebot an Porzellan-Tieren, als Waldemar Lindström weitere 160 Tierfiguren für Serienproduktion freigab, so dass jetzt ein rund 300 verschiedene Modelle umfassender Bestand vorhanden war. Im Rörstrand „Modellbuch" sind zirka 200 Tierfiguren verzeichnet – darunter auch einige von Alf Wallander, Karl Lindström und Nils Lundström. Später präsentierte Vicken von Post ihre eleganten kleinen Figurengruppen und Vögel in Porzellan mit zarten, nahezu süßlichen Unterglasurfarben, zeitgleich zu den ihrer Auffassung nach ähnlichen Arbeiten des aus Schweden gebürtigen Gerhard Henning[40] für die Königliche Porzellanfabrik in Kopenhagen. Im Rörstrand „Modellbuch" sind über 30 solcher Figuren verzeichnet.

Das „Rörstrand-Porzellan"

Die Kunstkeramik war zwar in wirtschaftlicher Hinsicht zunächst noch ohne größere Bedeutung, bildete aber bereits seit der Mitte des 19. Jahrhunderts einen festen Bestandteil der Produktion. Mit der Annäherung an die Jahrhundertwende gab es einen Markt für mehr exklusive Stücke, die insbesondere auf Ausstellungen präsentiert wurden, wo man in höherem Maße die anspruchsvollere Ware absetzen konnte. Die Stücke wurden zwar großenteils noch nach den traditionellen Vorlagen der 1890er Jahre gefertigt, fanden aber trotzdem den Zuspruch des Publikums. Erst in der Zeit um 1900 richtete sich die Aufmerksamkeit stärker auf die neuen stilistischen Tendenzen.

Das Erscheinungsbild des Rörstrand-Porzellans dieser Jahre, das auf den internationalen Präsentationen und insbesondere auf der Pariser Weltausstellung von 1900 eine große Beachtung fand, wurde durch das Feldspatporzellan mit seinen weichen Vasenformen und den entsprechenden plastischen Dekoren

which meant that some three hundred different models were now in stock. The Rörstrand 'model catalogue' lists approx. two hundred animal figurines – including some by Alf Wallander, Karl Lindström and Nils Lundström. Later Vicken von Post launched the elegant little groups of figures and birds in porcelain painted in delicate, albeit rather cloying, underglaze colours at the same time as what she believed were similar works by Gerhard Henning,[40] a Swedish national who worked for the Royal Porcelain Manufactory in Copenhagen. The Rörstrand model catalogue lists more than thirty figurines of this kind.

Rörstrand porcelain

At first insignificant as an economic factor, a line in art ceramics was firmly established at Rörstrand by the mid-nineteenth century. As the century came to a close, however, a market developed for more exclusive pieces, which were displayed at trade fairs especially where it was possible to sell more upmarket wares. Most of those pieces were still made from the traditional 1890's models yet nonetheless they appealed to the public. It was not until about 1900 that more attention was directed at the emergent stylistic trends.

During those years, the look of Rörstrand porcelain, which met with considerable acclaim at international launches, notably the 1900 Paris Exposition, was made possible by feldspathic paste, which could be shaped into softly fluid vase forms with sprigged decoration to match: motifs drawn from the terrestrial flora and fauna of Sweden, landscapes and underwater scenes with aquatic marine life, painted in mild, pure underglaze colours that were close to nature. Alf Wallander's contribution was crucial but other artists at Rörstrand also produced their share of ideas. A standard Rörstrand range, so to speak, was developed for serial production. It also included numerous works with motifs on vases taken from panel paintings and showy bowls as well as a series of experiments in glazes ranging from copper lustre and ox-blood to a wide variety of crystallising glazes. Another Rörstrand speciality, known as Rörstrand Black or Rörstrand Noir, is well worth mentioning here: vases that are black all over and boast vivid floral motifs in underglaze painting. The recipe book that has come down to us contains a great many glaze combinations as well as several firing processes and other technical details. In addition, there are also data on executing the standard models in lead-glazed earthenware and with simpler glazes.

As has already been mentioned, the large studio building housed a separate division for the making of art products. Leather hard but not yet fired vessels were brought there for finishing with the new freehand-modelled sprigging by Alf Wallander, Algot Eriksson, Nils Lundström and Waldemar Lindström and other, less well-known, Rörstrand employees. Decoration, and not just sprigging but also colour schemes,

bestimmt: Motive aus der Flora und Fauna Schwedens, Landschaften und Meeresszenen mit Tang und Wassertieren, gemalt in milden, reinen und naturnahen Unterglasurfarben. Alf Wallanders Beitrag war entscheidend, aber auch andere Künstler bei Rörstrand brachten eigene Ideen ein. In der Serienproduktion wurde eine Art „Standard-Rörstrand" geschaffen. Hierzu gehören auch die vielen Arbeiten mit Motiven aus der Tafelmalerei auf Vasen und Prunkschalen und eine Reihe von Glasur-Experimenten, von Kupferlüster und Ochsenblut bis zu den vielfältigen Varianten von kristallisierenden Glasuren. Eine besondere Erwähnung verdient auch eine Spezialität, die die Bezeichnung „Rörstrand-Schwarz" oder „Rörstrand Noir" erhalten hatte: ganz schwarze Vasen mit verschiedenen kraftvollen Blumenmotiven in Unterglasurbemalung. In dem erhaltenen „Rezeptbuch" gibt es eine sehr große Zahl von Glasurkombinationen, ebenso unterschiedliche Brennverfahren und andere technische Details. Daneben findet man auch Angaben zu den Ausführungen der Standardmodelle in Steingut und mit einfacheren Glasuren.

Wie schon erwähnt, gab es in dem großen Atelierhaus eine gesonderte Abteilung für die Herstellung der Kunstobjekte. Dorthin verbrachte man die getrockneten, aber noch ungebrannten Gefäßformen als Rohmaterial für die neue Freihand-Modellierung der plastischen Dekore von Alf Wallander, Algot Eriksson, Nils Lundström und Waldemar Lindström sowie einigen Mitarbeitern mit weniger bekannten Namen. Die Dekore konnten nicht nur in der Modellierung, sondern auch in der Farbgebung erheblich voneinander abweichen, von kräftigen Majolikafarben, die Wallander für seine ersten Keramiken verwendet hatte, bis zu einer zart abgestuften Unterglasurbemalung, lebhafterer Aufglasurmalerei und verschiedenen Experimentalglasuren.

Rörstrand hatte eine imponierende Schar von Künstlern und Keramikern unterschiedlicher Bedeutung. Zu den hervorragenden Vertreterinnen und Vertretern gehörten neben den bereits Genannten Astrid Ewerlöf, Anna Boberg und Pamela Anderberg, aber auch Hugo Tryggelin, Georg Asplund, Ruben Rising und für kürzere Zeit Helene Holck, Hilma Persson und Hjördis Nordin. Auch Harald und Knut Almström waren einige Jahre künstlerisch tätig, und Einzelstücke wurden nach Vorlagen von Ferdinand Boberg[41] und Prinz Eugén[42] ausgeführt. Dazu kam die große Anzahl der in der Fabrik beschäftigten qualifizierten Former, Porzellanmaler und Dekorateure. Gelegentlich traten auch begabte Porzellanmalerinnen, die mit besonderer Lohnzulage in den Lohnlisten aufgeführt sind, mit signierten Einzelarbeiten hervor; zu nennen sind hier Emma Lindberg, Jane Lindberg, Mathilda Gravenstein sowie Maria und Anna Pettersson.

could vary widely; painting could range from the vibrant majolica colours Wallander had used for his first pieces to subtly nuanced underglazed painting, more lively overglaze painting and any number of experimental glazes.

Rörstrand employed an impressive workforce of artists and ceramicists of varying stature. The outstanding artists included the above mentioned Astrid Ewerlöf, Anna Boberg and Pamela Anderberg and Hugo Tryggelin, Georg Asplund and Ruben Rising, as well as, over the shorter term, Helene Holck, Hilma Persson and Hjördis Nordin. Harald and Knut Almström also worked for Rörstrand for some years in an artistic capacity and one-off pieces were made from prototypes by Ferdinand Boberg[41] and Prince Eugén.[42] Rörstrand also employed a large number of qualified repairers, porcelain painters and decorators. Talented women porcelain painters who are also listed in the payrolls as receiving extra pay occasionally distinguished themselves with signed one-off pieces; the names to be reckoned with here were Emma Lindberg, Jane Lindberg and Mathilda Gravenstein as well as Maria Peterson and Anna Pettersson.

Faience and earthenware for a broad market

Rörstrand also produced an extensive range of ornamental earthenware vases decorated with transfer printing or monochrome glazes; they often bore the stamp 'Dessin Alf Wallander', to emphasise their claim to art status by naming the designer. It was an attempt at creating more inexpensive objets d'art in the modern style – that the general public could afford, hence entirely in Ellen Key's spirit (see fig. 6, p. 29). Some of those models were also shown in 1899 at the first one of what were known as her programme exhibitions in April 1899.

Even by the first half of the 1890s, there were several Rörstrand vase forms in earthenware, simple yet modern pieces probably designed by Hugo Hörlin. The earlier pieces sported conventional majolica glaze but the later ones were taken into the standard range with lustre and other glazes and this was, incidentally, also the practice at Arabia.

Wallander notably provided a series of one-off vase forms in earthenware featuring astringently executed floral motifs with bold outlines as his contribution to the manufacture of generally affordable art products. His first pieces in this line surfaced as early as 1897; later models were decorated with different glazes (see fig. 44).

Although Wallander concentrated on working with porcelain, he continued to be involved in designing more affordable vases in earthenware. Among them are, interestingly enough, pieces that were presumably inspired by the Austrian decorative arts and the new ceramics from Bing & Grøndahl, with crisply stylised floral decoration arranged in bands or medallions encir-

Fayencen und Steingut für jedermann

Rörstrand betrieb ebenfalls eine umfangreiche Serienproduktion von Steingut-Ziervasen, die mit Umdruckdekor, einfacher Bemalung oder einfarbigen Glasuren versehen waren; sie trugen oft den Stempel „Dessin Alf Wallander", um durch die Nennung des Entwerfers ihren künstlerischen Anspruch hervorzuheben. Es war ein Versuch zur Schaffung von billigeren Kunstwerken im modernen Stil – auch für die Allgemeinheit erschwinglich und damit ganz im Geiste von Ellen Key (siehe Abb. 6, Seite 29). Einige dieser Modelle wurden auch im April 1899 in ihren so genannten Programmausstellungen gezeigt.

Schon in der ersten Hälfte der 1890er Jahre gab es mehrere einfache, aber moderne gegossene Vasenformen in Steingut, die wahrscheinlich von Hugo Hörlin entworfen wurden. Sie hatten zunächst eine Majolikaglasur in herkömmlicher Art, wurden aber später mit Lüster- und anderen Glasuren in die Standardproduktion übernommen, übrigens auch von Arabia.

Vor allem Wallander lieferte eine Serie von einzelnen Vasenformen in Steingut mit straffen, umrissbetonten Blumenmotiven als seinen Beitrag zur Herstellung von allgemein erschwinglichen Kunstprodukten. Die ersten Exemplare tauchten schon 1897 auf, später wurden die Modelle mit unterschiedlichen Glasuren versehen (siehe Abb. 44).

Im Zentrum seiner Tätigkeit standen Porzellanarbeiten, doch befasste sich Wallander auch später noch mit Entwürfen für

cling vessel walls, an unequivocal rejection of the floral decorativeness of the Jugendstil/Art Nouveau style. In 1906/07 Wallander added a new series of ornamental vases notable for clear, shimmering nuances of underglaze yellows, blues, greens and reds. Motifs such as flowers, fruits, fish, birds, grapes, ornamental tendrils and osier decoration now appeared as decoration on this line in earthenware (see fig. 45).

The artists and their ceramics

Alf Wallander. For nearly twenty years beginning in 1895, Alf Wallander (1862–1940) was the leading Rörstrand artist. During his tenure, Wallander shaped the look of art ceramics at Rörstrand. His career began more or less by chance. In autumn 1894 he had modelled some pieces in clay and had Rörstrand fire them. In late summer 1895 he unexpectedly received an offer from Robert Almström to design a series of objets d'art for Rörstrand in preparation for the 1897 Stockholm exhibition. The sudden death of Hugo Hörlin in the summer of the previous year had left Rörstrand without an artistically qualified head designer. So Wallander began working as an artist for Rörstrand in autumn 1895.

At that time about thirty years old, Alf Wallander was still young but already an artist with a well-earned reputation, largely due to his pastel paintings informed by a strong social commitment (see fig. 46). He was also well trained from the industrial art standpoint. By 1882 he had graduated from the

Abb. // Fig. 44
Deckelurne und Vase, signiert // Covered urn and vase, signed 'DESSIN ALF WALLANDER', ca 1900

Steingut mit gedrucktem oder gemaltem Dekor. Mit dieser Serie, ab Ende des 19. Jhd., versuchte das Unternehmen billige Zierstücke in moderner Formgebung – ganz im Geiste Ellen Keys – herzustellen; die Produktion lief bis 1926.
// Lead-glazed earthenware with printed or painted decoration. With this series, starting in the late nineteenth century, Rörstrand tried to make inexpensive ornamental pieces in modern shapes – entirely in the spirit of Ellen Key; they were in production until 1926.
Private collection.

Abb. // Fig. 45
Alf Wallander: Steingut-Vase in kräftigen Majolikafarben // lead-glazed earthenware vase in vibrant majolica colours

Er entwarf in diesem Stil eine große Vasenserie, oft in klarem Gelb, Blau und Grün auf weißem Grund; ab 1907 in Serienproduktion. Häufig bezeichnet mit „DESSIN WALLANDER".
// He designed a large series of vases in this style, often in clear yellows, blues and greens on a white ground; produced serially from 1907. Often marked 'DESSIN WALLANDER'.

Abb. // Fig. 46
Oscar Björck: Porträt von Alf Wallander // Portrait of
Alf Wallander, 1893

Wallander, ein dynamischer und kreativer Künstler,
war einer der führenden Gestalten im neuen
schwedischen Kunsthandwerk.
// Wallander, a dynamic and creative artist, was one of
the leading figures in the new Swedish applied arts.

preiswertere Vasen in Steingut. Darunter befinden sich inter-
essanterweise auch einige Modelle, die mit ihren vermutlich
unter dem Einfluss des österreichischen Kunsthandwerks und
der neuen Keramik von Bing & Grøndahl entstandenen straff
stilisierten, als Band oder Medaillons rund um die Gefäßwan-
dungen angebrachten Blumenornamenten eine deutliche
Abkehr von dem floral-ornamentalen Jugendstil erkennen lassen. 1906/07 kam eine neue Folge von Ziervasen mit klaren,
schimmernden Nuancen von Gelb, Blau, Grün und Rot in
Unterglasurmalerei hinzu. Auf diesem Steingut-Programm
tauchten jetzt auch Blumen, Früchte, Fische, Vögel, Weintrauben, ornamentale Ranken und Korbgeflechte als Dekorations-
motive auf (siehe Abb. 45).

Die Künstler und ihre Keramik

Alf Wallander. Fast 20 Jahre lang, ab 1895, war Alf Wallander
(1862–1940) Rörstrands führender Künstler. In diesem Zeitraum drückte er der Kunstkeramik bei Rörstrand seinen Stempel auf. Seine Karriere begann mehr oder weniger zufällig. Im
Herbst 1894 modellierte er einige Stücke aus Ton und ließ sie
bei Rörstrand brennen. Im Spätsommer 1895 erhielt er dann
unvermittelt das Angebot von Robert Almström, eine Serie von
Kunstwerken für die Fabrik in Vorbereitung der Stockholmer
Ausstellung von 1897 zu entwerfen. Die Fabrik war nach Hugo
Hörlins plötzlichem Tod im Sommer des Vorjahres ohne eine
künstlerisch qualifizierte Führungspersönlichkeit. Im Herbst
1895 begann Wallander seine künstlerische Arbeit für Rörstrand.
Der gut 30jährige Alf Wallander war in dieser Zeit ein zwar noch
junger, aber schon bekannter Künstler, vor allem dank seiner
von einem starken sozialen Engagement geprägten Pastellma-
lerei (siehe Abb. 46). Auch unter kunstindustriellem Aspekt war

HKS at the Technical School in Stockholm (one of his teachers
there had been Hugo Hörlin) where he had also worked in
ceramics. He then finished his formal education at the Royal
Art Institute. After studies in Paris in the late 1880s, he returned
in autumn 1889 to Stockholm where he worked as a painter for
several years. Although Wallander had had several solo shows,
he did not succeed in breaking into the charmed circle of leading 1890s painters. Hence he was receptive to Ellen Key's mes-
sage of 'Beauty for all' and reports from his friend Erik Folcker
on the English Arts and Crafts movement. They provided Wallander with an incentive for switching to interior decoration
and making a name for himself with designs for furnishings,
textiles and interiors as well as ceramics and glass. In 1896, Alf
Wallander was working hard at AB Svensk Konstslöjdutställning Selma Giöbel (Swedish Artistic Crafts Selma Giöbel Inc.),
in Stockholm, a leading crafts and interior design business of
the day; at the close of 1898/99 he became head of Giöbels. That
position notwithstanding, Wallander continued to be employed
at Rörstrand, where he was not only the leading in-house artist
with a product line of his own but was also an artistic consultant and management representative responsible for preparing
and carrying out the Rörstrand share of trade-fair exhibitions
during those years.

Abb. // Fig. 47
Alf Wallanders Debut-Ausstellung im Haus des Gewerbevereins
// Alf Wallander's debut exhibition in the Swedish Association
of Applied Arts Building, Stockholm, April 1896.
Ord och Bild 1896.

Alf Wallander's first public appearance in April 1896 with a
collection comprising twenty-eight works at the Swedish Association of Applied Arts exhibition lead to what was virtually an
overnight transformation of Swedish ceramics. The impressive
collection represented the fruits of half a year's work. These
early pieces are distinguished mainly by powerful relief, often
fully in the round or spiralling in rampant movement on tautly
configured vessel walls, composed into an organic-looking aesthetic whole. The basic form of most of those vessels is either
bulbous or ovoid. The ornamental motifs are usually naturalistic in conception; this is equally true of both the sculpturally

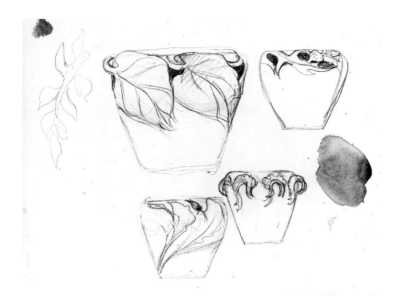
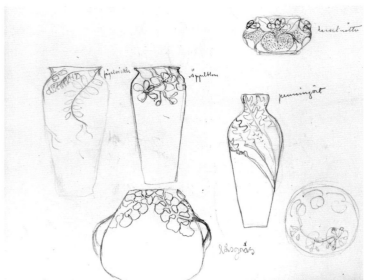

Abb. // Fig. 48, 49
Skizzen von Alf Wallander // Sketches of Alf Wallander's, ca 1896/97
National Museum Stockholm

er gut ausgebildet. Wallander hatte bereits 1882 Abschlüsse der HKS und der Technischen Schule in Stockholm (hier war u.a. Hugo Hörlin sein Lehrer) erworben, wo er auch mit Keramik gearbeitet hatte. Anschließend absolvierte er das Royal Art Institute. Nach Studien in Paris Ende der 1880er Jahre kehrte er im Herbst 1889 nach Stockholm zurück und arbeitete einige Jahre als Maler. Obwohl er mehrere Einzelausstellungen hatte, konnte er nicht zu den führenden Malern der 1890er Jahre aufschließen. So war er empfänglich für Ellen Keys Botschaft von der „Schönheit für alle" und die Berichte des Freundes Erik Folcker über die englische Arts-&-Crafts-Bewegung. Sie lieferten ihm den Anstoß, sich auf die Innendekoration zu verlegen und mit Entwürfen für Möbel, Textilien und Einrichtungen sowie für Keramik und Glas hervorzutreten. 1896 engagierte sich Alf Wallander in einem der führenden schwedischen Kunstgewerbe- und Einrichtungsunternehmen dieser Jahre, AB Svensk Konstslöjdutställning Selma Giöbel (Swedish Artistic Crafts Selma Giöbel Inc.) in Stockholm; am Jahresende 1898/99 übernahm er die Leitung von „Giöbels". Behielt aber in dieser Zeit seine Beschäftigung bei Rörstrand bei, wo er nicht nur führender Künstler mit eigener Produktion, sondern auch künstlerischer Berater und Beauftragter für die Vorbereitung und die Durchführung der Beteiligung des Unternehmens an der Mehrzahl der Ausstellungen dieser Jahre war.

Alf Wallanders erster öffentlicher Auftritt im April 1896 mit einer Kollektion von 28 Arbeiten im Ausstellungslokal des Gewerbevereins in Stockholm führte quasi über Nacht zu einer Neuorientierung der gesamten schwedischen Keramik. Die beeindruckende Schau war das Ergebnis der Arbeit eines halben Jahres. Diese frühen Arbeiten zeichnen sich vor allem durch kraftvolles Relief aus, oft freiliegend oder in spiralig wachsender Bewegung auf straff gespannten Gefäßwandun-

rendered and the painted decoration consisting of large clusters of flowers and leaves. Underglaze colours and occasionally also traditional majolica glazes underscore the naturalistic effect with vibrant shades of blue, green, yellow and red. The clay body is usually earthenware paste that fires white. We find parallels between what was happening in ceramics at the time in Paris and Copenhagen. There the first examples of relief decoration in association with underglaze painting were launched that would also be the dominant feature of art ceramics at Rörstrand for decades to come. Wallander had a section for art ceramics in the Art Hall at the 1897 Stockholm exhibition. That marked the first appearance of a Swedish ceramicist in a context of this kind.

An undated Wallander sketchbook (ca 1897) contains several examples of the work he was doing in the new ceramics and decoration in the new style (see fig. 48, 49).

In 1896, Rörstrand showed a collection of Wallander's new ceramics and other pieces at the grand 'Moderne Keramik' exhibition in Berlin. A smaller number of Wallander pieces had already been shown in December that year at the well-known Berlin art salon run by Fritz Gurlitt. Those shows earned Rörstrand considerable success and attracted the notice of the press. *Das Volk*, quoted in *Dagens Nyheter*, reported that the work was '*the most interesting that was to be seen in this field recently. Particularly successful was the organic aspect, which the artist skilfully realised in each case in conjunction with the basic vessel form and its representational decoration.*' The *Berliner Tageblatt* (quoted in *Svenska Dagbladet*) emphasises that '*the pieces are painted in delicate yet vivid colours, uniting purity of form with attractive richness of invention.*'[43] These were ceramics that would shape Rörstrand exhibition displays for many years to come. The new art porcelain at the exhibition

gen, komponiert zu einer organisch wirkenden Gesamtheit. Die Grundform der Gefäße ist meist zwiebel- oder eiförmig. Die dekorativen Motive sind in der Regel ganz naturalistisch aufgefasst; das gilt sowohl für die plastisch ausgebildeten als auch für die gemalten Dekore mit großen Blumentrauben und Blättern. Die Unterglasurfarben und mitunter auch die traditionellen Majolikaglasuren unterstützen den naturalistischen Effekt mit starken Nuancen von Blau, Grün, Gelb und Rot. Das Material ist in der Regel eine weißbrennende Steingutmasse. Parallelen finden wir in dem, was sich zur gleichen Zeit in Paris und Kopenhagen vollzog. Hier tauchten auch die ersten Beispiele für den plastischen Dekor in Verbindung mit Unterglasurmalerei auf, der in den kommenden Jahrzehnten Rörstrands Kunstkeramik beherrschen sollte. Wallander hatte auf der Ausstellung 1897 eine Abteilung mit Kunstkeramik in der Kunsthalle. Es war der erste Auftritt eines schwedischen Keramikers in einem solchem Rahmen.

Ein erhaltenes undatiertes Skizzenbuch von ca. 1897 weist mehrere Beispiele für seine Arbeit mit der neuen Keramik und den neuen Dekoren nach (siehe Abb. 48, 49).

Bereits 1896 hatte Rörstrand mit einer Kollektion von Wallanders neuer Keramik und anderen Exponaten an der großen Ausstellung „Moderne Keramik" in Berlin teilgenommen. Eine kleinere Anzahl von Arbeiten wurde schon im Dezember des gleichen Jahres in Fritz Gurlitts wohlbekanntem Berliner Kunstsalon gezeigt. Diese Auftritte waren mit einem beachtlichen Erfolg für die Fabrik verbunden und zogen auch die Aufmerksamkeit der Presse auf sich. „Das Volk", zitiert in „Dagens Nyheter", berichtete, es sei *das Interessanteste, was man in letzter Zeit auf diesem Gebiet gesehen hätte. Höchst geglückt sei vor allem das Organische, das der Künstler in jedem einzelnen Fall zu realisieren verstanden hätte, im Zusammenspiel zwischen der Grundform eines Gefäßes und dessen figuraler Ausstattung."* Das „Berliner Tageblatt" (zitiert nach „Svenska Dagbladet") hebt hervor, dass *die Stücke gehalten sind in zarten, jedoch hervortretenden Farben, die Formen-Reinheit mit anziehendem Erfindungsreichtum vereinen."*[43] Diese Keramik bestimmte für viele Jahre Rörstrands Auftritt auf Ausstellungen. Das neue Kunstporzellan auf der Ausstellung im dänischen Kunstindustriemuseum in Kopenhagen im Dezember 1897 verhalf der Fabrik zu einem großen internationalen Durchbruch. Zudem bedeutete die Ausstellung für Rörstrand einen bemerkenswerten Prestigegewinn, weil Pietro Krohn selbst die Teilnahme von Rörstrand erbeten hatte.

Wallander arbeitete auch mit einfachen Vasenformen in Steingut mit straff konturierten Blumenmotiven, um so seinen Beitrag zur Herstellung von preiswerteren Kunstwerken zu leisten. Diese Stücke tauchten schon 1897 auf, zur gleichen Zeit also, in der er auch mit Kupferlüster- und Kristallglasuren arbeitete und außerdem mit Steinzeug zu experimentieren begann.

Frühzeitig entwickelte Alf Wallander auch eine neue Facette in seiner Keramik, die eine deutliche Distanz zu dem ornamental-

mounted in December 1897 by the Industrial Art Museum in Copenhagen marked the international breakthrough for Rörstrand. Moreover, that show brought a remarkable gain in prestige because Pietro Krohn had personally invited Rörstrand to take part in it.

Wallander also worked with simple vase forms in earthenware decorated with astringently executed floral motifs as his contribution to the making of more affordable objets d'art. He had started making them by 1897, at the same time, therefore, as he was also working with copper lustre and crystal glazes and had even begun to experiment with fine stoneware.

At an early date Alf Wallander also developed a new facet of his ceramics that shows he had come a long way from the ornamental, vegetal Art Nouveau/Jugendstil. These works, featuring crisply stylised floral decoration in borders or medallions encircling the vessel clearly reveal the influence of the Austrian decorative arts and the new ceramics from Bing & Grøndahl. The year 1906/07 saw the launch of Wallander's pieces with high-fired colours in clear, shimmering shades of yellow, blue, green and red. Later he developed a technique based on decoration with the contours in relief. The body is invariably earthenware and the ornamental motifs were flowers, fruits, fish, birds, grapes, decorative tendrils and osier decoration (see fig. 45).

Hugo Tryggelin. Regardless of how many new ideas Alf Wallander launched with his new shapes and new palette, it was always possible for the other artists at Rörstrand to develop profiles of their own and express themselves through their art.

Hugo Tryggelin (1846–1924), an architect, had been hired as far back as 1872 to support Almström and Stråle as an art consultant (see fig. 40). Tryggelin worked chiefly in the tiled stove department; his work in this area was probably the main reason why he was designated *chefdessinateur* [head designer]. Later, however, his fields of activity also included the production of tableware. Hugo Tryggelin worked at Rörstrand until 1909, designing a great many patterns for services as well as some showy vases and, towards the turn of the century, also some pieces in the new style. A trailed (slip-painted) series in mild sepia and shades of blue is particularly interesting. Works by Tryggelin were shown in all Rörstrand sections at exhibitions until well after 1910.

Algot Eriksson. The most outstanding artist at Rörstrand after Alf Wallander was Algot Eriksson (1868–1937) (see fig. 50). He had grown up at Rörstrand, trained at the Technical School and was a Rörstrand employee from 1886 until 1912. Towards the close of the 1890s he was head of the underglaze painting division. During his tenure there, he organised the production of a very large number of ornamental vases with painted motifs and used underglaze painting in conjunction with softly naturalistic relief decoration. He also made use of various floral and faunal motifs, often composed in gently rhythmic movement around vase rims. Also noteworthy are some patterns for services that were made after his designs. His work is discernibly

Abb. // Fig. 50
Algot Eriksson, ca 1901

Abb. // Fig. 51
Nils Emil Lundström, 1901

Abb. // Fig. 52
Karl Lindström, ca 1901

vegetabilen Jugendstil erkennen lässt. Diese Arbeiten mit ihren scharf stilisierten Blumenornamenten in Band- oder Medaillon-ausführung rund um die Gefäßkörper zeigen deutlich den Ein-fluss des österreichischen Kunsthandwerks und der neuen Keramik bei Bing & Grøndahl. 1906/07 erschienen die Arbeiten Wallanders mit Scharffeuerfarben in klaren, schimmernden Nuancen von Gelb, Blau, Grün und Rot. Später entwickelte er eine Technik mit reliefkonturierten Dekoren. Das Material ist durchgehend Steingut, und die dekorativen Motive waren Blu-men, Früchte, Fische, Vögel, Weintrauben, ornamentale Ranken und Korbgeflechte (siehe Abb. 45).

Hugo Tryggelin. Ungeachtet der neuen Ideen Alf Wallanders, seines neuen Formenbestandes und seiner neuen Farbenpalette war es auch für die übrigen Künstler bei Rörstrand immer mög-lich, ein eigenes Profil zu entwickeln und ihre künstlerischen Ausdrucksmöglichkeiten zu entfalten. Der Architekt Hugo Tryggelin (1846–1924) war schon 1872 angestellt worden, um Almström und Stråle als künstlerischer Beistand zur Seite zu stehen (siehe Abb. 40). Er arbeitete vor allem in der Kachelofen-produktion, und vermutlich hängt die Bezeichnung „Chefdes-sinateur" hauptsächlich mit diesem Arbeitsfeld zusammen; später erfasste sie allerdings auch die Produktion von Service-waren. Hugo Tryggelin arbeitete bis 1909, entwarf eine große Zahl von Servicemustern, aber auch verschiedene Prachtvasen und gegen die Jahrhundertwende auch einige Stücke im neuen Stil. Besonders interessant ist eine Serie mit Schlickerbema-lung in milden Sepia- und Blau-Tönen. Seine Arbeiten waren Bestandteil aller Ausstellungsbeiträge von Rörstrand bis in die Zeit nach 1910.

Algot Eriksson. Der hervorragendste Künstler neben Alf Wal-lander war Algot Eriksson (1868–1937) (siehe Abb. 50). Er war

influenced by early 1890s Danish ceramics and by Alf Wal-lander. In 1912, Eriksson left Rörstrand; until 1916 he worked for the Lidköping Porcelain Manufactory and later also for the Karlskrona and Gävle factories.

Nils (Emil) Lundström (1865–1960). He, too, had a more inde-pendent position as a ceramicist at Rörstrand (see fig. 51). Lundström also worked in textiles. He had trained in Düssel-dorf, at the Royal Art Institute in Stockholm and in Berlin, where he evidently also took courses in ceramics. In 1896 he was hired by Rörstrand before the Stockholm exhibition and stayed at the factory until 1935, that is, even after it had moved to Göteborg. Nils Lundström's ceramics clearly show that he had trained as a painter. Apart from variants of Wallander pieces, he had a predilection for large vase forms and showy bowls decorated with floral and faunal motifs in the Danish Japonising manner. Large motifs tend to spread beyond the sides of a vessel. His palette is more decidedly naturalistic, how-ever, than that used by the Danish porcelain manufactories. Early in the twentieth century he was working with decoration in low relief. From 1910 he followed the prevailing trend and also experimented with high-fired fine stoneware and faience with distinctive, Japanese-inspired decoration. He designed several services in the modern Rococo style. Along with Edward Hald and Louise Adelborg, he was still a leading artist at Rörstrand in the 1920s.

Karl Lindström. He also grew up at Rörstrand, where several generations of Lindströms had been employed as factory fore-men and artisans. Karl Lindström (1865–1936) became one of the leading Rörstrand artists in porcelain (see fig. 52). He liked to work on ornamental plates and vases with the underglaze painting inspired by Arnold Krog, mainly naturalistically con-

Abb. // Fig. 53
Waldemar Lindström, ca 1901

Abb. // Fig. 54
Anna Boberg, ca 1901

bei Rörstrand aufgewachsen, ausgebildet an der Technischen Schule und von 1886 bis 1912 angestellt. Gegen Ende der 1890er Jahre stand er der Abteilung für Unterglasurmalerei vor. In dieser Zeit besorgte er die Ausführung einer sehr großen Anzahl von Ziervasen mit gemalten Motiven, und er benutzte die Unterglasurmalerei in Verbindung mit weichem naturalistischem Reliefdekor. Auch verschiedene Blumen- und Tiermotive, oft komponiert in weicher rhythmischer Bewegung rund um die Vasenmündungen, fanden Verwendung. Zu erwähnen sind auch einige Servicemuster, die nach seinen Entwürfen ausgeführt wurden. Seine Arbeiten sind stark beeinflusst von der dänischen Keramik vom Anfang der 1890er Jahre und von Alf Wallander. 1912 verließ er Rörstrand; er arbeitete bis 1916 an der Porzellanfabrik Lidköping und war später für die Porzellanfabriken Karlskrona und Gävle tätig.

Nils (Emil) Lundström (1865–1960). Auch er hatte eine selbst-ständigere Stellung als Keramiker in Rörstrand (siehe Abb. 51). Er war auch Textilkünstler, hatte in Düsseldorf, an der Kunsthochschule Stockholm und in Berlin studiert und dort offenbar auch Keramik als Studienfach belegt. 1896, vor der Stockholmer Ausstellung, fand er eine Anstellung bei Rörstrand und blieb dort bis 1935, also auch nach dem Umzug der Fabrik nach Göteborg. Dass Nils Lundström ausgebildeter Maler war, macht sich deutlich in seiner Keramik bemerkbar. Neben Varianten von Wallanderstücken galt seine Vorliebe großen Vasenformen und Prachtschalen, dekoriert mit Blumen- und Tiermotiven in japanisch-dänischer Art. Oft breiten sich dabei große Bildmotive über die Seiten des Gefäßes hinaus aus. Seine Farbskala ist stärker naturalistisch als die der dänischen Manufakturen. Zu Anfang des 20. Jahrhunderts arbeitete er mit flachem Reliefdekor. Ab 1910 folgte er der allgemeinen Entwicklung und ver-

ceived motifs such as crows, storks, other flora and fauna. Although very naturalistic in conception, they are painted in an equally naturalistic, albeit occasionally rather cloying, palette. In the manner typical of Rörstrand, he also worked in low relief and can be regarded as the creator of much of the factory output in this genre in his day. In collaboration with Waldemar, his younger cousin, who often drew the sculptural decoration, Karl Lindström ensured that most of Wallander's more ambitious models and prototypes were put into serial production.

Waldemar Lindström (1875–1941) was hired by Rörstrand in 1897 (see fig. 53). That same year he was mentioned in Copenhagen but his first public appearance on his own was at the 1900 Paris Exposition. There and at the 1903 Helsingborg trade fair, he showed, apart from quite a small collection of vases, a series of small animal figurines of the same kind as the popular pieces made in Copenhagen and Berlin. They are pieces that are entirely naturalistic in conception; following the trend prevailing at the time, they are painted in mild, naturalistic tints that occasionally verge on the cloying: slinky foxes, hares, bears and lynx, elks, deer, cats, dogs, many birds and even fish. Animal figurines were very popular then; the Rörstrand range embraced more than one hundred and sixty different models plus variants decorated with various glaze and paint options and they were in production until 1926. Waldemar Lindström often executed the sculptural decoration for vases after designs by several different artists while his older cousin Karl was responsible for the painted décor.

Anna Boberg and Helene Holck. Some artists were given special commissions from time to time, particularly for the 1897 Stockholm exhibition, but also on later occasions. The painter Anna Boberg (née Scholander, 1864–1935), wife of Ferdinand

suchte sich auch mit hochgebranntem Steinzeug und Fayencen mit besonderen, japanisch inspirierten Dekoren. Er entwarf mehrere Service im modernen Rokokostil. Neben Edward Hald und Louise Adelborg gehörte er auch in den 1920er Jahre zu Rörstrands führenden Künstlern.

Karl Lindström. Ebenfalls bei Rörstrand aufgewachsen, wo mehrere Generationen Lindström als Werkmeister und Künstler in der Fabrik beschäftigt waren, wurde Karl Lindström (1865–1936) zu einem der führenden Porzellankünstler der Fabrik (siehe Abb. 52). Er arbeitete gern mit der von Arnold Krog inspirierten Unterglasurbemalung auf Ziertellern und Vasen, überwiegend mit naturalistisch gestalteten Motiven wie Krähen, Störchen, anderen Tieren und Blumen. Sie sind ganz naturnah aufgefasst und in ebenso naturnaher, gelegentlich auch ein wenig süßlicher Farbskala bemalt. Wie für Rörstrand typisch, arbeitete auch er mit Flachrelief und kann für einen großen Teil der einschlägigen Produktion als verantwortlich angesehen werden. Zusammen mit seinem jüngeren Vetter Waldemar, der oft für den plastischen Dekor zeichnete, führte er die meisten von Wallanders anspruchsvolleren Modellen und Vorlagen zur Serienproduktion aus.

Waldemar Lindström (1875–1941) war bei Rörstrand 1897 eingestellt worden (siehe Abb. 53). Er wurde zwar schon im selben Jahr in Kopenhagen erwähnt, aber sein erstes selbstständiges Auftreten verbindet sich mit der Pariser Ausstellung von 1900. Dort und auf der Ausstellung in Helsingborg 1903 zeigte er neben einer kleineren Vasenkollektion vor allem eine Folge von kleinen Tierfiguren, gleich geartet wie die populären Gegenstücke aus Kopenhagen und Berlin. Es sind ganz naturalistisch aufgefasste Stücke, bemalt im Trend der Zeit mit naturnahen, milden und mitunter auch ein wenig süßlichen Farben: schleichende Füchse, Hasen, Bären und Luchse, Elche und Rehwild, Katzen und Hunde, viele Vögel und sogar Fische. Die Tierplastiken waren sehr gefragt; mit über 160 unterschiedlichen Modellen in verschiedenen Varianten unterschiedlicher Glasuren und Farben waren sie in dem Angebot von Rörstrand vertreten und wurden bis 1926 produziert. Oft führte Waldemar Lindström auch die plastischen Dekore für Vasen nach Entwürfen von unterschiedlichen Künstlern aus, während sein älterer Vetter Karl die Bemalung besorgte.

Anna Boberg und Helene Holck. Einige Künstler wurden gelegentlich für unterschiedliche Spezialaufgaben in Anspruch genommen, besonders vor der Stockholmer Ausstellung 1897, aber auch bei späteren Gelegenheiten. Größere Aufmerksamkeit erweckte die Malerin Anna Boberg (geb. Scholander, 1864–1935), die Ehefrau von Ferdinand Boberg (siehe Abb. 54). Ihre Anwesenheit in der Fabrik ist nur für 1897 belegt, doch kam es auch in den folgenden Jahren mehrfach zu einer kürzeren oder längeren Mitarbeit. Nach ihrem Entwurf wurde die berühmte *Pfauenvase* ausgeführt, eine 1,8 m hohe Vase mit vier Pfauen in freiem Relief, naturalistisch modelliert und mit Scharffeuerfarben bemalt. Das imponierend große Stück beherrschte die

Boberg, met with considerable acclaim (see fig. 54). Her presence at Rörstrand is only verified for 1897 but she was also employed in later years for several brief stints or longer-lasting projects. She designed the celebrated Peacock Vase, a vessel 1.8 metres high featuring four peacocks fully in the round, naturalistically modelled and painted with high-fired colours. This grandly imposing piece reigned supreme in the 1897 Stockholm exhibition display cases and did so again in Paris in 1900. Anna Boberg also designed several smaller vases and dishes in the Rörstrand style, which are distinguished by a finely attuned correspondence of form and colour.

Helene Holck (1867–1922), porcelain painter and miniaturist, had submitted designs to Rörstrand since 1893 but worked more closely with the manufactory in 1896 and 1897 before the Stockholm exhibition; in later years she would retain her links with Rörstrand. Helene Holck had a studio of her own, in which she also worked on porcelain painting, and showed a selection of her own works at Malmö in 1904.

Harald and Knut Almström. Robert Almström's sons collaborated on the artistic side of production for many years. Their ornamental vases were exhibited in 1897 and 1900 and their hands-on approach from the outset can also be viewed as preparation for taking over their father's position. Between 1896 and 1903 Harald Almström designed a number of ornamental vases, most of them fairly small, to match the Rörstrand standard product line. Knut Almström spent some time on applying glazes such as *rouge flambé*, crystallising and lustre to ornamental vases which were either designed by Wallander or came from the standard range. Most of them had been developed in collaboration with, and under the supervision of, works foreman Axel Lindström and it is fairly safe to assume that they were results from Knut Almström's 1895 study trip. Taking such one-off pieces with art glazes into the Rörstrand range turned out to be decidedly prescient. Comparable objects that are easily recognisable as Japanese or Chinese inspired, were very similar to pieces produced at the same time by the Sèvres, Berlin, Meißen and Copenhagen porcelain factories. Wallander, later followed by Nils Lundström and Karl Lindström, pursued the trend with models of their own glazed to match.

Ewerlöf, Anderberg, Asplund et al. Astrid Ewerlöf (1876–1927) was for several years one of the best known women artists at Rörstrand. She designed quite small vases and bowls in the Rörstrand manner, many of them notable for stringency of form, decoration and colour. After completing her studies at the Industrial Art School (HKS) in 1899, she was hired at Rörstrand and remained there as an employee until about 1914. Between 1896 and 1909 Mela (Pamela) Anderberg (1865–1927) designed several vases in the Rörstrand style, harmonious in decoration and colour but not particularly original, as well as some tableware services. She was subsequently made head of the underglaze painting division at Rörstrand. Georg Asplund (1879–ca 1930) was another of the many artists at Rörstrand. Probably

Ausstellungsvitrinen in Stockholm 1897 und auch noch einmal 1900 in Paris. Sie entwarf auch verschiedene kleinere Vasen und Schalen im Stil der Fabrik, die sich durch eine feine Abstimmung in Form und Farbe auszeichnen.

Einzelne Entwürfe der Porzellan- und Miniaturmalerin Helene Holck (1867–1922) entstanden schon ab 1893 für Rörstrand; zu einer intensiveren Zusammenarbeit kam es 1896 und 1897 vor der Stockholmer Ausstellung, und auch in den Folgejahren blieb die Verbindung bestehen. Helene Holck beschäftigte sich auch in ihrem eigenen Atelier mit Porzellanmalerei und zeigte 1904 in Malmö eine Auswahl eigener Arbeiten.

Harald und Knut Almström. Robert Almströms Söhne waren viele Jahre lang an der künstlerischen Produktion beteiligt. Ihre Ziervasen wurden 1897 und 1900 ausgestellt, und ihre praktische Mitarbeit kann auch als Vorbereitung auf die Übernahme der väterlichen Position gelten. Harald Almström gestaltete zwischen 1896 und 1903 eine Anzahl meist kleinerer Ziervasen in der Art des „Standard-Rörstrand"-Programms. Knut Almström befasste sich zeitweise mit Ziervasen, die von Wallander entworfen waren oder aus der Standardproduktion stammten und von ihm mit verschiedenen Glasuren versehen wurden, u. a. rouge flambé sowie kristallisierende und Lüsterglasuren. Sie waren zum großen Teil gemeinsam mit und unter der Leitung von Werkmeister Axel Lindström entwickelt worden und können als Verarbeitung der Erfahrungen seiner Studienreise von 1895 gelten. Die Aufnahme derartiger Einzelstücke mit Kunstglasuren in das Herstellungsprogramm erwies sich als ausgesprochen zukunftsträchtig. Vergleichbare Gegenstände, die unschwer die Verarbeitung japanisch-chinesischer Vorbilder erkennen ließen, kamen der etwa gleichzeitig in den Porzellanfabriken von Sèvres, Berlin, Meißen und Kopenhagen entstandenen Produktion sehr nahe. Wallander, später auch Lundström und Karl Lindström folgten mit eigenen Modellen, auf die entsprechende Glasuren aufgebracht wurden.

Ewerlöf, Anderberg, Asplund u. v. a. Astrid Ewerlöf (1876–1927) war für mehrere Jahre eine der bekanntesten Künstlerinnen bei Rörstrand. Sie entwarf in Art der Fabrik kleinere Vasen und Schalen, oft sehr konzentriert in Form, Dekor und Farbe. Nach ihrem Abschluss an der Höheren Kunstschule (HKS) 1899 wurde sie bei Rörstrand angestellt, wo sie bis ca. 1914 tätig war.

Zwischen 1896 und 1909 gestaltete auch Mela (Pamela) Anderberg (1865–1927) verschiedene Vasen im Stil der Fabrik, stimmig in Dekor und Farbe, aber nicht von allzu selbstständigem Charakter, dazu auch einige Service. Anschließend wurde sie mit der Verantwortung für die Unterglasurmalerei-Abteilung der Fabrik betraut.

Zu den zahlreichen Fabrikkünstlern gehörte auch Georg Asplund (1879–ca. 1930), angestellt wahrscheinlich von der Mitte der 1890er Jahre bis in das zweite Jahrzehnt des 20. Jahrhunderts; er wechselte später zur Gävle Porslinsfabrik in Gävle. Bei Rörstrand gestaltete er Kachelöfen, Kacheln und Ziergegenstände, u. a. die wohlbekannten Piedestale mit Seerosen 1895 (siehe Abb. 55).

Abb. // Fig. 55
Georg Asplund: Piedestal (Blumensäule), Zeichnung // Pedestal (floral column), drawing, 1896

hired in the mid-1890s, he seems to have remained at the factory until the second decade of the twentieth century; later he transferred to the Gävle Porslinsfabrik in Gävle. At Rörstrand he designed tiled stoves, tiles and objets d'art, including the celebrated pedestal with water lilies (1895) (see fig. 55).

Ruben Rising (1869–1929) was the creator of a number of vases made at the turn of the century; he also designed quite a few successful models of sculptural design for serial production.

In the early years of the new century, Hilma Persson (1877–1953), employed from 1900 to 1906, brought an array of figurines and ornamental pieces into the Rörstrand range (see fig. 56). In 1906/1907, works by Hjördis Norden, a sculptor and painter, were also added. From 1904 Hilma Persson was responsible for decorating the first Rörstrand Christmas plates. In 1906/07 she went home to her native Rackstad, where she soon set up a ceramics workshop with her husband Rolf Hjelm. Another porcelain painter was Gerda Zielfelt (1893–1947), who worked at Rörstrand from 1913 until 1921.

One-off pieces designed by the architect Ferdinand Boberg, who had been hired in 1897 to design a series of new tiled stove models, were also made. Prince Eugén also designed a service and some ornamental pieces to be made at Rörstrand. From 1915 Vicken von Post-Börjesson (1886–1950) too worked for some years there. She designed several series of small figurines

Abb. // Fig. 56
Hilma Persson, ca 1910

Auf Ruben Rising (1869–1929) geht eine Reihe von Vasen zurück, die um die Jahrhundertwende entstanden; er entwarf auch eine Anzahl erfolgreicher Modelle mit skulpturaler Formgebung für die Serienproduktion.

Am Anfang des neuen Jahrhunderts kam eine Reihe von Kleinplastiken und Zierkeramik von Hilma Persson (1877–1953) in das Produktionsprogramm, die von 1900 bis 1906 bei Rörstrand angestellt war, dazu 1906/1907 auch Arbeiten der Bildhauerin und Malerin Hjördis Norden (siehe Abb. 56). Hilma Persson dekorierte seit 1904 die ersten Weihnachtsteller bei Rörstrand; 1906/07 zog sie sich in ihre Heimat nach Rackstad zurück und richtete hier eine eigene Keramikwerkstatt ein, die sie in der Folgezeit gemeinsam mit ihrem Ehemann Rolf Hjelm betrieb. Eine weitere Porzellanmalerin war Gerda Zielfelt (1893–1947), bei Rörstrand tätig von 1913 bis 1921.

Einzelstücke wurden nach Entwürfen des Architekten Ferdinand Boberg hergestellt, der 1897 eigentlich für eine Serie von neuen Kachelofenmodellen engagiert worden war. Auch Prinz Eugén ließ in Rörstrand ein Service und einige Zierstücke anfertigen. Ab 1915 arbeitete Vicken von Post-Börjesson (1886–1950) hier für einige Jahre. Sie entwarf mehrere Serien von kleinen Figuren, die in der Nachfolge der Arbeiten standen, die der schwedische Bildhauer und Keramiker Gerhard Henning, bei dem sie mehrere Jahre studiert hatte, für die Königliche Porzellanfabrik Kopenhagen gestaltet hatte.

Die Glasuren und das Steinzeug

Zu dem kunstkeramischen Programm des Unternehmens gehörten auch die vielen Arbeiten mit unterschiedlichen Glasuren, von Kupferlüster und Ochsenblut bis zu den aufregenden Varianten kristallisierender Glasuren, von denen sich viele mit dem Namen Knut Almström verbinden. Das Experimentieren mit verschiedenen Glasuren war um die Jahrhundert-

influenced by works designed for the Royal Copenhagen Manufactory by Gerhard Henning, a Swedish sculptor and ceramicist with whom she had studied for several years.

Glazes and fine stoneware

The Rörstrand art ceramics range also included numerous works featuring distinctive glazes ranging from copper lustre and ox-blood to exciting variants of crystallising glazes, many of them associated with Knut Almström. Experimenting with glazes was the order of the day at many large porcelain manufactories at the turn of the century. That Rörstrand was no exception is shown by the numerous recipes contained in what is known as the recipe book.

At that time interest in working on an artistic level with fine stoneware was growing apace at both Rörstrand and Gustavsberg, Rörstrand's main competitor. Alf Wallander executed several pieces in that material, some of them for his first collection in 1895/96 and the others in 1900. Numerous other artists would follow him into fine stoneware, including Nils Lundström, and distinguish themselves in that medium.

Luxury art services and tiled stoves

The Rörstrand line in utilitarian ceramics included a large number of services in a wide variety of forms and styles. The number of individual pieces belonging to each service was large and richly varied, far from being merely modern tableware made for everyday use. The 1897 Rörstrand price lists for 'faience and genuine porcelain' contain one hundred and sixty-

Abb. // Fig. 57
Objekte mit Uranglasur // Objects with uranium glaze, ca 1910
Rörstrand Museum.

wende in vielen großen Fabriken an der Tagesordnung. Dass Rörstrand dabei keine Ausnahme bildete, lässt sich auch den zahlreichen Rezepten in dem so genannten „Rezeptbuch" entnehmen.

In diesem Zeitraum gab es bei Rörstrand und auch beim Konkurrenten Gustavsberg ein gesteigertes Interesse an der Arbeit mit künstlerischem Steinzeug. Alf Wallander führte mehrere Stücke in diesem Material aus, teils für seine erste Kollektion 1895/96, teils um 1900. In der Folgezeit griffen zahlreiche andere Künstler, darunter auch Nils Lundström, diese Anregungen auf und traten ebenfalls mit Steinzeugarbeiten hervor.

Künstlerische Luxusservice und Kachelöfen

Das Rörstrand-Angebot an Gebrauchskeramik umfasste eine große Zahl von Servicen in höchst unterschiedlichen Formen und Stilrichtungen. Auch die Anzahl der einzelnen Serviceteile war groß und variantenreich und damit weit davon entfernt, nur als modernes Geschirr für den alltäglichen Gebrauch zu dienen. Rörstrands Preisverzeichnisse von 1897 für „Fayence und echtes Porzellan" enthalten auf 167 Seiten 27 verschiedene Servicemodelle. Das älteste von ihnen, das Dacca-Modell = Modell A, stammt aus den 1830er Jahren, die fünf Modelle B – G aus der Zeit um 1860/70 und die übrigen aus den 25 Folgejahren. Man konnte sie aus verschiedenen Massen gefertigt finden: *gewöhnliche Masse* (Steingut), *Perlmasse, Ironstone China, Opak, Ivory* (= Elfenbein), *Äkta* (= Echt, Feldspatporzellan) und *Stenmassa*, verziert mit Umdruckdekor oder mit unterschiedlichen Randverzierungen und Bändern in mehreren Farben oder auch mit Goldrand. In dem großen Angebot an Serviceteilen standen Teller, ovale und runde Schüsseln in unterschiedlicher Größe, Fischplatten mit Sieb, Roastbeafplatten, Ragoutschüsseln, Karotten und Terrinen, Saucen- und Pastetenschalen, Satten, Salatschüsseln, Obst- und Dessertschalen sowie Frühstücksserviceteile zur Auswahl. Es gab Empfehlungen für die geeignete Zusammensetzung von Servicen für 6, 12, 18 und 24 Personen. Dazu kamen eine große Menge von Tee- und Kaffeeservicen, einzelne Angebote für andere Gegenstände und Waschservice.

Zu den künstlerisch spektakulären Geschirren im Art-Nouveau-Stil zählten in diesen Jahren Alf Wallanders Service mit neuen Formen und dekorativen Mustern wie *Lilien* (auch Iris genannt) bzw. *Tulpe* und *Blasentang*, die 1897 in Stockholm und 1900 in Paris gezeigt wurden. Sie entsprachen mit ihren stilisierten floralen Dekoren, dem leichten Relief und der Bemalung in zarten Unterglasurtönen ganz den Gestaltungsprinzipien der von ihm zu dieser Zeit entworfenen Ziergegenstände. Diese Service waren aus Feldspatporzellan. Die späteren Entwürfe von Wallander, beispielsweise die Service *Trollslända* (= Dragon Fly,

Abb. // Fig. 58
Rörstrand-Tafelservice mit Jugendstil-Dekoren // Rörstrand tableware service with Art Nouveau decoration.

seven pages devoted to twenty-seven different service models. The oldest model, Dacca = Model A, dates from the 1830s, the five models B–G from about 1860/70 and the others from the twenty-five years that followed. They were made from various pastes: *common paste* (earthenware), *pearl paste, ironstone china, Opak* (= *Opaque*), *Ivory, Äkta* (= true porcelain, i.e. feldspar porcelain) and *Stenmassa*, (a kind of hard porcelain) decorated with transfer printing or with a variety of ornamental borders and bands in several colours or also gilt-edged. The large number of individual pieces in each service included plates, oval and round dishes of various sizes, fish platters with strainers, platters for serving roast meat, ragout tureens, deep disches and soup tureens, sauce-boats and tureens for pâté, salad bowls, fruit and dessert bowls and breakfast service pieces. Recommendations were made for the most suitable types of pieces to be included in 6, 12, 18 and 24-piece place settings. There were also a large number of tea and coffee services, individual objets d'art and basins and ewers for washstands.

Among the most stunning sets of tableware in the aesthetic sense of the Art Nouveau style then were those designed by Alf Wallander featuring new forms and ornamental patterns such as *Lilies* (also known as *Iris*), *Tulip* and *Bladderwrack*, which were shown in Stockholm in 1897 and Paris in 1900. With their stylised floral decoration, low relief and painting in delicate underglaze tints, they perfectly matched the design principles informing the objets d'art Wallander designed at that time. Those Wallander services were of feldspar porcelain. His later designs, such as the *Trollslända* (= Dragon Fly, 1908) and *Fjäril* (= Butterfly, 1911) tableware service, are distinguished by a new, more stringent conception of form. The lily pattern was also used for coffee and tea services. Algot Eriksson also designed some decoration for the 1900 Paris Exposition in the Wallander

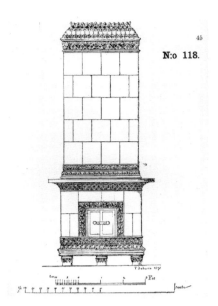

N:o 118.

Abb. // Fig. 59
Ferdinand Boberg:
Kachelofen-Modell // *tiled
stove model.*
Preisliste // price list, 1904

1908) *Fjäril* (= Schmetterling, 1911), zeichneten sich demgegenüber durch eine neue, straffere Formgebung aus. Das Lilienmuster wurde auch für Kaffee- und Teeservice benutzt. Auch Algot Eriksson entwarf für die Weltausstellung 1900 in Paris in Wallanders Stil einige Dekore, jedoch mit stärker naturalistisch aufgefassten Zweigen und Blüten, u.a. Gröna blad (= Grünes Blatt, 1900) und Alpviol (= Alpenveilchen, ebenfalls 1900, jedoch erst ab 1902 in der Produktion).

Einige Motive im neuen Stil waren für ein breiteres Publikum zur Ausführung in billigerer Porzellanqualität vorgesehen. Dazu gehörten u.a. *Blåsippa* (= Märzenbecher) von Alf Wallander (1897–1908 in der Produktion) und mehrere, keinem bestimmten Entwerfer zuzuweisende Muster wie *Tage* (1908), *Göta* (1911), *Greta* (1911) und *Helga* (1915). Einige Dekore lassen in ihren dekorativen Blütenarrangements fernöstliche Einflüsse erkennen, z.B. Svala (= Schwalbe, 1897) und Tärna (= Seeschwalbe, 1911), und bei anderen finden sich Anklänge an den Empirestil mit klassischer Formgebung und einfachen Randbetonungen (siehe Abb. 58).

Mit der Übernahme der Fabrikleitung durch die Söhne Almström kam es allerdings zu einer Bereinigung und Reduzierung des mittlerweile überreichen Sortiments, und auch in den Jahren nach 1910 setzte sich diese Entwicklung, verbunden mit einer deutlichen Anpassung an neue stilistische Tendenzen, in größerem Umfang, fort.

Rörstrand blieb auch in dieser Zeit einer der größten Hersteller von Kachelöfen in Schweden, und in den Jahren um die Jahrhundertwende wurden mehrere führende Architekten zur Mitarbeit herangezogen. Berühmt sind insbesondere Ferdinand Bobergs Kachelöfen von 1897, aber auch Hugo Tryggelin und die Architekten Bror Almqvist, Gustaf Clason und Axel Lindegren steuerten verschiedene Modelle in dem neuen Stil bei (siehe Abb. 59).

style yet with more naturalistically conceived boughs and flowers, including *Gröna blad* (= Green Leaf, 1900) and *Alpviol* (= Alpine Violet, also 1900, although not in production until 1902).

Some patterns in the new style were reserved for the broader public, hence were executed in less expensive porcelain. These patterns include *Blåsippa* (= Daffodils) by Alf Wallander (in production 1897–1908) and several patterns that cannot be attributed to any particular designer, including *Tage* (1908), *Göta* (1911), *Greta* (1911) and *Helga* (1915). The decorative foliate arrangements featured in some patterns reveal Far Eastern inspiration, for instance *Svala* (= Swallow, 1897) and *Tärna* (= Tern, 1911), and still others are notable for echoes of the Empire style with neo-Classical forms and simple, emphasised borders (see fig. 58).

When the Almström sons became managers at Rörstrand, they reduced the number of items in production, which had become too numerous to handle, and this development, concomitantly with a noticeable adaptation to new style trends, continued for the most part even after 1910.

During this period, Rörstrand remained one of the largest Swedish tiled-stove manufacturers and in the turn-of-the-century years hired several leading architects. The most famous architect-designed Rörstrand products are the tiled stoves by Ferdinand Boberg (1897) although Hugo Tryggelin and architects Bror Almqvist, Gustaf Clason and Axel Lindegren also contributed models in the new style (see fig. 59).

1 Arvid Bernard Horn, Graf af Ekebyholm (1664–1742), schwedischer Offizier und Politiker; nach dem Tod Kaiser Karls XII. an der Beseitigung der absoluten Monarchie beteiligt und in der Folgezeit der eigentliche Herrscher Schwedens.

2 HKS: Högra Konstindustriella Skolan (Höhere Schule für Dekorative Kunst an der Technischen Schule).

3 Jacobsson, Ernst. 1900. *Konstslöjden.* Allmänna Konst- & Industriutställningen i Stockholm 1897. Officiell berättelse. II, 507–613.

4 Frykholm, Sunny. 1898. *Glass industry and ceramics in Sweden.* The Artist. 1898 December, vol. XXIII, 198–203.

5 *L'Art Decoratif* 1898:1.

6 Nach der 1825 erteilten Genehmigung wurde 1827 auf der Insel Värmdö im Stockholmer Stadtgebiet Gustavsberg die Herstellung von Steingut aufgenommen. Nach mehrfachem Besitzerwechsel erfolgte 1875 die Umwandlung in die *Aktiebolaget Gustafsberg Fabriks Interessenter, Gustafsberg.* Um die Jahrhundertwende war das Unternehmen mit nahezu eintausend Beschäftigten hinter Rörstrand der zweitgrößte Keramikhersteller in Schweden. Das Angebot umfaßte Gebrauchsgeschirr und Sanitärkeramik in Steingut sowie Zier- und Kunstgegenstände in Parian und Steingut. Künstlerischer Leiter war von 1897 bis 1908 Gunnar Wennerberg. Die vorwiegend nach seinen Entwürfen ausgeführten Ziergegenstände mit mehrfarbigem Sgraffitodekor erlangten eine beträchtliche Popularität. Auf der Weltausstellung in Paris 1900 erhielt die Firma eine Goldmedaille.

7 Arnold Krog (1856–1931), Architekt, Maler, Graphiker, Keramiker und Kunsthandwerker. Von 1884 bis 1916 Künstlerischer Leiter der *Königlichen Porzellanmanufaktur* Kopenhagen. Krog führte hier die Unterglasurmalerei mit einer großen Skala farblicher Abstufungen ein und konnte zahlreiche Künstler als Mitarbeiter gewinnen. Er wurde damit auch für Rörstrand zum Vorbild.

8 Gegründet 1797 als *Gustav IV Adolfs Stenkohlsverk*; firmierte bis 1903 als *Höganäs Stenkohlsverk* und danach als *Höganäs-Billesholms Aktiebolaget.* 1832 begann man mit der Herstellung von Gebrauchs- und Zierkeramik. In den Jahren um die Jahrhundertwende entstanden unter der künstlerischen Leitung des Malers und Keramikers Helmer Osslund (auch Åslund, 1866–1938) Zierobjekte im Stil des Art Nouveau; sie fanden außerhalb Skandinaviens allerdings nur wenig Beachtung.

9 *P. H. Lundgrens Kakelfabrik*, gegründet in den 1860er Jahren von Bror Hjalmar Lundgren. Unter seinem Sohn P. H. Lundgren wurde das Programm um Gebrauchs- und Zierkeramik erweitert. Die Firma wurde 1911 geschlossen.

10 *Kosta Glasbruk*, die älteste schwedische Glasfabrik, gegründet 1742, trat seit 1897 mit einem größeren Angebot von Kunstgläsern hervor, die in den Dekoren und der Technik eine Beeinflussung durch die französische Glaskunst der Zeit, insbesondere durch die Arbeiten von Emile Gallé, erkennen ließen.

11 *Reijmyre Glasbruk*, 1810 zur Herstellung von Fensterglas gegründete schwedische Glashütte. Um 1900 Aufnahme der Herstellung von Kunstgläsern nach französischem Vorbild.

12 Pudor, Heinrich, in: Dokumente des modernen Kunstgewerbes, Serie A, 1902, Heft 2, S. 57

13 Sandier, Alexandre. 1900. *Ceramique à l'Exposition.* Art et Decoration, 8, 1900, S. 183–96.

14 Ring, Herman A. 1900. *Paris och världsutställningen 1900.* Dagens Nyheter 1/5 1900.

15 Holt, E Gilmore. 1988. *The Expanding World of Art, 1874–1902.* Vol. 1 Universal Expositions and State-Sponsored Fine Arts Exhibitions.

16 Jens Ferdinand Willumsen (1863–1958), Maler; beschäftigte sich bereits von 1890 bis 1894 in Paris mit Keramik; von 1897 bis 1900 war er künstlerischer Leiter der Porzellanfabrik Bing & Grøndahl in Kopenhagen und bestimmte die für Jahre charakteristische Dekorationsweise der Manufaktur.

17 Die Bezeichnung „Feldspatporzellan" (schwedisch: fältspatporslin) für das europäische Hartporzellan nach chinesischem Vorbild war (in Abgrenzung zu der 1708 von Böttger entwickelten Variante, bei der zunächst Calciumverbindungen Verwendung fanden) noch bis in die erste Hälfte des vergangenen Jahrhunderts auch in Deutschland üblich. In Meißen war man allerdings schon 1727 oder wenig später zum Feldspatporzellan übergegangen, nachdem man im Lande geeignete Vorkommen gefunden hatte. Demgegenüber wurde in Frankreich die ergänzende Beimischung von Kalk zu den auch dort verwendeten feldspathaltigen Rohstoffen noch bis in das 20. Jahrhundert beibehalten. Die Hervorhebung der Bezeichnung bei Rörstrand dient nicht nur der Abgrenzung zu dem französischen Porzellan, sondern ist auch insofern von Bedeutung, als Schweden über Feldspatvorkommen von besonderer Qualität verfügt und die reinste und beste Qualität aus der Grube Ytterby auf der Insel Resarö kommt, die sich im Besitz von Rörstrand befand, so dass sie unter der Handelsbezeichnung „Rörstrand-Feldspat" geführt wurden. In

1 Arvid Bernard Horn, Graf af |Count| Ekebyholm (1664–1742), Swedish officer and statesman; after the death of King Charles XII, Horn played a role in abolishing the absolute monarchy in Sweden, after which he de facto ruled the country.

2 HKS: Högra Konstindustriella Skolan (Higher School of Industrial Arts).

3 Jacobsson, Ernst. 1900. *Konstslöjden.* Allmänna Konst- & Industriutställningen i Stockholm 1897. Officiell berättelse. vol. II, p. 507–613.

4 Frykholm, Sunny. 1898. 'Glass industry and ceramics in Sweden', in *The Artist.* 1898 December, vol. XXIII, p. 198–203.

5 *L'Art Decoratif* 1898:1.

6 After the first letter of patent was granted in 1825, ordinary stoneware began to be made in 1827 on the island of Värmdö within the Stockholm district of Gustavsberg. After the factory changed hands several times, the business was turned into a private company, registered as Aktiebolaget Gustavsberg Fabriks Interessenter, Gustavsberg. Towards the turn of the century, Gustavsberg employed a workforce of nearly a thousand, making it, after Rörstrand, the second largest ceramics manufacturer in Sweden. The Gustavsberg range comprised tableware for everyday use, stoneware bathroom fixtures, and ornaments and objets d'art in Parian porcelain and stoneware. Gunnar Wennerberg was leading artist at Gustavsberg from 1897 until 1908. Ornamental objects boasting polychrome sgraffito decoration, most of them made after his designs, became enormously popular. Gustavsberg was awarded a gold medal at the 1900 Paris World Exposition.

7 Arnold Krog (1856–1931), architect, painter, printmaker, ceramicist and craftsman. Art director of the Royal Copenhagen Porcelain Factory from 1884 to 1916. Krog was the one to introduce underglaze painting in a wide range of colour shades there and employed numerous artists, becoming an example for Rörstrand.

8 Est. 1797 as Gustav IV Adolfs Stenkohlsverk; registered until 1903 as Höganäs Stenkohlsverk and after that as Höganäs-Billesholms Aktiebolaget. The manufacture of everyday tableware and decorative ceramics began in 1832. In the years before the turn of the century, Helmer Osslund (also Åslund, 1866–1938), a painter and ceramicist, made a collection for the 1897 Stockholm exhibition. Ornamental objects in the Art Nouveau style were made under his supervision but they were little appreciated.

9 P. H. Lundgrens Kakelfabrik, established in the 1860s by Bror Hjalmar Lundgren. Under his son, P. H. Lundgren, the range was widened to include utilitarian and decorative ceramics. The firm closed down in 1911.

10 Kosta Glasbruk, the oldest Swedish glassworks (est. 1742), produced a wide range of art glass products from 1897, which reveal the influence of contemporaneous art glass, especially the work of Émile Gallé, in respect of decoration and technique.

11 Reijmyre Glasbruk, Swedish glassworks established in 1810 to make window glass. Ca 1900 began to make art glass in the French manner.

12 Pudor, Heinrich, in: Dokumente des modernen Kunstgewerbes, Serie A, 1902, Heft 2, p. 57.

13 Sandier, Alexandre. 1900. *Ceramique à l'Exposition.* Art et Decoration, 8, 1900, p. 183–96.

14 Herman A. Ring. 1900. "Paris och världsutställningen 1900". *Dagens Nyheter* 1/5 1900.

15 E Gilmore Holt. 1988. *The Expanding World of Art, 1874-1902.* vol. 1 Universal Expositions and State-Sponsored Fine Arts Exhibitions.

16 Jens Ferdinand Willumsen (1863–1958), painter; as early as 1890 to 1894 studied ceramics in Paris; from 1897 until 1900 he was artistic director of the Bing & Grøndahl Porcelain Manufactory in Copenhagen, where he was the one to define the type of decoration that was characteristic of that factory for years.

17 The term 'feldspar porcelain' (Swedish: *fältspatporslin*) was applied to European hard-paste porcelain modelled after Chinese porcelain (as distinct from the variant developed by Böttger in 1708, for which calcines were at first used) even on into the first half of the 20th cent. in Germany as well. At Meißen, however, the transition to feldspar porcelain had been made as early as 1727 or not much later after enough of the raw material was found in the region. In France, on the other hand, the practice of mixing calcine with the feldspathic raw materials which were also used there persisted on into the 20th cent. The emphasis laid on the term at Rörstrand not only serves to distinguish Rörstrand porcelain from French porcelain but is also significant because Sweden boasts feldspathic rock of particularly high quality: the best superior quality feldspar comes from the Ytterby pit on the island of Resarö, which used to belong to Rörstrand so that it was traded as 'Rörstrand feldspar'. In porcelain paste, feldspar makes the body dense and transparent; the particular toughness thus achieved increases durability and prevents the body from being warped during firing – a property that is of the utmost impor-

der Porzellanmasse bewirkt der Feldspat das Dichtwerden und die Transparenz des Scherbens; seine besondere Zähigkeit erhöht die Standfestigkeit und verhindert die Deformation des Scherbens im Brand – eine Eigenschaft, die angesichts der durchbrochenen Rörstrand-Objekte mit ihren feinen plastischen Auflagen von größter Bedeutung ist, so dass die Beibehaltung der Bezeichnung für ihre immer wieder variierten Massemischungen gerechtfertigt ist.

18 Auf den Scherben aufgetragene und mit der sie überziehenden farblosen Glasur eingebrannte Farben von großer Leuchtkraft, allerdings von eingeschränkter Farbpalette, da nur wenige Farben den sehr hohen Brenntemperaturen standhalten.

19 An Kameen erinnernde Dekortechnik; bei der langwierigen und diffizilen Herstellung wird ein relativ dünner Massebrei nach und nach auf den aus der gleichen Masse bestehenden Grund aufgetragen, so dass ein weißer oder farbiger Reliefdekor entsteht.

20 Metallisch schimmernde farbige Glasuren, die in einem rauchigen Brand unter Sauerstoffentzug eine metallische Farbigkeit der Oberfläche bewirken. Durch Eintauchen in ein Säurebad kann eine Mattätzung erreicht werden.

21 Auf Porzellan und Steinzeug (seltener auch auf Steingut) aufgebrannte Glasur, die Ausscheidungen von Kristallen entwickelt, die sich in Größe, Farbe und Verteilung deutlich unterscheiden. Wegen der aufwendigen und leicht störbaren Herstellung recht selten.

22 Auch China-Rot, Sang-de-bœuf oder Ochsenblut, ein durch Kupferoxidzusatz zu leichtflüssigen Glasuren im abwechselnd reduzierenden und oxidierenden Brand erreichtes intensives Blutrot. Das in China seit langem bekannte Verfahren wurde gegen Ende der 1870er Jahre fast gleichzeitig an verschiedenen Stellen in Europa wiederentdeckt.

23 Ein heller bis farbiger poröser Scherben, überzogen mit einer weißdeckenden Zinnglasur, auf die in ungebranntem Zustand die Bemalung aufgetragen wird. Der Name ist abgeleitet von der italienischen Stadt Faenza. Die oft synonym gebrauchte Majolika zeichnet sich bei gleicher Dekorationsart durch eine deckende farbige Glasur aus. Bei den von Rörstrand in dem behandelten Zeitraum unter der Bezeichnung Fayence angebotenen Artikeln handelt es sich häufig um Aufglasur-Fayencen, bei denen die Dekore auf die bereits glattgebrannte Glasur in Handmalerei oder als Farbdruck aufgebracht werden.

24 Gunnar Gunnarsson Wennerberg (1863–1914). Schwedischer Maler, Graphiker und Kunsthandwerker. Studierte in Paris und absolvierte anschließend eine Ausbildung in der Manufacture Nationale in Sèvres. Von 1895 bis 1908 war er leitender Künstler der Gustavsberg Porslinsfabrik. Außerdem lieferte er Entwürfe für die Kosta Glasbruk und war von 1902 bis 1908 Lehrer für Malerei an der Tekniska Skolan in Stockholm. Wennerberg war in der Epoche des Jugendstils neben Wallander der bedeutendste Keramik-Gestalter in Schweden.

25 Bei den Sgraffito-Arbeiten von Wennerberg wurde der weiße oder eingefärbte Scherben mit einer andersfarbigen Engobe überzogen; durch deren partielles Entfernen entstanden Dekore. Abschließend wurde die gesamte Oberfläche mit einer farblosen, transparenten Glasur überzogen.

26 Briefe Robert Almström an Pietro Krohn 20.4.1897 und 15.2.1898. Archiv des Kunstindustriemuseums Kopenhagen.

27 Siegfried Bing (1838–1905). Geboren in Hamburg. Nach kaufmännischer Tätigkeit in der elterlichen Porzellanmanufaktur in Paris gründete er dort 1863 die Porzellanhandlung Leullier & Bing. Später verlegte er sich auf den Handel mit fernöstlicher Kunst, baute eine umfassende Sammlung auf und trat seit 1883 auch mit Veröffentlichungen hervor, darunter der Serie „Le Japon Artistique". 1895 richtete er in Paris seine Galerie „L'Art Nouveau" ein, in der Spitzenwerke der Kunst und des Kunsthandwerks des neuen Stils, dem sie seinen Namen gab, angeboten wurden. 1904 wurden die Galerie und die ihr angeschlossenen Werkstätten aufgelöst.

28 Kaolin (nach dem chinesischen Berg Kaoling), Porzellanerde; eine vorwiegend aus dem Mineral Kaolinit, einem Aluminiumsilikat, bestehende weiche, formbare Tonsubstanz. Hauptbestandteil des Porzellans.

29 Almström, Robert. 1903. *Lervarorna och deras tillverkning*. Särtryck Uppfinningarnas Bok, Bd. VII.

30 Masse, aus Ton oder tonhaltigen Stoffen bestehende, mit Wasser aufbereitete Substanz unterschiedlicher Konsistenz, die sich beliebig gestalten lässt. Im Brand entsteht aus ihr der Scherben.

31 Eindrehen (auch: Einformen), maschinelles Formgebungsverfahren, bei dem die (Gips-)Form die äußere, die Schablone die innere Seite eines keramischen Gebildes (Tasse, Schüssel, usw.) formt.

32 Schlickermalerei, Oberflächendekoration keramischer Gegenstände mit Malschlicker, einem mit Wasser angerührten, naturbelassenen oder eingefärbtem Tonbrei.

33 Lüsterfarben, schimmernde Überzüge, die eine metallische Farbigkeit der Oberfläche bewirken; der eigentliche Effekt wird meist in einem rauchigen Brand unter Sauerstoffentzug bewirkt.

34 Ekerot, Gunnar. 1899. Rörstrands Porslinsfabrik. Svenska Industriella Verk och Anläggningar. 1899:1, 1–12.

tance for ensuring the stability of pierced Rörstrand objects with fine sprigging; hence retaining the term for their paste mixtures, which were often varied, was justified.

18 Very vibrant colours, albeit available in only a limited range since only a very few colours stand firing at very high temperatures, applied directly to the body and coated in colourless glaze.

19 A decoration technique reminiscent of cameo; the time-consuming and difficult process of executing it entails gradually applying relatively thin white slip to a porcelain paste ground of the same composition to create white or coloured relief decoration.

20 Metallic iridescent glazes that create a metallic coloured surface. A matt surface was produced by dipping the workpiece in an acid bath.

21 A glaze fired on porcelain and fine stoneware (less often also on earthenware), which precipitates crystals that vary widely in size, colour and surface distribution. Quite rare because making it was difficult and could easily go wrong.

22 Also known as Chinese Red, *sang-de-bœuf* or ox-blood, a brilliant blood-red colour produced by adding copper oxide as a colouring agent to fluid glazes and firing them alternately in a reducing and an oxidising atmosphere. Long known in China, the process was rediscovered almost simultaneously in various places in Europe towards the close of the 1870s.

23 Porous earthenware body ranging from light to coloured, coated in an opaque white tin glaze, on to which painting is applied before firing. The name derives from the city of Faenza in Italy. Majolica, often used synonymously is decorated in the same way but the ground is an opaque coloured glaze. The articles called faience at Rörstrand during the period discussed here are often overglaze faience, with the decoration applied by hand or printed on in colour on to glaze that had already been hardened on.

24 Gunnar Gunnarsson Wennerberg (1863–1914). Swedish painter, graphic artist and craftsman. Studied in Paris, and then completed training at the Manufacture Nationale in Sèvres. From 1895 until 1908 he was the leading artisan at the Gustavsberg Porslinsfabrik. He also submitted designs to the Kosta Glasbruk and taught painting at the Tekniska Skolan in Stockholm from 1902 to 1908. In the Art Nouveau/Jugendstil era Wennerberg was, along with Wallander, the leading ceramics designer in Sweden.

25 Wennerberg's sgraffito pieces featured a white or stained body coated in engobe of a different colour; decoration was created by removing the engobe in places. Then the whole surface was coated in a colourless transparent glaze.

26 Letters written by Robert Almström to Pietro Krohn on 20 Apr. 1897 and 15 Feb. 1898. Archives of the Danish Museum of Art and Design in Copenhagen.

27 Siegfried Bing (1838–1905). Born in Hamburg. After on-the-job training at his father's porcelain factory in Paris, Siegfried Bing established Leullier & Bing, dealers in porcelain, in 1863. Later he switched to dealing in East Asian art, building up a comprehensive collection. From 1883 he also began to publish, including the series entitled *Le Japon Artistique*. In 1895 he established the Paris gallery L'Art Nouveau, in which he displayed and sold top-quality art works and pieces of decorative art in the new style, which was named after the gallery. The gallery and the associated workshops were disbanded in 1904.

28 Kaolin (after the Chinese mountain Kaoling): earth used in making porcelain; a soft, ductile clay substance consisting chiefly of the mineral kaolinite, an aluminium silicate. The main ingredient of porcelain paste.

29 Robert Almström. 1903. 'Lervarorna och deras tillverkning' (The making of ceramics). Separate print from *Uppfinningarnas Bok (The book of inventions)*, vol. VII.

30 Paste, consisting of clay or substances containing clay, prepared with water to a varying consistency, which can be worked as desired. Firing turns it into body.

31 Turning (also: moulding), mechanical shaping process by which the (plaster) mould shapes the outside while a stencil shapes the inside of a ceramic piece (cup, bowl, etc.).

32 Trailing (French: *pastillage*), decorating the surface of ceramic objects with slip, potter's clay mixed with water to a creamy consistency, either left in its natural colour or tinted.

33 Lustre colours, an iridescent coating that lends a metallic sheen to surfaces; the actual effect is usually created by firing in a smoky reducing (rich in carbon monoxide instead of oxygen) atmosphere.

34 Gunnar Ekerot. 1899. *Rörstrands Porslinsfabrik. Svenska Industriella Verk och Anläggningar (Industrial works in Sweden)*. 1899:1, 1–12.

35 Aventurine glaze, an alkaline glaze rich in borium with an iron oxide content of up to 30%; while the glaze is cooling after firing, clearly discernible, glittery crystalline spangles of iron are formed.

36 Crystal glaze, a glaze fired on to porcelain and fine stoneware (more rarely also earthenware), which precipitates as crystals that vary considerably in size, colour and distribution.

35 Aventuringlasur, quarzreiche Alkali-Borglasur mit Zusatz von bis zu 30% Eisenoxid; beim Abkühlen der Glasur nach dem Brand bilden sich deutlich erkennbare, kristallin-metallisch glitzernde Eisenflitter.

36 Kristallglasur, auf Porzellan und Steinzeug (seltener auch auf Steingut) aufgebrannte Glasur, die Ausscheidungen von Kristallen entwickelt, die sich in Größe, Farbe und Verteilung deutlich unterscheiden.

37 Uranglasur, tomatenrote, bleireiche Glasur, eingefärbt mit bis zu 10% Uranoxid; heute wegen der radioaktiven Strahlung nicht mehr eingesetzt.

38 Norrlandsposten, 10/11, 1897.

39 Göteborgs Morgonspost, 26/10, 1935.

40 Gerhard Henning (1880–1967), schwedischer Bildhauer und Keramiker. Nach der Ausbildung an der Valands Konstskola in Göteborg und einem Studienaufenthalt in Italien ging er nach Dänemark und wurde dort Mitarbeiter von Arnold Krog. Er lieferte zahlreiche Entwürfe für die Königliche Porzellanfabrik in Kopenhagen.

41 Ferdinand Boberg (1860–1945); Architekt, Graphiker und Kunsthandwerker; Ehemann der auch für Rörstrand tätigen Malerin Anna Boberg. Lieferte Entwürfe für Rörstrand und zwischen 1909 und 1914 auch für den Konkurrenten Gustavsberg.

42 Prinz Eugén (1865–1947), Sohn von König Oscar II; Maler und Kunsthandwerker; lieferte Entwürfe für Gustavsberg und Rörstrand und trat auch mit keramischen Einzelarbeiten hervor.

43 Die Texte sind einer von Alf Wallander angelegten Mappe mit Zeitungsausschnitten entnommen.

37 Uranium glaze, a tomato-red glaze rich in lead, tinted by the admixture of up to 10%; nowadays no longer used because of its radioactivity.

38 Norrlandsposten, 10/11, 1897.

39 Göteborgs Morgonspost, 26/10, 1935.

40 Gerhard Henning (1880–1967), Swedish sculptor and ceramicist. After training at Valands Konstskola in Göteborg and a stay in Italy for study purposes, he went to Denmark, where he was employed by Arnold Krog. He submitted numerous designs to the Royal Copenhagen Porcelain Manufactory.

41 Ferdinand Boberg (1860–1945), architect, graphic artist and craftsman. Husband of the painter Anna Boberg, who also worked for Rörstrand. Designed for Rörstrand and, between 1909 and 1914, also for Gustavsberg, Rörstrand's main competitor.

42 Prince Eugén (1865–1947), son of King Oscar II, painter and craftsman. Submitted designs to Gustavsberg and Rörstrand and also made a name for himself with one-off ceramics.

43 The texts have been taken from a portfolio of newspaper cuttings collected by Alf Wallander.

Rörstrand
Porzellan-Objekte // Porcelain-Objects

1 Vase, ca 1899

plastisch üppige Ausformung einer Mohnblüte, die den gesamten Mündungsrand umfasst und formt. Von zwei gegenseitig aufsteigenden Stängeln zweigt jeweils ein weiterer Stängel mit leicht geöffneter Knospe ab, der sich um den Vasenkorpus legt. // with sumptuously three-dimensional moulded poppy bloom encircling and shaping the entire mouth of the vase. Two stalks rising in mirror image, each branching off into another stalk bearing a slightly opened bud to encircle the vase wall.

Diese Vase wurde auf mehreren Ausstellungen gezeigt, u.a. auf der Weltausstellung 1900 in Paris. // This vase was shown at several trade fairs, including the 1900 Paris World Exposition.

Entwurf // Design **Alf Wallander**

H 30.5 cm

3 Kronen-Marke und *A. Wallander 1900* in grüner Farbe // *3 coronets mark* and *A. Wallander 1900* in green

VORBEMERKUNG:
PRELIMINARY REMARKS:

Alle Objekte sind aus hochgebranntem Porzellan mit Unterglasur-Bemalung. Die Rörstrand-Marke (3 Kronen und Schriftzug) sowie **die Künstler-Signatur sind überwiegend in grüner Farbe mit Pinsel aufgetragen.**
// All objects are of high-fired porcelain. Painting is always underglaze. The Rörstrand mark (3 coronets and writing) and artist signatures are usually applied by brush in green.

Die Proportionen der abgebildeten Objekte sind unterschiedlich. Die genauen Größenangaben entnehmen Sie bitte der jeweiligen Objektbeschreibung.
// The proportions of objects in the figures vary. The exact sizes should be taken from the corresponding object's description.

2 Vase, ca 1905/1910

konisch aufsteigender Korpus mit sechs auf der Schulter liegenden, stark reliefierten Alpenveilchen. Der Hals ist mit geometrischen Formen gleichförmig und umlaufend durchbrochen. // with bevel tapering upwards with six cyclamen blooms in high relief on the shoulder of the vase. The neck is uniformly pierced all round with geometric forms.

Bemalung // Painting Nils Emil Lundström
H 45 cm
3 *Kronen-Marke* und *NL* in grüner Farbe, blind *JK, C* und 55
// *3 coronets mark* and *NL* in green, blind-stamped *JK, C* and 55

3   Vase, ca 1905

an Bauch und Hals mit reliefierten Wildrosen, sowie mit drei aufsteigenden, zu Henkeln ausgeformten Zweigen auf tief-dunkelblauem Fond dekoriert. // decorated with wild roses in relief on wall and neck as well as three vertical twigs moulded into handles on deep dark blue ground.
Bemalung // Painting Karl Lindström
H 38 cm
3 Kronen-Marke und *KL* in grüner Farbe, blind *H.P.* und *15302*
// *3 coronets mark* and *KL* in green, blind-stamped *H.P.* and *15302*

4 *Vase, ca 1905/1910*

bauchig-flacher Fuß, zur Mündung konisch
zulaufend. Basis und Hals mit reliefierten
Herzlöffelblättern und -blüten dekoriert.
// with low, swelling foot, vase tapering
conically towards the mouth. Base and
neck decorated with foliage and flowers of
Caldesia parnassiifolia [no English common name].
Bemalung // Painting Algot Eriksson
H 37 cm
3 Kronen-Marke und *AE* in grüner Farbe,
blind *20521* // *3 coronets mark* and *AE* in
green, blind-stamped *20521*

5 *Vase, ca 1898*

mit aus zwiebelförmigem Körper aufwachsenden, einen hohen Halskelch bildenden
Blättern und mit drei reliefiert aufliegenden Blüten. // with leaves growing up out of
bulbous vase to form a high neck with
flaring rim and three flowers in relief on
the wall of the vase.
Bemalung // Painting Nils Emil Lundström
H 38 cm
3 Kronen-Marke, NEL (ligiert) und *755*
in grüner Farbe // *3 coronets mark, NEL*
(monogram) and *755* in green

6 *Vase, vor // before* 1902

mit drei gleich dekorierten Seiten: Erbsen-
ranke in kräftig ausgeformtem Relief.
// with three identically decorated sides:
pea tendrils in high relief.
Modelliert und bemalt // Modelled and
painted Anna Boberg, 1897
H 10.8 cm
3 Kronen-Marke und • *AB* • (ligiert) in grüner
Farbe, blind *AB* (ligiert), *11094* und *3*
// *3 coronets mark* and • *AB* • (monogram)
in green, blind-stamped *AB* (monogram),
11094 and *3*

7 *Vase, ca* 1900

mit Kapuzinerkresse, drei größere Blätter
jeweils mit einem Stiel verbunden, von
diesem hängen je drei kleinere Blätter
herab. // with nasturtiums: three quite
large leaves linked with stem from which
three smaller leaves dangle.
Modelliert und bemalt // Modelled and
painted Astrid Ewerlöf
H 7.5 cm
3 Kronen-Marke und · *E* · in grüner Farbe,
blind · *E* · und *13927* // *3 coronets mark* and
· *E* · in green, blind-stamped · *E* · and *13927*

8 *Vase, ca* 1900

mit großer reliefierter Mohnblüte,
umrahmt von zwei langstieligen Knospen,
die andere Vasenseite gleich dekoriert.
// with large poppy in relief, flanked by
two buds on long stems; the other side
identically decorated.
Modelliert // Modelled Ruben Rising;
Bemalung // Painting Nils Emil Lundström
H 9 cm
3 Kronen-Marke und *NL* in grüner Farbe,
blind *RR* und *8954* // *3 coronets mark* and
NL in green, blind-stamped *RR* and *8954*

9 Vase, vor // *before* 1900

mit drei gleich dekorierten Seiten: Distel mit je zwei reliefierten
Blüten. // with three identically decorated sides: thistles, each with
two blooms in relief.
Bemalung // Painting Mela Anderberg
H 27.5 cm
3 Kronen-Marke, MA und 6063 in grüner Farbe, blind L und 1
// 3 coronets mark, MA and 6063 in green, blind-stamped L and 1

10   Vase, ca 1902/1909

mit zwei gegenständig aufwachsenden, von je einem Blatt begleiteten Stängeln, die unterhalb der durchbrochen gearbeiteten, aus je drei Blüten gebildeten Vasenöffnung zu einem kleinen Henkel geformt sind. // with two three-dimensional stalks accompanied by one leaf each forming a small handle below the pierced vase mouth, which is composed of three flowers to each stalk.

Bemalung // Painting Nils Emil Lundström
H 25.5 cm
3 Kronen-Marke und *NL* in grüner Farbe, blind *M.P.* (Maria Pettersson?), *J, 50095* und *32* // *3 coronets mark* and *NL* in green, blind-stamped *M.P.* (Maria Pettersson?), *J, 50095* and *32*

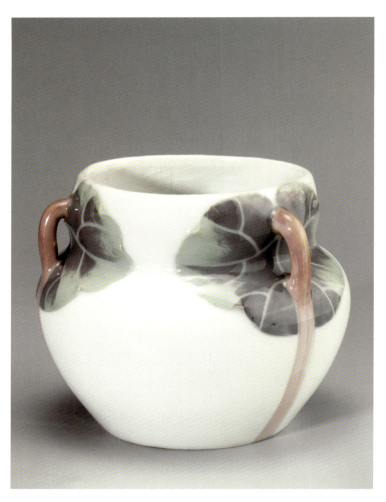

11   *Vase, ca 1902*

mit auf drei Seiten gleichem Dekor: Blatt
der Kapuzinerkresse, reliefiert, der Blattstiel ist als Griff geformt. // with identical
decoration on three sides: nasturtium leaf
executed in relief; the stem is formed into
a handle.
Modelliert und bemalt // Modelled and
painted Georg Asplund
H 11 cm
3 Kronen-Marke und • G • in grüner Farbe,
blind • G •, 30765 und 3 // 3 coronets mark
and • G • in green, blind-stamped • G •,
30765 and 3

12   *Vase, ca 1900*

mit reliefierten und durchbrochenen See-
rosenblättern, am Vasenrand umgelappt.
// with water lily leaves executed in relief
and pierced, overlapping at vase rim.
Modelliert und bemalt // Modelled and
painted Anna Boberg
H 13 cm
3 Kronen-Marke und • AB • (ligiert) in grüner
Farbe, blind • AB • (ligiert), JL, 10693 und 15
// 3 coronets mark and • AB • (monogram)
in green, blind-stamped • AB • (monogram),
JL, 10693 and 15

13 Vase, ca 1905/1909

mit am Rande reliefierten Stiefmütterchen-
blättern, am Hals drei Blüten. // with pansy
leaves in relief on the rim, three flowers on
the neck.
Bemalt // Painting Georg Asplund
H 22 cm
3 Kronen-Marke und • *G* • in grüner Farbe,
blind *H.S.* und *85* // *3 coronets mark* and
• *G* • in green, blind-stamped *H.S.* and *85*

14 Vase, ca 1905

mit Blättern und leicht reliefierten Blüten,
auf beiden Seiten gleich. // with foliage and
blossoms executed in low relief; identical
on both sides.
Bemalung // Painting Georg Asplund
H 13 cm
3 Kronen-Marke und • *G* • in grüner Farbe,
blind *M.P.* (Maria Pettersson?), *.B.* und *1838*
// *3 coronets mark* and • *G* • in green, blind-
stamped *M.P.* (Maria Pettersson?), *.B.* and
1838

15 Vase, vor // before 1902

an der Schauseite mit zwei jungen Kiefern-
zapfen, reliefiert, und Nadelbüscheln.
// with two young pine cones executed in
relief and tufts of pine needles on the main
viewing side.
Bemalung // Painting Anna Boberg
H 11.5 cm
3 Kronen-Marke und *AB* in grüner Farbe,
blind *E. G.* und *1552* // *3 coronets mark* and
AB in green, blind-stamped *E. G.* and *1552*

16 Vase, ca 1900

Die berühmte Schwanenvase, hier Unikat von Alf Wallander (unten
an der Wandung signiert/eingeritzt A. Wallander), entstanden vor
1897. // The celebrated Swan Vase, here a one-off by Alf Wallander
(near the bottom of the wall signed/carved A. Wallander), made before
1897 (siehe // see: *Keramische Monatshefte*, 1903, Heft [No.] 7, p. 111).
Diese Vase wurde erstmals 1897 auf der Industrieausstellung Stockholm, dann 1900 auf der Weltausstellung Paris und 1909 auf der
Stockholm-Ausstellung gezeigt. // This vase was first shown at the
1897 Stockholm General Art and Industrial Art Exhibition, then at the
1900 Paris World Exposition and at the 1909 Stockholm Exhibition.
H 41 cm
3 Kronen-Marke zweifach in grüner Farbe, blind *APZ* und *S2*
// *3 coronets mark* twice in green, blind-stamped *APZ* and *S2*

17 Vase, ca 1902/1905

mit Sumpfdotterblume (Blätter und Blüten) umlaufend dekoriert. // decorated all round with marsh marigold (leaves and flowers).
Modelliert und bemalt // Modelled and painted Georg Asplund
H 13 cm
3 Kronen-Marke und *· G ·* in grüner Farbe, blind *· G ·* und *30444* // *3 coronets mark* and *· G ·* in green, blind-stamped *· G ·* and *30444*

18 Vase, nach // after 1910

mit fliegenden Schwänen am abendlichen Himmel. // with swans in flight against an evening sky.
Bemalung // Painting Nils Emil Lundström
H 24 cm
3 Kronen-Marke und *NEL* (ligiert) in grüner Farbe, blind *BMN, S7* und *28* // *3 coronets mark* and *NEL* (monogram) in green, blind-stamped *BMN, S7* and *28*
Stimmungsvoll bemalte Vase im Stil der Kopenhagener Manufaktur // Atmospheric painting in the style of the Royal Copenhagen Manufactory

19 Vase, ca 1900

mit drei Schirmkiefern bei Dämmerlicht, auf der anderen Seite zwei Kiefern.
// featuring three umbrella pines at dusk, two pines on other side.
Bemalung // Painting Nils Emil Lundström
H 15 cm
3 Kronen-Marke, NEL (ligiert) und *1735* in grüner Farbe, blind *J* // *3 coronets mark, NEL* (monogram) and *1735* in green, blind-stamped *J*

20 Vase, ca 1898

mit blühendem Mohn in verschwommenen Konturen, auf der anderen Vasenseite ebenfalls, aber einfacher ausgeführt.
// with poppy blooms in blurred contours; similar on the other side but more simply executed.
Bemalung // Painting Algot Eriksson
H 14 cm
3 Kronen-Marke, AE und *668* in grüner Farbe, blind *I* und *AAC* // *3 coronets mark, AE* and *668* in green, blind-stamped *I* and *AAC*

21 Vase, ca 1897/1899

mit blühendem Mohn in verschwommenen Konturen, auf der anderen Vasenseite ebenfalls, aber einfacher ausgeführt.
// with poppy in full bloom, contours blurred; similar on other side of vase but more simply executed.
Bemalung // Painting Algot Eriksson
H 25.5 cm
3 Kronen-Marke, AE und *468* in grüner Farbe, blind *J* // *3 coronets mark, AE* and *468* in green, blind-stamped *J*

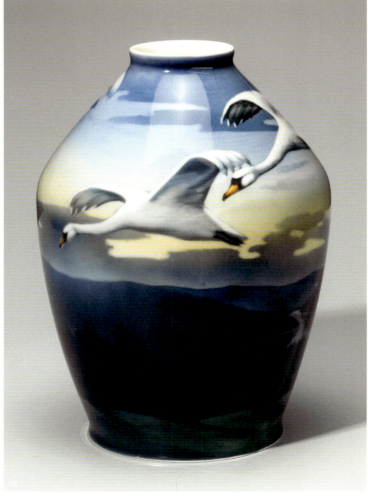

mit reliefierten Algen auf drei gleich dekorierten Seiten. // with three
identically decorated sides with seaweed executed in relief.
Modelliert // Modelled **Waldemar Lindström**
H 23 cm
3 Kronen-Marke in grüner Farbe, blind *W.L., 2850* und *1* // *3 coronets
mark* in green, blind-stamped *W.L., 2850 and 1*

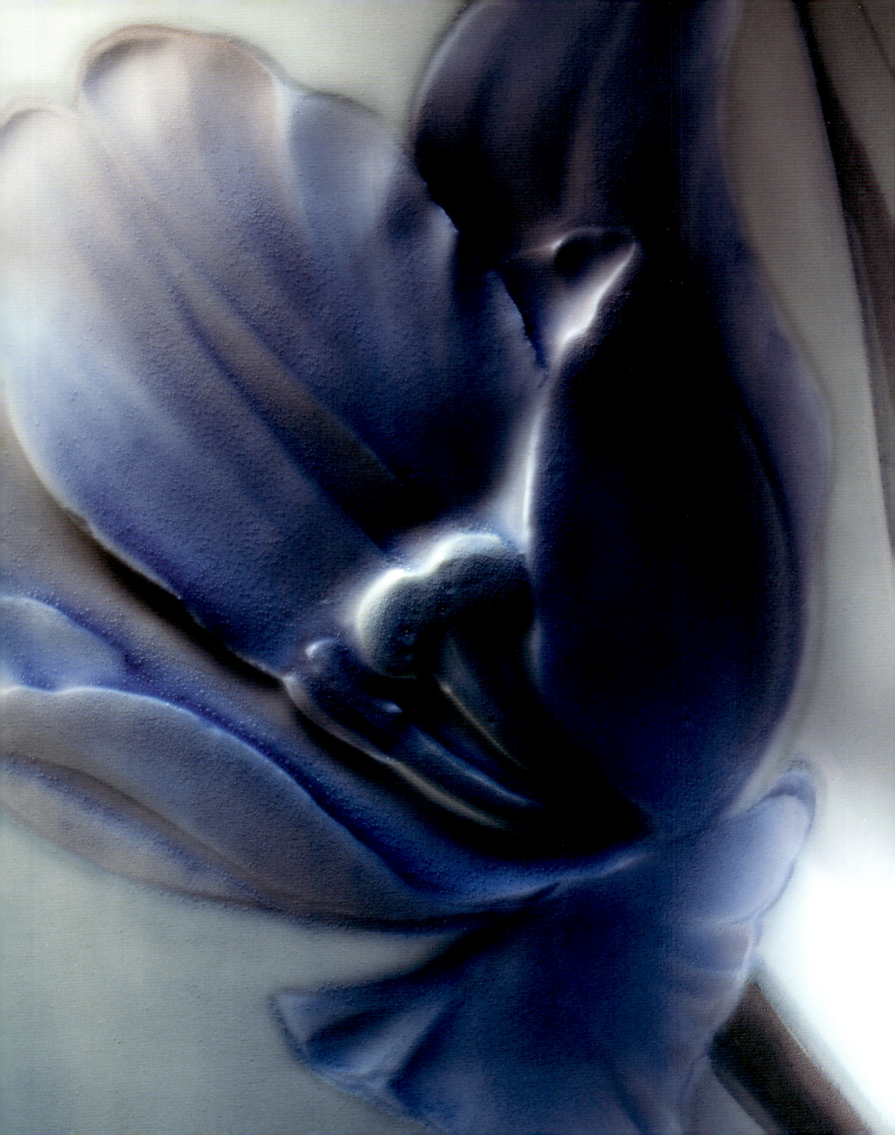

23 Vase, ca 1910

mit vier Tulpenblüten in geöffnetem Hüllblatt, dazwischen vier
weitere, schräg stehende Blüten. // with three tulip flowers in opened
enveloping leaf, between them four more flowers standing obliquely.
Bemalung // Painting Algot Eriksson
H 48 cm
3 Kronen-Marke und *AE* in grüner Farbe, blind *45* und *J* // *3 coronets
mark* and *AE* in green, blind-stamped *45* and *J*

24 Vase, ca 1905/1910

mit auf drei Seiten gleichem Dekor: reliefierte Heckenrosenblüten, dazwischen je ein herabhängendes Blatt, der schmale Vasenrand ist geschwungen und eingekerbt. // with identical decoration on three sides: dog roses executed in relief, alternating with one dangling leaf; narrow vase rim wavy and notched.
Modelliert // Modelled Ruben Rising; Bemalung // Painting Nils Emil Lundström
H 20 cm
3 Kronen-Marke und *NL* in grüner Farbe, blind *RR, J, A 1103* und *23* // *3 coronets mark* and *NL* in green, blind-stamped *RR, J, A 1103* and *23*

25 Vase, ca 1902/1905

konisch aufsteigende Form, im oberen Drittel bauchig ausladend mit drei aufsteigenden Stängeln und sechs leicht reliefierten, blaufarbigen Rosenblüten mit Blättern. // in conical form tapering upwards; in the upper third globular with three vertical flower stalks and six blue roses in low relief with leaves.
Modelliert // Modelled Ruben Rising; Bemalung // Painting Nils Emil Lundström
H 21 cm
3 Kronen-Marke und *NL* in grüner Farbe, blind *RR* und *5702* // *3 coronets mark* and *NL* in green, blind-stamped *RR* and *5702*

26 Vase, ca 1905/1910

mit eingeschnürt abgesetztem Hals aus drei reliefierten Mohnblüten, deren Stiele und Blätter dem Vasenkörper aufliegen. // with nipped-in recessed neck composed of three poppy blooms executed in relief, sprigged poppy stems and leaves on the vase wall.
Modelliert // Modelled Ruben Rising; Bemalung // Painting Karl Lindström
H 21 cm
3 Kronen-Marke und *KL* in grüner Farbe, blind *RR* // *3 coronets mark* and *KL* in green, blind-stamped *RR*

27 *Vase, ca 1905/1909*

mit auf drei Seiten gleichem Dekor: geflügelte Ahornfrüchte, reliefiert, mit großem und herabhängendem kleinerem Blatt.
// with identical decoration on three sides: winged maple seeds, executed in relief, with a large leaf and a dangling smaller leaf.
Modelliert // Modelled Ruben Rising; Bemalung // Painting Astrid Ewerlöf
H 26 cm
3 Kronen-Marke und *· E ·* in grüner Farbe, blind *RR, A 1435* und *J* // *3 coronets mark* and *· E ·* in green, blind-stamped *RR, A 1435* and *J*

28 *Vase, ca 1900*

mit auf drei Seiten gleichem Dekor: dreiblättriges Kleeblatt reliefiert, der Blattstiel ist aus dem nach außen gestellten Vasenrand herabgebogen und als Griff geformt.
// identical decoration on three sides: trilobate clover leaf in relief; the stem bends out from the everted rim of the vessel to form a handle.
Modelliert // Modelled Ruben Rising; Bemalung // Painting Nils Emil Lundström
H 15 cm
3 Kronen-Marke und *NL* in grüner Farbe, blind *RR* und *1118* // *3 coronets mark* and *NL* in green, blind-stamped *RR* and *1118*

29 *Vase, ca 1902*

mit auf drei Seiten gleichem, leicht reliefierten Dekor: Blätter des Pfennigkrauts. // with identical decoration on three sides in light relief: moneywort leaves.
Modelliert // Modelled Astrid Ewerlöf; Bemalung // Painting Nils Emil Lundström
H 8.8 cm
3 Kronen-Marke und *NL* in grüner Farbe, blind *· E ·, •1902 •* und *13* // *3 coronets mark* and *NL* in green, blind-stamped *· E ·, •1902 •* and *13*

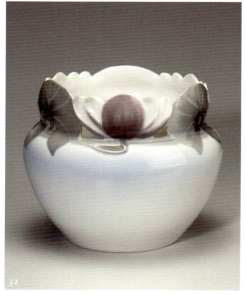

30 Vase, ca 1902/1905

mit durchbrochenem Hals aus drei
reliefierten Clematisblüten mit
herabhängenden Blattranken. // with
pierced neck formed of three clematis flowers in relief with trailing sprays of leaves.
Modelliert // Modelled **Ruben Rising;**
Bemalung // Painting **Nils Emil Lundström**
H 18 cm

3 Kronen-Marke und *NL* in grüner Farbe,
blind *RR, 20962* und *21* // *3 coronets mark*
and *NL* in green, blind-stamped *RR, 20962*
and *21*

31 Vase, ca 1905

bauchige Form, von der Mündung aus
umlaufend herabhängende Brombeer-
Ranken mit Früchten, reliefiert, am Hals
mehrfach durchbrochen. // swelling form,
fruit-laden blackberry canes all round
in relief trailing from mouth; pierced in
several places on the neck.
Modelliert // Modelled **Ruben Rising**
H 15 cm

3 Kronen-Marke in roter Farbe, blind *RR*
und *A2481* // *3 coronets mark* in red, blind-
stamped *RR* and *A2481*

32 Vase, ca 1902

mit aus Seerosenblüten und -blättern
geformtem, durchbrochenem Kragen.
// with pierced collar formed of water lilies
and leaves.
Modelliert // Modelled **Ruben Rising;**
Bemalung // Painting **Nils Emil Lundström**
H 14.5 cm

3 Kronen-Marke und *NL* in grüner Farbe,
blind *RR* und *20622* // *3 coronets mark* and
NL in green, blind-stamped *RR* and *20622*

33 *Vase, ca 1900/1905*

mit durchbrochen gearbeitetem Algen-
dekor und drei Fischen. // with pierced
seaweed decoration and three fishes.
Bemalung // Painting Nils Emil Lundström
H 12 cm
3 Kronen-Marke und *NL* in grüner Farbe,
blind *B.M.P., J, 215* und *13* // *3 coronets
mark* and *NL* in green, blind-stamped
B.M.P., J, 215 and *13*

34 Deckelvase // Covered vase, ca 1902

mit drei gleich dekorierten Seiten: ein fast ornamental gemalter Stiel trägt eine in Relief ausgeführte, der durchbrochenen Wandung aufliegende Iris-Blüte; auf dem Deckel eine weitere, vollplastisch modellierte Blüte, deren drei äußere Kronblätter dem Deckel aufliegen, während die drei inneren den knospenförmigen Knauf bilden. // with three identically decorated sides: rather ornamentally painted stalk bearing iris flower executed in relief on pierced wall; another bloom modelled in full relief with three outer petals lying on the lid while the three inner petals form the bud-shaped knop.
Modelliert // Modelled **Waldemar Lindström**; Bemalung // Painting **Karl Lindström**
H 30 cm
3 Kronen-Marke und *KL* in grüner Farbe, blind • *WL* • (ligiert), *12537, I und 6* // *3 coronets mark* and *KL* in green, blind-stamped • *WL* • (monogram), *12537, I* and *6*

35 Vase, ca 1899

mit drei weißen Irisblüten auf milchigblauem Grund.
// with three white irises on a milky-blue ground.
Entworfen wohl // Probably designed **Alf Wallander**
H 20.5 cm
3 Kronen-Marke in grüner Farbe, blind *D.J.,1626* und *J*
// *3 coronets mark* in green, blind-stamped *D.J.,1626* and *J*

36 Vase, ca 1907

mit stilisierten Blättern und Blüten. // with stylised foliage
and flowers.
Bemalung // Painting **Erik Hugo Tryggelin**
H 15 cm
3 Kronen-Marke und *TEH.* (ligiert) in grüner Farbe, blind *80187*
und *17* // *3 coronets mark* and *TEH.* (monogram) in green, blind-
stamped *80187* and *17*

37 Vase, ca 1905

mit Pfennigkrautranken, die einander dreifach überkreuzen und den reliefierten Hals bilden. // with triple-crossed moneywort tendrils worked in relief to form the neck of the vase.
Modelliert // Modelled Ruben Rising; Bemalung // Painting Astrid Ewerlöf
H 7.5 cm
3 Kronen-Marke und · *E* · in grüner Farbe, blind *RR* // *3 coronets mark* and · *E* · in green, blind-stamped *RR*

38 Vase, ca 1900/1905

mit blauer Knospe und Blüte der Sumpfgladiole mit aufsteigend länglichem Blatt, das den Mündungsrand umlaufend bildet. // with blue bud and bloom of the Marsh Gladiolus (*Gladiolus palustris*) and elongated vertical leaf that edges the entire mouth of the vessel.
Modelliert // Modelled Waldemar Lindström; Bemalung // Painting Karl Lindström
H 16.5 cm
3 Kronen-Marke und *KL* in grüner Farbe, blind • *WL* • (ligiert) und *6797* // *3 coronets mark* and *KL* in green, blind-stamped • *WL* • (monogram) and *6797*

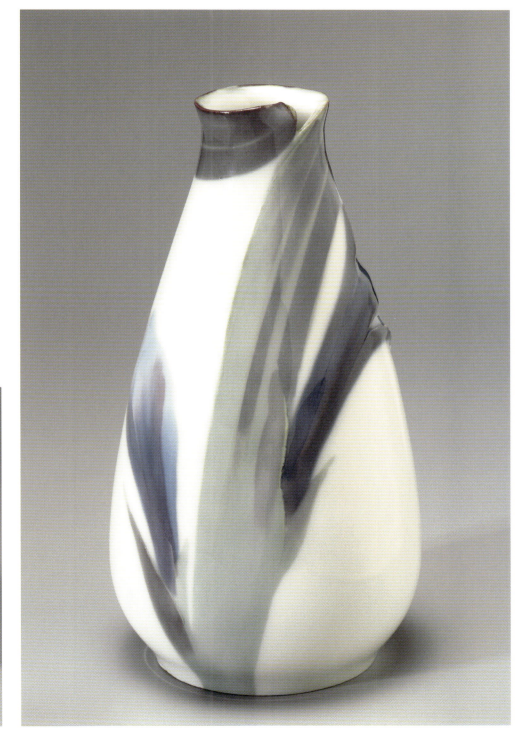

mit drei in weitem Bogen in den Vasenrand auslaufenden Pfeilkraut-
stängeln, die reliefierten Blüten stehen am Vasenhals abwechselnd
einzeln und zu zweit. // with three arrowhead stalks terminating
in a wide arc at the vase rim; alternating one and two flowers in relief
at the neck of the vessel.
Entwurf wohl // Probably designed **Alf Wallander**
H 22.5 cm
3 Kronen-Marke in grüner Farbe, blind *AFH, AS, I, JS* und *2676*
// *3 coronets mark* in green, blind-stamped *AFH, AS, I, JS* and *2676*

40 Vase, ca 1898/1899

mit reichem Kirschblütenrelief. // with elaborate cherry blossoms
in relief.
Bemalung // Painting Algot Eriksson (zugeschrieben anhand
eines Vergleichsstückes der Sammlung Robert Schreiber // attributed
to him by comparison with a piece in the Robert Schreiber Collection,
in: Bengt Nyström. *Rörstrand Porcelain, Art Nouveau Master Pieces,*
Abbeville Press, 1996, S. 63.)
H 26.5 cm
3 Kronen-Marke und *520* in grüner Farbe // *3 coronets mark
and 520 in green*

41 Vase, ca 1902

mit auf beiden Seiten gleichem Dekor:
zwei reliefierte Heckenrosenblüten. // with
identical decoration on both sides: two dog
rose blooms executed in relief.
Bemalung // Painting Anna Boberg
H 15 cm
3 Kronen-Marke und *AB* in grüner Farbe,
blind *11015* und *I* // *3 coronets mark* and
AB in green, blind-stamped *11015* and *I*

42 Vase, ca 1900–1905

mit versetzt gruppierten, reliefierten
Blüten. // with staggered clusters of flowers
executed in relief.
H 21 cm
3 Kronen-Marke in grüner Farbe, blind *D.J.,
7371, 4* und *I* // *3 coronets mark* in green,
blind-stamped *D.J., 7371, 4* and *I*

43 Vase, ca 1900/1902

mit drei von der Mündung herabhängenden weißen Alpenveilchen-Blüten auf
seladonfarbigem Fond. // with three white
cyclamen flowers drooping from the
mouth of the vessel on celadon ground.
Modelliert wohl // Probably modelled
Ruben Rising; Bemalung // Painting
Nils Emil Lundström
H 15 cm
3 Kronen-Marke und *NL* in grüner Farbe,
blind *R* und *11989* // *3 coronets mark* and
NL in green, blind-stamped *R* and *11989*

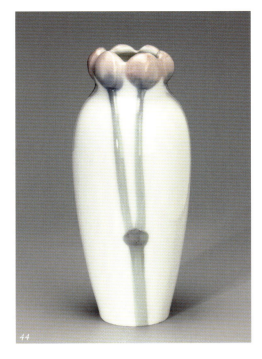

44 *Vase, ca 1900/1905*

drei aufsteigende, im unteren Drittel sich doppelt verzweigende Stängel vom Schwanenliesch mit sechs umlaufenden, den Mündungsrand bildenden Knospen. // with three vertical stalks of *Butomus umbellatus* (flowering rush) forking in lower third of vase, with six buds forming the rim of the vase.
Bemalung // Painting Karl Lindström
H 18 cm
3 Kronen-Marke und *KL* in grüner Farbe, blind *D.J., 6156, 14* und *I* // *3 coronets mark* and *KL* in green, blind-stamped *D.J., 6156, 14* and *I*

45 *Vase, ca 1902/1905*

mit drei reliefierten Narzissenblüten. // with three narcissus blooms in relief.
Bemalung // Painting Karl Lindström
H 18 cm
3 Kronen-Marke und *KL* in grüner Farbe, blind *LC* (oder *LG*), *90124* und *21* // *3 coronets mark* and *KL* in green, blind-stamped *LC* (or *LG*), *90124* and *21*

46 *Vase, ca 1905*

mit auf beiden Vasenseiten gleichem Blütenstand, der durchbrochene Vasenhals ist aus einem Kranz von sechs Blüten geformt. // with identical inflorescence on both sides; the pierced neck of the vase is formed of a wreath of six blossoms.
Bemalung // Painting Nils Emil Lundström
H 21.5 cm
3 Kronen-Marke und *NL* in grüner Farbe, blind *M.P.* (Maria Pettersson?), *.B.* , *J* und *1* // *3 coronets mark* and *NL* in green, blind-stamped *M.P.* (Maria Pettersson?), *.B.* , *J* and *1*

47 Vase, 1901

in Form eines von einer weiblichen Figur gehaltenen Gefäßes. // in the shape of a female figure.
Entworfen und ausgeführt // Designed and executed Alf Wallander 1901
H 31.5 cm
3 Kronen-Marke und *A. WALLANDER 1901* in grüner Farbe, blind *1* // *3 coronets mark* and *A. WALLANDER 1901* in green, blind-stamped *1*
Im Nationalmuseum Stockholm befindet sich eine offenbar etwas kleinere Variante // What is evidently a slightly smaller variant is in the Stockholm National Museum
(Bengt Nyström, Konsten till industrin, Abb. S. 29)

48   Schale // Bowl, ca 1899

stark reliefierte Schale mit wellenartig ausgeformtem Rand. An einer
Seite plastisch modelliertes Tritonmuschelgehäuse, aus dem der
Oberkörper einer liegenden Meernixe herausragt. Weißlich-silbrige
Kristallglasur. // bowl decorated in high relief with undulating rim.
On one side triton shell in relief, rising from the torso of a reclining
mermaid. Silvery white crystal glaze.

B 20.5 cm, L 22.5 cm

Auf dem Standring eine Widmung *TILL ELLEN KEY MED
BEUNDRAN FRÅN ALF WALLANDER*, blind *SP KK1* // Dedication
on the foot-ring *TILL ELLEN KEY MED BEUNDRAN FRÅN ALF
WALLANDER*, blind *SP KK1*

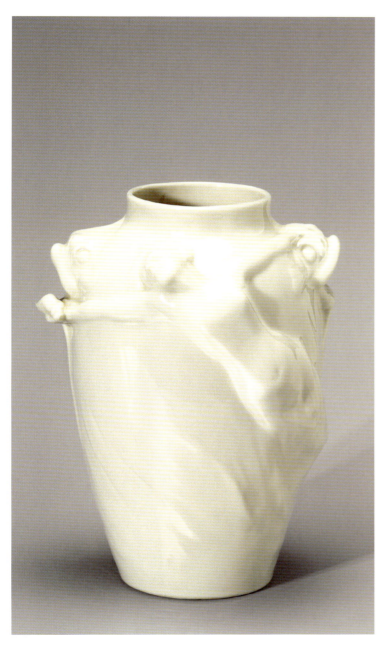

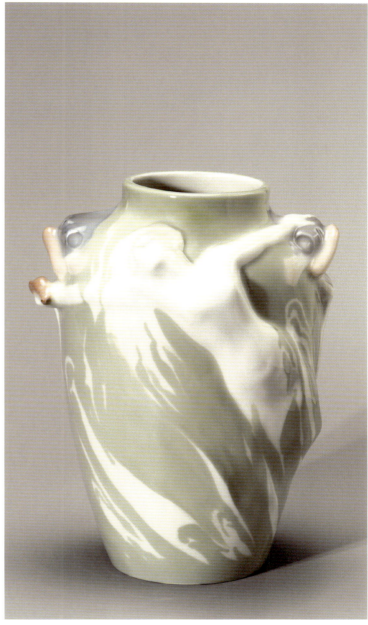

49   *Vase, späte 1890er // late 1890s*

weiß, unbemalt, mit plastisch modellierter Meernixe, die sich mit der linken Hand auf den Kopf eines Seeteufels stützt und in der rechten Hand eine Muschel hält. // white, unpainted, with mermaid executed fully in the round; she is leaning on her left hand, which rests on a monkfish's head, and is holding a shell in her right hand.
Entworfen // Designed (model) Alf Wallander in 1896
H 22 cm
3 Kronen-Marke in grüner Farbe, blind *AS* und *PF* // *3 coronets mark* in green, blind-stamped *AS* and *PF*

50   *Vase, 1898/1900*

mit plastisch modellierter Meernixe, die sich mit ihrer linken Hand auf den Kopf eines Seeteufels stützt und in ihrer rechten eine Muschel hält. // with mermaid modelled in the round: she is leaning on her left hand, which rests on a monkfish's head, and is holding a shell in her right hand.
Entwurf // Designed (model) Alf Wallander in 1896
H 21 cm
3 Kronen-Marke in grüner Farbe, blind *W, J* und *XZ* // *3 coronets mark* in green, blind-stamped *W, J* and *XZ*

mit reliefierten Blättern und über die gesamte leicht reliefierte
Wandung gestreuten Blüten. // with foliage in relief and flowers
strewn over the whole wall, which is in light relief.
Bemalung // Painting Algot Eriksson
H 18 cm
3 Kronen-Marke und *AE* in grüner Farbe, blind *B.M.P., 843, J* und *34*
// *3 coronets mark* and *AE* in green, blind-stamped *B.M.P., 843, J* and *34*

52 Vase, ca 1897/1899

mit Lindenblüten und -blättern. // with lime flowers and leaves.
Bemalung // Painting Erik Hugo Tryggelin. Wohl für die Weltausstellung Paris 1900. // Probably for the 1900 Paris World Exposition.
H 43 cm
3 Kronen-Marke, 1900 und *TH* (ligiert) in weißer Farbe, blind 3
// *3 coronets mark*, 1900 and *TH* (monogram) in white, blind-
stamped 3

53 Vase, ca 1905

Pfeilkraut mit drei Blüten an der Mündung und umlaufenden Blättern auf dem Korpus. // Arrowhead with three blooms on the mouth of the vessel and wall encircled by foliage.
Modelliert // Modelled Ruben Rising; Bemalung // Painting Astrid Ewerlöf
H 7.5 cm
3 Kronen-Marke und · E · in grüner Farbe, blind RR und A2075 // 3 coronets mark and · E · in green, blind-stamped RR and A2075

54 Vase, ca 1902/1905

mit drei Pfeilkrautblättern und aus drei reliefierten Blüten gebildeter, durchbrochen gearbeiteter Vasenöffnung. // with three arrowhead leaves and pierced mouth formed of three flowers executed in relief.
Bemalung // Painting Karl Lindström
H 19 cm
3 Kronen-Marke und KL in grüner Farbe, blind E.G., 40907 und 23 // 3 coronets mark and KL in green, blind-stamped E.G., 40907 and 23

55 Vase, ca 1905

mit aus drei Pfeilkrautblüten geformtem Hals, am Vasenkörper schlanke Blütenstängel mit je einem Blatt. // with neck formed of three arrowhead blooms; on the body of the vase one slender flower stalk with one leaf each.
Bemalung // Painting Astrid Ewerlöf
H 10 cm
3 Kronen-Marke und · E · in grüner Farbe, blind GH und 1145 // 3 coronets mark and · E · in green, blind-stamped GH and 1145

56 Vase, ca 1905/1909

mit einem Rochen auf der Schauseite, reliefiert. // with a skate executed in relief on the main viewing side.
Bemalung // Painting Nils Emil Lundström
H 14 cm
3 Kronen-Marke und NL in grüner Farbe, blind M.P. (Maria Pettersson?), B, 277 und 16 // 3 coronets mark and NL in green, blind-stamped M.P. (Maria Pettersson?), B, 277 and 16

57 Vase, vor // before 1900

mit drei diagonal aufliegenden Reliefblättern // with three diagonally arranged leaves in relief
Bemalung // Painting Algot Eriksson
H 25 cm
3 Kronen-Marke und AE in grüner Farbe, blind J // 3 coronets mark and AE in green, blind-stamped J

58 Vase, ca 1902/1905

mit zwei breiten, von schmalen Linien begleitenden Dekorstreifen mit Fischen, Quallen und Seegras // decorated with two broad strips accompanied by narrow lines and featuring fish, jellyfish and seaweed
Entworfen und ausgeführt // Designed and executed Alf Wallander
H 44 cm
In der Rörstrand-Abteilung auf der Allgemeinen Schwedischen Ausstellung für Kunsthandwerk und Kunstindustrie in Stockholm 1909 ausgestellt // Exhibited in the Rörstrand section at the Universal Swedish Trade Fair for the Applied Arts and Industrial Art, Stockholm 1909
3 Kronen-Marke in grüner Farbe, blind RW, AZ, S2 und I, seitlich am Vasenkörper AW (ligiert) // 3 coronets mark in green, blind-stamped RW, AZ, S2 and I; on the side of the vase wall AW (monogram)

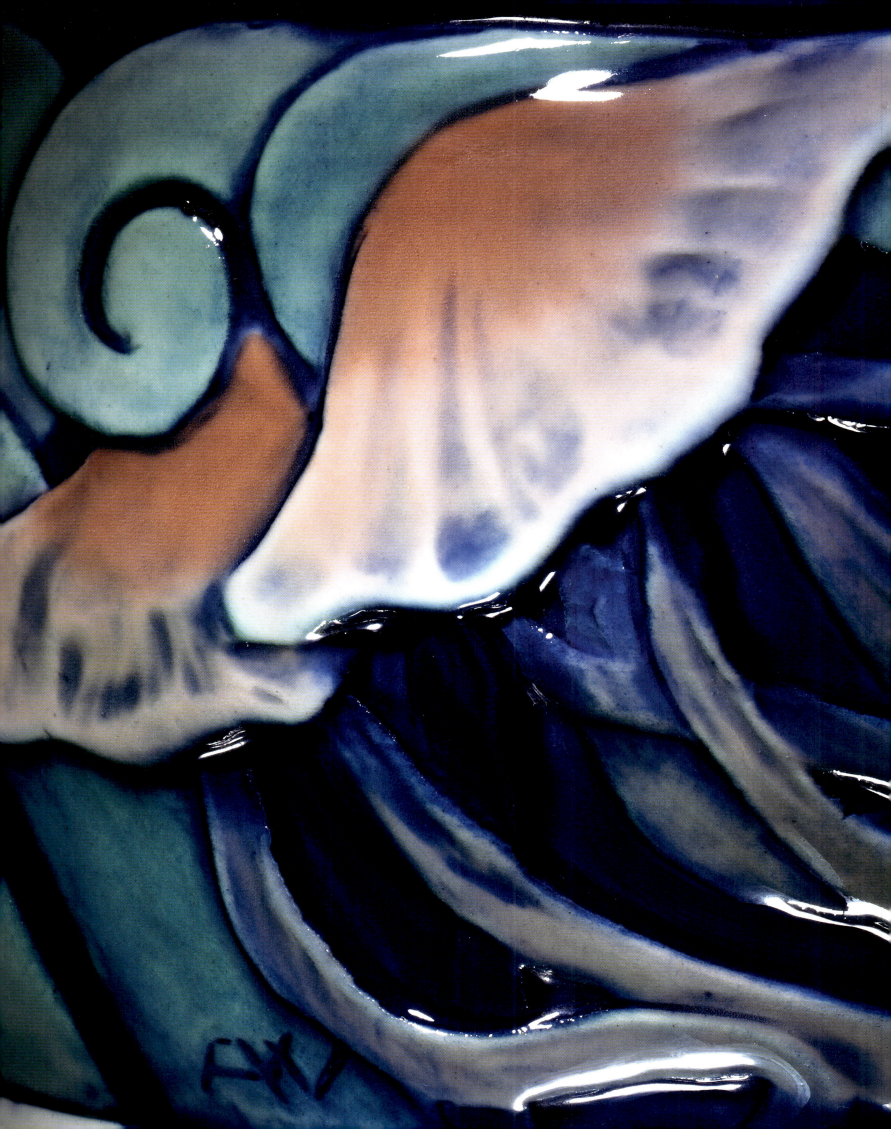

59 *Brosche // Brooch,*
ca 1900/1902

Flache, fast kreisrunde Porzellan-Scheibe
mit zwei reliefierten, sich überlagernden
Blüten. Die Halterung an der Rückseite der
Brosche ist in Silber ausgeführt.
Ø 6 cm
*A.B · N, nicht identifizierbares Beschau-
zeichen, 07 (oder 97) // A.B · N, unidentifi-
able assay mark 07 (or 97)*

60 *Knauf // Knob, ca 1900*

Porzellan-Kugel mit applizierter Blüte und
Knospe, leicht reliefiert. Metallschraube
fest mit der Porzellanmasse verbunden.
Vermutlich für kleinere Möbelstücke verwendet worden. // Porcelain ball with
sprigged flower and bud, low relief. Metal
screw embedded in porcelain fabric. Presumably used for small pieces of furniture.
Ø 3 cm
Unsigniert // Unsigned

61 *Vase, ca 1905*

mit drei gleich dekorierten Seiten: Veil-
chenblätter und kaum reliefierte Blüten
bedecken die Schulter und den durchbrochenen Hals der Vase. // with three
identically decorated sides: violet leaves
and looms executed in barely perceptible
relief cover the shoulder and pierced neck
of the vase.
Bemalung // Painting Nils Emil Lundström
H 25.5 cm
3 Kronen-Marke und *NL* in grüner Farbe,
blind *B.MP., 552* und *31* // *3 coronets mark*
and *NL* in green, blind-stamped *B.MP., 552*
and *31*

62   *Vase, ca 1900/1905*

hochschultrige, sich nach unten verjün-
gende Form mit von der Mündung herabhängenden reliefierten Ahornfrüchten
und umlaufend durchbrochen gearbeitetem Hals. // in high-shouldered form tapering to the bottom with maple seeds trailing
from the mouth and neck pierced all
round.
Modelliert // Modelled **Waldemar Lindström**; Bemalung wohl // Painting probably
Karl Lindström
H 31 cm
3 Kronen-Marke in grüner Farbe, blind
W.L., 2872 und I // *3 coronets mark* in
green, blind-stamped *W.L., 2872 and I*

63   *Dose* // *Jar, ca 1901*

mit floralem Dekor auf dem Deckel, Silber-
montierung von Eugène Lefèbvre, Paris.
// with floral decoration on the lid; silver
mount by Eugène Lefèbvre, Paris.
Bemalung // Painting **Emma Lindberg**
Ø 10 cm
*3 Kronen-Marke, L und 9031 in grüner
Farbe, blind 1 und 2* // *3 coronets mark,
L and 9031 in green, blind-stamped 1 and 2*
Vgl. // Cf. Kat. Bröhan V/2, 1996, Nr. 196

64   *Flakon* // *Flagon, ca 1905*

birnenförmig, mit plastisch ausgeformtem
Stöpsel, leicht reliefiertem und umlaufendem Kranz von Veilchenblüten und
-blättern im unteren Drittel auf der Wandung aufliegend. // pyriform, with sculpturally moulded stopper; wreath of violets
and violet leaves in low relief encircling
the lower third of the vessel wall.
Ausführende Künstler unbekannt //
Artist(s) unknown
H 12.3 cm
3 Kronen-Marke in grüner Farbe, blind
B.M.P. und 1520 // *3 coronets mark* in
green, blind-stamped *B.M.P. and 1520*

65   Vase, ca 1902/1905

mit drei Orchideenstängeln und reliefierten, am Hals durchbrochen
gearbeiteten Blüten auf blassblauem Fond. // with three orchid stalks
and pierced flowers in relief on the pale blue ground of the neck.
Bemalung // Painting Nils Emil Lundström
H 49 cm
3 Kronen-Marke und NEL (ligiert) in grüner Farbe, blind L und 50
// 3 coronets mark and NEL (monogram) in green, blind-stamped L
and 50

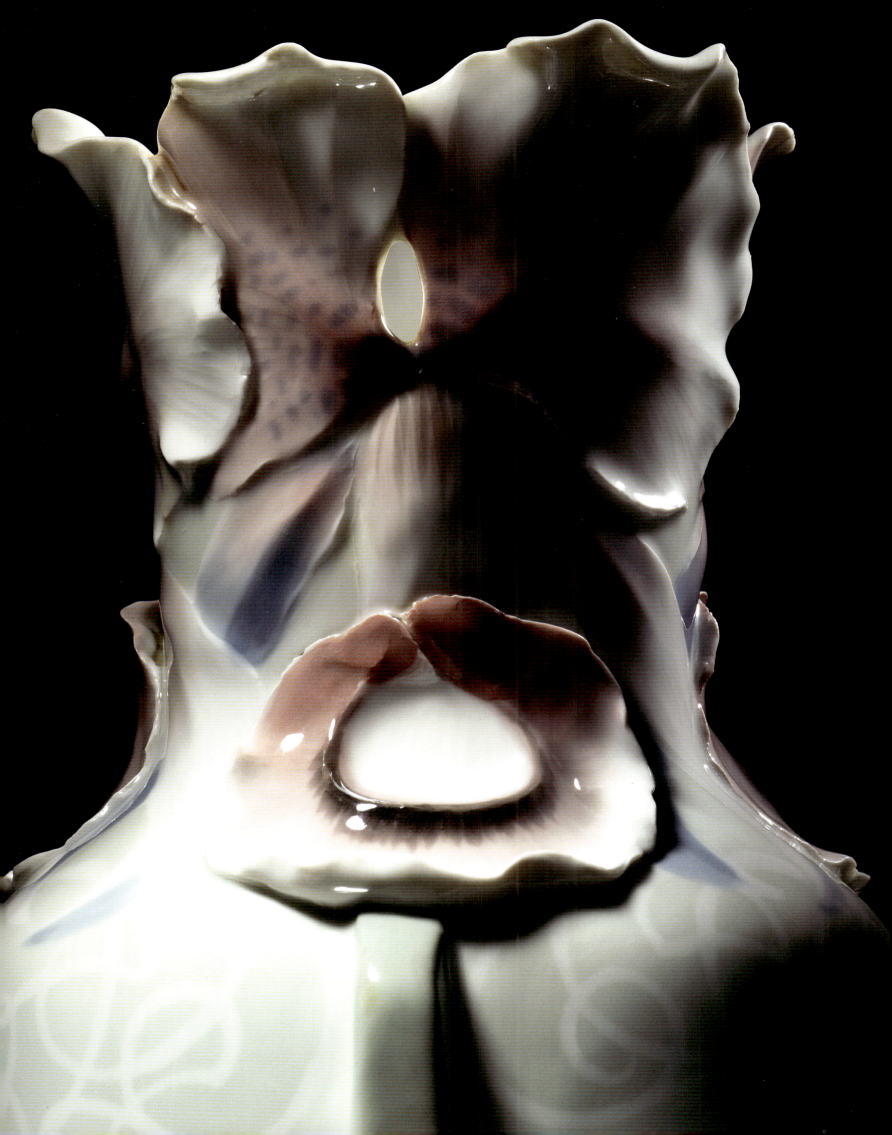

66   Vase, vor // *before* 1900

mit drei gleich dekorierten Seiten: reliefiert ausgeführte Blüten der
Sonnenblume. // with three identically decorated sides: blossom of
sunflowers executed in relief.
Entworfen wohl // Probably designed **Alf Wallander**
H 23 cm
3 Kronen-Marke in grüner Farbe, blind *1* und *I* // *3 coronets
mark* in green, blind-stamped *1* and *I*

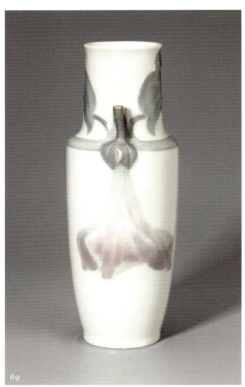

67 Vase, ca 1915

mit Blattwerk und drei Stängeln mit je zwei reliefierten Blüten, die sich am Vasenrand zu einem Blattkranz schließen. // with foliage and three stalks, each bearing two flowers executed in relief, enclosing the rim of the vase with a foliate wreath.
Modelliert und bemalt // Modelled and painted by Gerda Zielfeldt
H 18 cm
3 Kronen-Marke und • *Z* • in grüner Farbe, blind *Z* und *F 17*. // *3 coronets mark* and • *Z* • in green, blind-stamped *Z* and *F 17*.

68 Vase, ca 1905

mit reliefierten Blüten und Blättern. // with blossoms and leaves executed in relief.
Modelliert // Modelled Anna Boberg
H 20 cm
3 Kronen-Marke in grüner Farbe, blind • *AB* • (ligiert), *10574, 4* und *I* // *3 coronets mark* in green, blind-stamped • *AB* • (monogram), *10574, 4* and *I*

69 Vase, ca 1905

mit zwei gegenständig herabhängenden Blüten, deren Stängel zu zwei kleinen Henkeln geformt sind. // with two dangling blossoms executed in relief, their stems forming two small handles.
Bemalung // Painting Karl Lindström
H 27 cm
3 Kronen-Marke und *KL* in grüner Farbe, blind *M.P.* (Maria Pettersson?), *38084, JL, 31* und *4* // *3 coronets mark* and *KL* in green, blind-stamped *M.P.* (Maria Pettersson?), *38084, JL, 31* and *4*

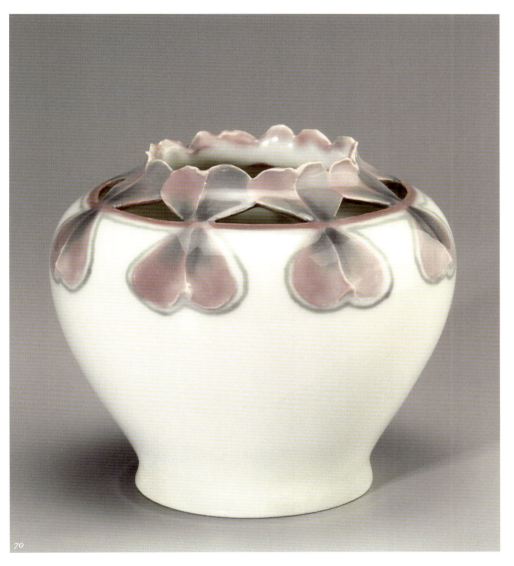

70 *Vase, ca 1902/1905*

mit einem Kranz von acht reliefierten
Blättern am Vasenrand. // with a wreath
composed of eight leaves executed in relief
on the rim of the vase.
Bemalung // Painting Astrid Ewerlöf
H 10 cm
3 Kronen-Marke und • *E* • in grüner Farbe,
blind *11823* // *3 coronets mark* and • *E* • in
green, blind-stamped *11823*

71 *Vase, ca 1902/1905*

mit aus drei Pfeilkrautblüten geformtem
Hals, die kräftigen Blütenstängel über-
schneidend, am Vasenkörper jeweils ein
schräg stehendes Blatt. // with neck formed
of three arrowhead blooms, sturdy stalks
overlapping, on the body of the vase one
diagonal vertical leaf for each bloom.
H 18.5 cm
3 Kronen-Marke in grüner Farbe, blind *M.P.*
(Maria Pettersson?) und *30* // *3 coronets
mark* in green, blind-stamped *M.P. (Maria
Pettersson?)* and *30*

72 *Vase, ca 1900*

mit vier Zweigen mit reliefierten Blüten-
kätzchen. // with four branches bearing
catkins in relief.
Modelliert // Modelled Anna Boberg
H 18.5 cm
3 Kronen-Marke in grüner Farbe, blind
• *AB* • (ligiert) und *7615* // *3 coronets mark*
in green, blind-stamped • *AB* • (monogram)
and *7615*

73 *Vase, um 1910 oder später // around 1910 or later*

in Vierkantform mit durchbrochenem Gezweig von Blättern und Beeren, darin einige Singvögel. // four sided with pierced leafy branch with berries and some songbirds.
Bemalung // Painting Nils Emil Lundström
H 47 cm
3 Kronen-Marke und *NL* in grüner Farbe, blind *OL, BEN* und *S2*
// 3 coronets mark and *NL* in green, blind-stamped *OL, BEN* and *S2*

74 Vase, ca 1900

im oberen Drittel mit durchbrochen gearbeitetem Hals, vier reliefierten Hundsrosen mit Blättern und vier kurzen Stängeln. // in the upper third with pierced neck, four dog roses in relief with leaves and four short stems.
Bemalung // Painting Mela Anderberg
H 34 cm
3 Kronen-Marke, • M • A • und *5840* in grüner Farbe, blind *12*
// *3 coronets mark*, • M • A • and *5840* in green, blind-stamped *12*

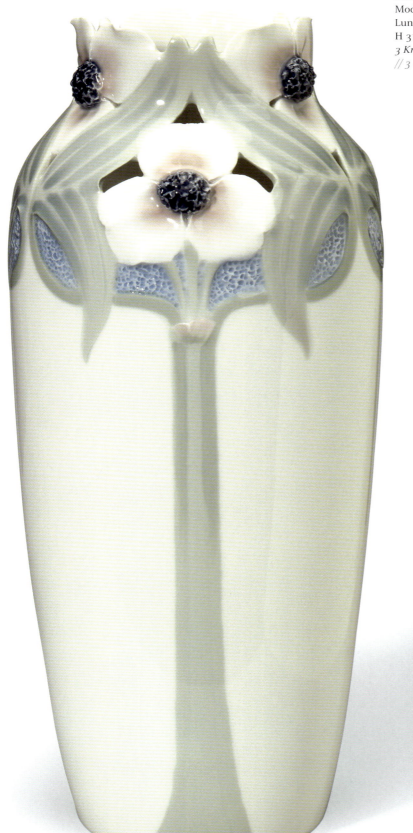

Vase, ca 1902

mit aus drei Pfeilkrautblüten geformtem Hals, auf der Vasenschulter
große Blätter mit drei kleineren Blüten. // with neck formed of three
arrowhead blooms; on the vase shoulder large leaves with three
smaller flowers.
Modelliert // Modelled Ruben Rising; Bemalung // Painting Nils Emil
Lundström
H 31 cm
3 Kronen-Marke und *NL* in grüner Farbe, blind *RR, 20764* und *35*
// *3 coronets mark* and *NL* in green, blind-stamped *RR, 20764* and *35*

76 *Vase, ca 1905*

mit Nadelbüscheln und plastisch auf-
gelegten jungen Zapfen. // with bunches
of needles and sprigged with young pine
cones.
Modelliert // Modelled Ruben Rising;
Bemalung // Painting Astrid Ewerlöf
H 9 cm
3 Kronen-Marke und · *E* · in grüner Farbe,
blind *RR, J, I* und *3980* // *3 coronets mark*
and · *E* · in green, blind-stamped *RR, J, I*
and *3980*

77 *Vase, ca 1902*

mit drei gleich dekorierten Seiten: reliefiert
ausgeführte Blüten. // with three identically decorated sides: blossoms executed in
relief.
Bemalung // Painting Astrid Ewerlöf
H 9 cm
3 Kronen-Marke und · *E* · in grüner Farbe,
blind *13359* // *3 coronets mark* and · *E* · in
green, blind-stamped *13359*

78 *Vase, ca 1905*

mit vier reliefierten Mohnblüten, deren
Blätter den Vasenhals bilden. // with four
poppies executed in relief, their foliages
forming the neck of the vase.
Modelliert // Modelled Ruben Rising;
Bemalung // Painting Karl Lindström
H 23 cm
3 Kronen-Marke und *KL* in grüner Farbe,
blind *RR* und *20912* // *3 coronets mark* and
KL in green, blind-stamped *RR* and *20912*

79 *Vase, ca 1905*

mit durchbrochen gearbeitetem Hals,
reliefierten Blättern und drei Blüten, deren
Stängel zu drei kleinen Henkeln geformt
sind. // with pierced neck, foliage executed
in relief and three flowers, their stems
forming small handles.
Bemalung // Painting **Karl Lindström**
H 18 cm
3 Kronen-Marke und *KL* in grüner Farbe,
blind *M.P.* (Maria Pettersson?), *70947* und
21 // *3 coronets mark* and *KL* in green,
blind-stamped *M.P.* (Maria Pettersson?),
70947 und *21*

80 *Vase, ca 1902*

mit auf beiden Seiten gleichem Dekor:
drei Stiefmütterchenblüten, reliefiert.
// with identical decoration on both sides:
three pansies, executed in relief.
Modelliert und bemalt // Modelled and
painted **Astrid Ewerlöf**
H 14.5 cm
3 Kronen-Marke und *· E ·* in grüner Farbe,
blind *· E ·*, *13899* und *13* // *3 coronets mark*
and *· E ·* in green, blind-stamped *· E ·*,
13899 and *13*

147

81 Vase, ca 1905/1910

vom Fußrand aufwärts von zwei Blasen-
tangstreifen, die am Hals zwei kräftig
reliefierte Henkel bilden, in zwei Bildhälften
geteilt: auf der einen Seite sechs Pinguine,
auf der anderen zwei Eisbären und eine
Seerobbe. // divided equally into two
pictures from the foot ring upwards by two
strips of bladderwrack that form two handles in high relief at the neck: on one side,
six penguins, on the other two polar bears
and a seal.
Bemalung // Painting Algot Eriksson
H 55 cm
3 Kronen-Marke und *AE* in grüner Farbe,
Original-Papieretikett mit Preisangabe
// 3 coronets mark and *AE* in green; original
paper label indicating price SKr. 400,- (?)

82 *Vase, vor // before* 1903

mit leicht reliefiertem Kranz von Lorbeer-
blättern und herabhängenden Früchten,
Wandung oberhalb des Dekors und Innen-
seite schwarz glasiert. // with laurel wreath
in low relief with pendant fruits; wall
above decoration and interior glazed black.
Bemalung // Painting Karl Lindström
H 12 cm
3 Kronen-Marke und *KL* in grüner Farbe,
blind *E.G., JL 40230* und *13* // *3 coronets
mark* and *KL* in green, blind-stamped *E.G.,
JL 40230* and *13*

83 *Vase, ca* 1910

ovale Flaschenform mit auf beiden Seiten
gleichem Dekor: gefiedertes Blatt und
herabhängende Blütentraube. // ovoid flask
form with identical decoration on both
sides: feathery leaf and dangling flower
raceme.
Bemalung // Painting Nils Emil Lundström
H 32 cm
3 Kronen-Marke und *NL* in schwarz-brauner
Farbe, blind *BFX*, altes unbeschriftetes
Papieretikett // *3 coronets mark* and *NL* in
black-brown, blind-stamped *BFX*, old paper
label with no writing on it

84 *Vase, ca* 1905/1910

flache Ovalform mit Schwertlilien auf
verlaufend blau getöntem Grund, die
andere Vasenseite gleich dekoriert.
// flattened oval form with irises on trickle-
glazed, blue-tinted ground; the other side
identically decorated.
Bemalung // Painting Nils Emil Lundström
H 34 cm
3 Kronen-Marke und *NL* in schwarz-brauner
Farbe, blind *S2, BFL* und *36* // *3 coronets
mark* and *NL* in black-brown, blind *S2, BFL*
and *36*

85 *Vase, ca 1910 oder später*
// or later

am oberen Rand drei plastisch ausge-
formte Fischköpfe mit weit geöffneten
Mäulern, aus denen Flüssigkeit über den
Vasenkorpus bis zur Basis hinab fließt.
// with three fish heads on upper rim
moulded in the round with wide-open
maws, from which liquid is depicted as
flowing down the vase to the plinth.
Ausführende Künstler unbekannt
// Artist(s) unknown
H 69.5 cm
3 Kronen-Marke in blau-grüner Farbe, blind
AK und *DM* // *3 coronets mark* in blue-green,
blind-stamped *AK* and *DM*

86 *Vase, ca 1900/1910*

aus bauchiger Basis mittig aufragender
schmaler Stangenhals mit dunkelbräun-
lich-grünlicher Glasur und geätzten
Pflanzenornamenten, die in eine in Silber
applizierte Blüte münden. Vasenmündung
mit schmalem Silberrand umfasst.
// of slender stalk neck rising, centred,
from swelling base; dark brownish/green-
ish glaze and etched plant decoration
ending in floral appliqué in silver. Vase
mouth with narrow silver rim mount.
H 14 cm
3 Kronen-Marke in schwarzer Farbe
// *3 coronets mark* in black

87 *Vase, ca 1899/1905*

mit streifiger Laufglasur und großen,
leuchtend blauen Kristallflecken. *// with*
streaky trickle glaze and flecked with large,
vibrant blue crystals.
H 16 cm
3 Kronen-Marke und *18* in grüner Farbe,
blind *KK* und *1* // *3 coronets mark* and *18*
in green, blind-stamped *KK* and *1*

88 Vase, ca 1900

mit drei gleich gestalteten Seiten: an henkelförmig modelliertem Stiel hängendes, leicht reliefiertes Kleeblatt auf herzförmig durchbrochener Wandung. // with three identically decorated sides: clover leaf in light relief dangling from stem formed into a handle on heart-shaped pierced wall.

Entworfen // Designed Alf Wallander.
Für die Weltausstellung Paris 1900. // For the 1900 Paris World Exposition.
H 35 cm
3 Kronen-Marke, A. Wallander und *1900.* in grüner Farbe, blind *6552* // *3 coronets mark, A. Wallander* and *1900.* in green, blind-stamped *6552*
Vgl. kleinere Variante dieser Vasenform mit Pfeilkrautblättern von Nils Emil Lundström: Kat. Bröhan V/2, 1996, Nr. 209 // Cf. smaller variant of this vase form with arrowhead leaves by Nils Emil Lundström: Cat. Bröhan V/2, 1996, No. 209

89 Vase, ca 1905

mit umlaufendem Dekor: schwimmende Barsche im Wasser,
Vasenöffnung mit wellenförmigem Rand. // with decoration
all round: perch swimming in water; vase rim wavy.
Bemalung // Painting Nils Emil Lundström
H 27 cm
3 Kronen-Marke und NL in grüner Farbe, blind B.MP., 342
und 31 // 3 coronets mark and NL in green, blind-stamped
B.MP., 342 and 31

mit schwimmender Meernixe, deren menschlicher Oberkörper von den Wellen getragen wird, mit vollplastisch modelliertem Kopf eines Seeteufels mit weit geöffnetem Schlund. // with bathing mermaid, her human torso buoyed by the waves, with the head of a monkfish modelled fully in the round, its maw wide open.
Entworfen // Designed Alf Wallander
∅ 36 cm
3 Kronen-Marke und *A. Wallander* in grüner Farbe, blind *I*
// *3 coronets mark* and *A. Wallander* in green, blind-stamped *I*

91 Vase, späte 1890er // late 1890s

an der Schulter zwei plastisch gestaltete Seeteufel mit henkelartig
ausgeformten Körpern. // with two Monkfish in the round on the
shoulder with bodies moulded into handle-like shapes.
Modelliert // Modelled Waldemar Lindström; Bemalung // Painting
Algot Eriksson
H 32.8 cm
3 Kronen-Marke und *AE* in grüner Farbe, blind *W.L.* und *6600*
// *3 coronets mark* and *AE* in green, blind-stamped *W.L.* and *6600*

mit Seetang und zwei plastisch modellierten Seeteufeln. // with seaweed and two
Monkfish, modelled almost in the round.
Bemalung // Painting Karl Lindström
H 52 cm
3 Kronen-Marke und *KL* in grüner Farbe,
blind *65* und *1* // *3 coronets mark* and *KL*
in green, blind-stamped *65* and *1*

93 *Vase, ca 1902/1905*

mit durchbrochenem Hals und reliefierten Brombeerranken. // with pierced neck and sprays of blackberries in relief.
Modelliert // Modelled Ruben Rising; Bemalung // Painting Astrid Ewerlöf
H 13.5 cm
3 Kronen-Marke und · E · in grüner Farbe, blind *RR, 2321* und *A* // *3 coronets mark and · E · in green, blind-stamped RR, 2321 and A*

94 *Vase, ca 1905/1909*

mit drei gleich dekorierten Seiten: Wicken-blätter, am Vasenhals reliefierte Blüten. // three identically decorated sides: sweet pea leaves, sweet pea blooms in relief on the neck of the vase.
Modelliert // Modelled Ruben Rising; Bemalung // Painting Astrid Ewerlöf
H 10.5 cm
3 Kronen-Marke und · E · in grüner Farbe, blind *RR, A 1472* und *1* // *3 coronets mark and · E · in green, blind-stamped RR, A 1472 and 1*

95 *Vase, ca 1899*

in Zwiebelform mit naturalistisch model-lierten Hüllblättern. // in bulb form with naturalistically modelled husks.
Bemalung // Painting Nils Emil Lundström
H 8 cm
3 Kronen-Marke und *NL* in grüner Farbe, blind *O.B., 5657, I* und *1* // *3 coronets mark and NL in green, blind-stamped O.B., 5657, I and 1*

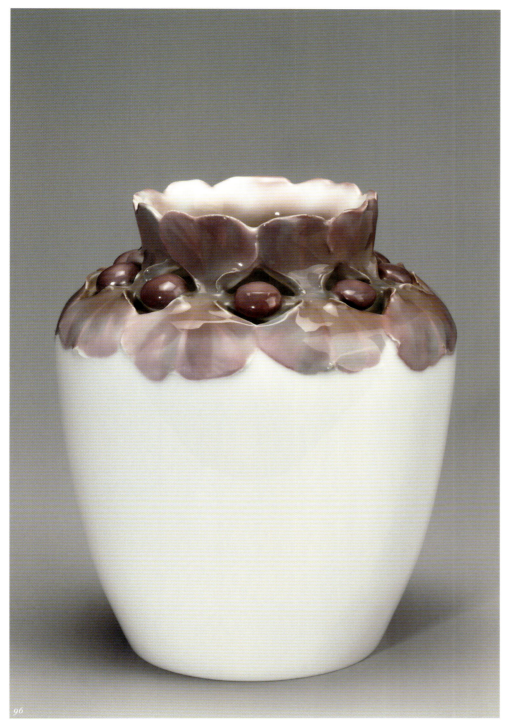

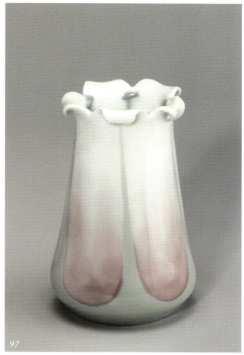

96 Vase, ca 1905/1910

mit reliefiertem Blätterkranz und reliefierten Früchten (Pfennigkraut und Erbsen). // with wreath of leaves and legumes in relief (arrowhead and peas).
Bemalung // Painting Algot Eriksson
H 15 cm
3 Kronen-Marke und *AE* in grüner Farbe, blind *IL* und *17* // *3 coronets mark* and *AE* in green, blind-stamped *IL* and *17*

97 Vase, ca 1902

in Fruchtform mit fünffach gelappter Mündung. // in the shape of a fruit with five-fold lobed mouth.
Bemalung // Painting Algot Eriksson
H 10 cm
3 Kronen-Marke und *AE* in grüner Farbe, blind *14833* // *3 coronets mark* and *AE* in green, blind-stamped *14833*

98 Vase, ca 1903/1906

in Form einer Fruchtkapsel, fünffach gekerbt. // in the shape of a seed capsule with five longitudinal ridges.
Modelliert // Modelled Ruben Rising; Bemalung // Painting Nils Emil Lundström
H 14 cm
3 Kronen-Marke und *NL* in grüner Farbe, blind *RR, 20596* und *16* // *3 coronets mark* and *NL* in green, blind-stamped *RR, 20596* and *16*

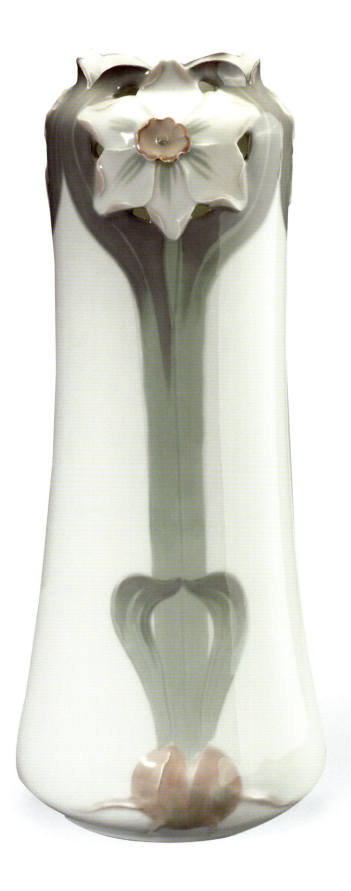

99 Vase, ca 1905

mit ornamental stilisiertem Dekor: drei, jeweils aus einer leicht reliefierten Zwiebel emporwachsende, reliefierte und unterhalb der Vasenöffnung durchbrochene Narzissenblüten. // ornamentally stylised decoration: three narcissi, each growing up from bulbs executed in light relief and pierced below the vase rim.
Entworfen wohl // Probably designed **Alf Wallander**
H 36 cm
3 Kronen-Marke in grüner Farbe, blind *EG., 80009* und *45*
// *3 coronets mark* in green, blind-stamped *EG., 80009* and *45*

100 *Vase, ca 1902/1905*

mit drei Lilienblüten, deren reliefierte Kronblätter der Vasenschulter aufliegen, die kräftigen Blütenstempel mit den Staubgefäßen führen henkelförmig empor und formen den Vasenrand. // with three lilies, their outer petals worked in relief on the shoulder of the vase; sturdy pistils and stamens rise handle-shaped to form the rim of the vase.

Modelliert // Modelled **Waldemar Lindström**; Bemalung // Painting **Karl Lindström**

H 36.5 cm

3 Kronen-Marke und *KL* in grüner Farbe, blind • *WL* • (ligiert), *12638* und *8* // *3 coronets mark* and *KL* in green, blind-stamped • *WL* • (monogram), *12638* and *8*

101 Vase, ca 1905

mit drei plastisch modellierten fliegenden
Kranichen auf der Vasenschulter.
// with three cranes in flight, modelled
almost fully in the round, on the shoulder
of the vase.
Entwurf // Designed Alf Wallander (siehe
// see: Keramische Monatshefte, 1902,
Heft 9, Seite 137)
Modelliert // Modelled Waldemar
Lindström; Bemalung // Painting Karl
Lindström
H 52 cm
3 Kronen-Marke und *KL.* in grüner Farbe,
blind *W.L, 4749* und *I* // *3 coronets mark*
and KL. in green, blind-stamped *W.L,*
4749 and *I*

102 *Vase, ca 1905*

mit drei reliefierten Schmetterlingen,
deren Fühler den Vasenrand bilden. // with
three butterflies executed in relief, their
feelers forming the rim of the vase.
Bemalung // Painting Nils Emil Lundström
H 13 cm
3 Kronen-Marke und *NL* in grüner Farbe,
blind *M.P.* (Maria Pettersson?), *.B.* und *219*
// *3 coronets mark* and *NL* in green,
blind-stamped *M.P.* (Maria Pettersson?),
.B. and *219*

103 *Vase, ca 1905/1909*

mit Libelle auf der Schauseite, die Flügel
leicht reliefiert, und herabhängenden
Pflanzen. // with dragonfly on the principal
side, with wings in low relief and dangling
plants.
Bemalung // Painting Nils Emil Lundström
H 12 cm
3 Kronen-Marke und *NL* in grüner Farbe,
blind *M.P.* (Maria Pettersson?), *.B.* und *631*
// *3 coronets mark* and *NL* in green,
blind-stamped *M.P.* (Maria Pettersson?),
.B. and *631*

104 *Vase, ca 1905/1910*

mit zwei gegenüberliegenden, an der
Vasenschulter aufgetragenen Tagschmet-
terlingen mit ausgebreiteten Flügeln,
vierfach eingedellte Mündung. // with two
diurnal butterflies, their wings outspread,
across from each other on the shoulder
of the vase; quatrefoil rim.
Modelliert und bemalt // Modelled and
painted Astrid Ewerlöf
H 11 cm
3 Kronen-Marke und *· E ·* in grüner Farbe,
blind *· E ·,13968* und *12* // *3 coronets mark*
and *· E ·* in green, blind-stamped *· E ·,*
13968 and *12*

105 *Vase, ca 1900*

mit fünf sternförmigen hellen Blüten auf
zartblau gewölbtem Grund, der mit leicht
reliefiertem Rand gegen den weißen, zur
Mündung hin grün schimmernden Vasenhals abgesetzt ist. // with five star-shaped
light-coloured flowers on cloudy light blue
ground, which is set off from the green
lustrous neck of the vessel in light relief
Bemalung // Painting **Algot Eriksson**
H 11 cm
3 Kronen-Marke, AE und *121* in grüner
Farbe, blind *J* // *3 coronets mark, AE* and
121 in green, blind-stamped *J*

106 *Vase, ca 1902/1905*

großflächige durchbrochene Schwimm-
blätter einer Wasserpflanze mit zwei von
der Basis gegenständig aufwachsenden
Stängeln. // with large pierced floating
leaves of an aquatic plant with two stems
in relief growing up from the base.
Modelliert // Modelled **Waldemar Lindström**; Bemalung // Painting **Karl Lindström**
H 29.5 cm
3 Kronen-Marke und *KL* in grüner Farbe,
blind · *WL* · (ligiert), *12869* und *35*
// *3 coronets mark* and *KL* in green, blind-
stamped · *WL* · (monogram), *12869* and *35*

107 Vase, ca 1903

mit drei gleich dekorierten Seiten: reliefierte Heckenrosen, Wandung
zwischen den Blüten durchbrochen. // with three identically decorated
sides: dog roses in relief; wall pierced between the flowers.
Bemalung // Painting Mela Anderberg
H 18 cm
3 Kronen-Marke, • M •A • und 60314 in grüner Farbe, blind 21
// 3 coronets mark, • M •A • and 60314 in green, blind-stamped 21

172

108 Vase, ca 1902/1909

mit zwei reliefierten Mohnblüten am durchbrochen gearbeiteten Hals und zwei am Vasenkörper herabhängenden Knospen. // with two poppy blooms worked in relief on the pierced neck and two buds hanging down on to the vase itself.

Modelliert // Modelled Ruben Rising; Bemalung // Painting Karl Lindström

H 22.5 cm

3 Kronen-Marke und KL in grüner Farbe, blind RR, 20953 und 26 // 3 coronets mark and KL in green, blind-stamped RR, 20953 and 26

109 *Vase, späte 1890er*
// late 1890s

in Form einer blühenden Artischocke mit
reliefierten Blattschuppen. // in the form of
an artichoke with imbricated leaves in
relief.

Entworfen wohl // Probably designed Alf
Wallander; Modelliert // Modelled Ruben
Rising

H 18 cm

3 Kronen-Marke in grüner Farbe, blind *RR,
J* und *21* // *3 coronets mark* in green, blind-
stamped *RR, J* and *21*

110 *Vase, ca 1910*

sechskantig, mit auf drei Seiten gleichem
durchbrochenen Reliefdekor: Mohnblüten
und –blätter. // hexagonal in section, with
identical pierced relief decoration on three
sides: poppy blooms and foliage.

Bemalung // Painting Georg Asplund

H 22 cm

3 Kronen-Marke und · *G* · in grüner Farbe,
blind *HP.* (ligiert), *J, AU2* und *51062*
// *3 coronets mark* and · *G* · in green, blind-
stamped *HP.* (monogram), *J, AU2* and
51062

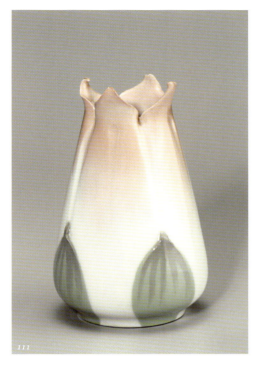

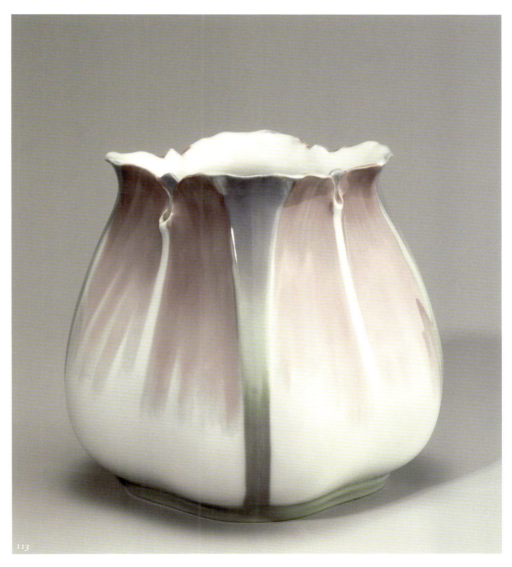

111 Vase, ca 1905/1909

in Fruchtform mit vier Hüllblättern.
// in the shape of a fruit with quadrilobate husk.
Modelliert wohl // Probably modelled Ruben Rising
H 11 cm
3 Kronen-Marke in grüner Farbe, blind *R* und *12* // *3 coronets mark* in green, blind-stamped *R* and *12*

112 Vase, ca 1900/1905

hellblau und rosafarben mit fünf blüten-artigen Blättern, die den betont plastischen Mündungsrand bilden. // in light blue and pink with five flower-like leaves forming the boldly sculptural rim of the mouth.
Modelliert wohl // Probably modelled Ruben Rising; Bemalung // Painting Karl Lindström
H 9 cm
3 Kronen-Marke und *KL* in grüner Farbe, blind *R* // *3 coronets mark* and *KL* in green, blind-stamped *R*

113 Vase, ca 1905

in Form einer vierseitigen beutelförmigen Blüte. // in the form of a quadrilobate pouch-shaped flower.
Modelliert // Modelled Waldemar Lind-ström; Bemalung // Painting Karl Lind-ström
H 13 cm
3 Kronen-Marke und *KL* in grüner Farbe, blind • *WL* • (ligiert), *AVA, J* und *90019*
// *3 coronets mark* and *KL* in green, blind-stamped • *WL* • (monogram), *AVA, J* and *90019*

114 Vase, ca 1900/1905

mit drei gleich dekorierten Seiten: Löwenzahnblatt mit rechts und
links je einem Stängel mit Blütenknospen. // with three identically
decorated sides: dandelion leaf each flanked by one bud-bearing stem.
Bemalung // Painting Waldemar Lindström
H 36 cm
3 Kronen-Marke und *W.L* in grüner Farbe, blind *6550, 8 und I*
// *3 coronets mark* and *W.L* in green, blind-stamped *6550, 8 and I*

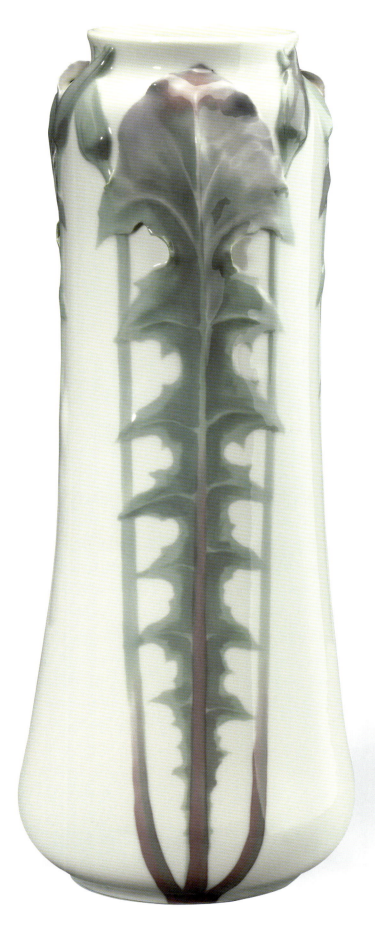

115 Vase, ca 1902/1905

mit zwei gegenständig aufwachsenden Stängeln und durchbrochenem, aus reliefierten Blüten gebildetem Hals. // with two rising stalks
in relief and pierced neck formed of flowers in relief.
Modelliert // Modelled Ruben Rising; Bemalung // Painting Algot
Eriksson
H 47 cm
3 Kronen-Marke und *Algot Eriksson* in grüner Farbe, blind *RR* und
11910 // *3 coronets mark* and *Algot Eriksson* in green, blind-stamped
RR and *11910*

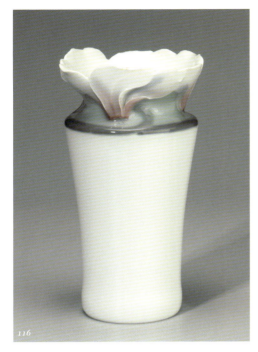

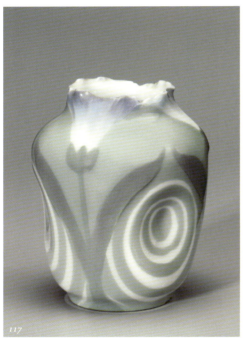

116 Vase, ca 1902/1907

von der Schulter aufsteigend drei Blüten mit reliefierten Alpenveilchen, die umlaufend die unregelmäßig geformte Mündung bilden. // with three cyclamen blooms rising from the vase shoulder in relief forming the irregularly shaped mouth of the vessel.
Bemalung // Painting Karl Lindström
H 15 cm
3 Kronen-Marke und *KL* in grüner Farbe, blind *E.G.* und *40003* // *3 coronets mark and KL in green, blind-stamped E.G. and 40003*

117 Vase, ca 1899

dreiseitig abgeflachte Form mit weiß ausgesparten Kreisen, dazwischen je eine Pflanze mit lanzettförmigen Blättern und reliefierter Blüte, Vasenrand unregelmäßig geformt. // form flattened on three sides with white reserve on circles; between each circle plant with lanceolate foliage and flower in relief; vase rim irregular in form.
Bemalung // Painting Algot Eriksson
H 11 cm
3 Kronen-Marke und *AE* in grüner Farbe, blind *O.B.* und *4369* // *3 coronets mark and AE in green, blind-stamped O.B. and 4369*

118 Vase, ca 1905

mit eingeschnürt abgesetztem Hals mit reliefiertem Dekor aus Fliederblättern und drei Blüten. // with nipped-in recessed neck with lilac leaves and three flower panicles executed in relief.
Bemalung // Painting Karl Lindström oder // or Nils Emil Lundström
H 15 cm
3 Kronen-Marke und *KL* oder (NL) in grüner Farbe, blind *B.M.P.* und *798* (unvollständig, Boden restauriert) // *3 coronets mark and KL or (NL) in green, blind-stamped B.M.P. and 798 (not complete: bottom restored)*

119 Vase, ca 1900/1905

mit umlaufend sechs aus einem schmalen Blattkranz wachsenden Pfeilkrautblüten. *// encircled by six arrowhead flowers growing out of a narrow wreath of arrowhead leaves.*
Bemalung // Painting Mela Anderberg
H 15 cm
3 Kronen-Marke, • M • A • und 5455 in grüner Farbe, blind 1 und 3 // 3 coronets mark, • M • A • and 5455 in green, blindstamped 1 and 3

120 Vase, ca 1902/1905

mit drei gleich dekorierten Seiten: je zwei reliefierte Glockenblumen auf der Vasenschulter. *// with three identically decorated sides: two bell-flowers in relief on each side of the vessel shoulder.*
Modelliert und bemalt // Modelled and painted Astrid Ewerlöf
H 17.5 cm
3 Kronen-Marke und · E · in grüner Farbe, blind · E ·, 143 D und 21 // 3 coronets mark and · E · in green, blind-stamped · E ·, 143 D and 21

121 Vase, ca 1900/1905

mit zwei gegenständig aufwachsenden Campanula-Stängeln mit reliefierten Blättern, einer hängenden und zwei aufgerichteten Blüten. *// with two rising campanula stalks in relief: leaves in relief and one drooping and two vertical flowers.*
Bemalung // Painting Nils Emil Lundström
H 17.5 cm
3 Kronen-Marke und NL in grüner Farbe, blind H.P. und 12422 // 3 coronets mark and NL in green, blind-stamped H.P. and 12422

122 Vase, ca 1900

in Kugelform mit kaum reliefierten Mohnblütenknospen und weit geöffneter frei modellierter Mohnblüte als Vasenmündung. // in spherical form with poppy buds in barely perceptible relief; mouth of vase formed by a freehand-modelled poppy in full bloom.
Modelliert // Modelled **Ruben Rising**; Bemalung // Painting **Nils Emil Lundström**
H 17 cm
3 *Kronen-Marke* und *NL* in grüner Farbe, blind *RR, 5752, 4* und *I*
// *3 coronets mark* and *NL* in green, blind-stamped *RR, 5752, 4* and *I*

123 Vase, ca 1900

mit drei reliefierten Pfeilkrautblüten am durchbrochenen Vasenrand, die Blätter sind am Vasenkörper ornamental stilisiert. // with three arrowhead flowers on pierced rim; leaves are decoratively stylised on wall of vase.
Bemalung // Painting Karl Lindström
H 35 cm
3 Kronen-Marke und *KL* in grüner Farbe, blind *D.J.* und *11281*
// *3 coronets mark* and *KL* in green, blind-stamped *D.J.* and *11281*

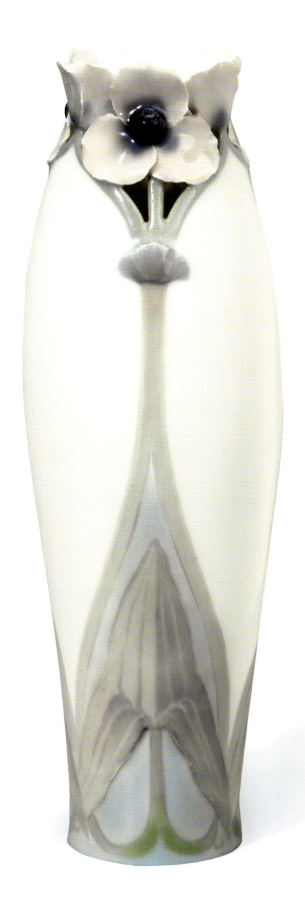

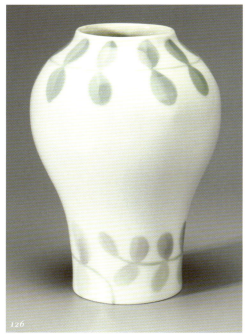

124 Vase, 1901/1902

mit drei gleich dekorierten Seiten: leicht reliefierte Blätter und Blütenkränzchen der Haselnuss. // with three identically decorated sides: foliage in low relief and hazelnut catkins.
Modelliert und bemalt // Modelled and painted Astrid Ewerlöf
H 19 cm
3 Kronen-Marke und • *E* • in grüner Farbe, blind • *E* • , *J, 13864* und *26* // *3 coronets mark* and • *E* • in green, blind-stamped • *E* •, *J, 13864* and *26*
Vgl. kleinere Rörstrand-Vase mit gleichem Dekor: Kat. Bröhan V/2, 1996 // Cf. smaller Rörstrand vase with identical decoration: Cat. Bröhan V/2, 1996

125 Vase, ca 1902/1909

mit Blättern und Blüten, auf der anderen Vasenseite nur zwei Blätter. // with foliage and blossoms; only two leaves on the other side of the vase.
Bemalt und wohl auch modelliert // Painted and probably also modelled Georg Asplund
H 12 cm
3 Kronen-Marke, • *G* • und • *7116* • in grüner Farbe, blind *I* // *3 coronets mark*, • *G* • and • *7116* • in green, blind-stamped *I*

126 Vase, ca 1900

an Basis und Mündung jeweils umlaufende Ranke mit Fliederblättern. // with base and mouth each surrounded by tendrils with lilac leaves.
H 16 cm
3 Kronen-Marke in grüner Farbe, blind *D.J.* und *4059* // *3 coronets mark* in green, blind-stamped *D.J.* and *4059*

127 Vase, ca 1905

birnenförmig, mit reliefiertem Knotentang auf wellenförmiger Bemalung. // pyriform, with matted seaweed in relief on wavy painted decoration.
Modelliert // Modelled Ruben Rising; Bemalung // Painting Astrid Ewerlöf
H 13 cm
3 Kronen-Marke und · *E* · in grüner Farbe, blind *RR* und *A1705* // *3 coronets mark* and · *E* · in green, blind-stamped *RR* and *A1705*

128 Vase, späte 1890er
// late 1890s

Korpus mit zartrosa Fond, vierseitig leicht eingedellt. Hals mit Blütenblättern umlaufend reliefiert und mit schwarz abgesetztem Mündungsrand. // with wall with delicate pink ground, slightly quatrefoil. Neck surrounded by flower leaves in relief and rim of mouth set off in black.
Modelliert // Modelled Ruben Rising. Künstlerinitialen nicht zu entschlüsseln // Artist initials indecipherable
H 10 cm
3 Kronen-Marke in grüner Farbe, blind *RR* und *2218* // *3 coronets mark* in green, blind-stamped *RR* and *2218*

129 Vase, ca 1902

mit drei gleich dekorierten Seiten: Glyzinien mit herabhängenden
Blütentrauben, in kräftigem Relief ausgeführt. // three identically
decorated sides: wisteria with pendulous racemes executed in
high relief.
H 26 cm
Ohne Stempel, Boden restauriert // No stamp, floor restored

130 *Vase, ca 1902*

mit auf beiden Seiten gleichem Dekor: Mohn mit zwei reliefierten, durchbrochenen Blüten, deren obere Ränder den Vasenrand bilden.
// with identical decoration on both sides: two poppies executed in relief and pierced, the upper edges of which form the vase rim.
Bemalung // Painting Nils Emil Lundström
H 31 cm
3 Kronen-Marke und *NL* in grüner Farbe, blind *D.J., 6779, 1 und 2*
// *3 coronets mark* and *NL* in green, blind-stamped *D.J., 6779, 1 and 2*

131 Vase, ca 1900

mit auf drei Seiten gleichem Reliefdekor: Lilienblüte und -blatt.
// with identical decoration in relief on three sides: lily and leaf.
Modelliert // Modelled Ruben Rising
H 31 cm
3 Kronen-Marke in grüner Farbe, blind R.R. und 2200 // 3 coronets
mark in green, blind-stamped R.R. and 2200

132 Vase, ca 1905/1909

mit auf beiden Seiten gleicher Stiefmütter-
chenblüte, dazwischen jeweils ein Blatt.
// with an identical pansy on both sides,
between the blooms one leaf each.
Bemalt und wohl auch modelliert
// Painted and probably also modelled
Georg Asplund
H 11.5 cm
3 Kronen-Marke und · *G · in grüner Farbe,
blind 719 // 3 coronets mark* and · *G · in
green, blind-stamped 719*

133 Vase, ca 1905/1910

mit zwei in leichtem Relief ausgeführten
Margaritenblüten. // with two daisies
executed in low relief.
Bemalung // Painting Nils Emil Lundström
H 10 cm
3 Kronen-Marke und *NL* in grüner Farbe,
blind 13 (?) // 3 coronets mark* and *NL* in
green, blind-stamped 13 (?)*

134 Vase, ca 1905/1909

mit Fußteller und ornamentalisiertem
Dekor: am zylindrischen Vasenkörper
sechs tulpenartige Blüten, auf dem Fußteller drei zwiebelförmige Gebilde. // with
en suite plate and stylised decoration:
six tulip-like blooms on the cylindrical
vase; on the plate three bulb-shaped con-
figurations.
Bemalung // Painting Astrid Ewerlöf
H 12 cm
3 Kronen-Marke, · *E* · und *8258* in grüner
Farbe, blind *I* // 3 coronets mark*, · *E* · and
8258 in green, blind-stamped I

135 Vase, ca 1902/1905

mit blassblauem Fond, leicht reliefierter Calla-Blüte und großem Calla-Blatt. // with calla lily in low relief and large calla leaf on pale blue ground.
Bemalung // Painting Karl Lindström
H 11 cm
3 Kronen-Marke und *KL* in grüner Farbe, blind *M.P.* (Maria Pettersson?) und *30587* // *3 coronets mark* and *KL* in green, blind-stamped *M.P.* (Maria Pettersson?) and *30587*

136 Vase, ca 1898/1899

mit mehreren Blüten, auf der anderen Vasenseite nur eine Blüte. // with several flowers; on the other side only one flower.
Bemalung // Painting Algot Eriksson
H 16.5 cm
3 Kronen-Marke, *AE* und *5153* in grüner Farbe // *3 coronets mark*, *AE* and *5153* in green

137 Vase, ca 1902/1909

mit drei gleich dekorierten Seiten: Blütenblätter in leichtem Relief. // with three identically decorated sides: petals in low relief.
Bemalung // Painting Nils Emil Lundström
H 11 cm
3 Kronen-Marke und *NL* in grüner Farbe, blind *M.P.* (Maria Pettersson?) und *7697* // *3 coronets mark* and *NL* in green, blind-stamped *M.P.* (Maria Pettersson?) and *7697*

138 Vase, vor // before 1900

mit drei gleich dekorierten Seiten: ornamental stilisierte Tulpen in transparentem
Weiß auf grau eingefärbter Porzellanmasse. // with three identically decorated
sides: decoratively stylised tulips in transparent white on grey-tinted porcelain body.
Bemalung // Painting Erik Hugo Tryggelin.
Wohl für die Weltausstellung Paris 1900. //
Probably for the 1900 Paris World Exposition.
H 31.5 cm
3 Kronen-Marke, TH. (ligiert) und Rörstrand
1900 in weißer Farbe, blind C.L. à 3, I und
2, an der unteren Vasenwandung Papieretikett „Rörstrands-Samling Nr. 607"
// 3 coronets mark, TH. (monogram) and
Rörstrand 1900 in white, blind-stamped
C.L. à 3, I and 2; on the lower vessel wall
paper label 'Rörstrands-Samling Nr. 607'

139 Vase, ca 1900/1905

mit ochsenblut-grauer Laufglasur und drei
wulstigen Ringen, an einer Seite von
einem blau-lilafarbigen breiten Glasurtrop-
fen überflossen. // with oxblood and grey
trickle glaze and three bulky rings; on one
side overlaid with a broad blue and purple
swathe of glaze.
H 28 cm
3 Kronen-Marke in grüner Farbe, blind F
// 3 coronets mark in green, blind-stamped F

140 Vase, ca 1900

mit Narzissenblüte in ausgesparter schwarzer Glasur. // with narcissus bloom in reserve on black glaze.
Bemalung // Painting Nils Emil Lundström
H 25 cm
3 Kronen-Marke, NL und *13547* in grüner Farbe, blind *I* // *3 coronets mark, NL* and *13547* in green, blind-stamped *I*

141 Vase, ca 1900

in Balusterform mit großer Mohnblüte in ausgesparter schwarzer Glasur. // balustershaped with large poppy in reserve on black glaze.
Bemalung wohl // Painting probably Algot Eriksson
H 46 cm
3 Kronen-Marke und *6064* in grüner Farbe, blind *3-Kronen-Marke* // *3 coronets mark* and *6064* in green, blind-stamped *3 coronets mark*

142 Vase, ca 1900

mit Schneeballblüten in ausgesparter
schwarzer Glasur. // with snowball flower
corymbs in reserve on black glaze.
Bemalung wohl // Painting probably
Algot Eriksson
H 27.5 cm
3 Kronen-Marke und *13546* in grüner
Farbe, Boden restauriert (weitere Zeichen
nicht erkennbar) // *3 coronets mark* and
13546 in green; bottom restored (no other
discernible marks)

143 Vase, ca 1900

mit zwei Mohnblüten in ausgesparter
schwarzer Glasur. // with two poppies in
reserve on black glaze.
Bemalung // Painting Algot Eriksson
H 15 cm
3 Kronen-Marke und *AE* in grüner Farbe
// *3 coronets mark* and *AE* in green

144 Vase, ca 1900

großflächig gemalte Mohnblüten auf
Rörstrand-schwarzem Fond. // Large-scale
poppy blooms painted on Rörstrand black
ground.
Bemalung // Painting Algot Eriksson
H 40 cm
3 Kronen-Marke und *AE* in grüner Farbe,
blind *50* // *3 coronets mark* and *AE* in
green, blind-stamped *50*

145 *Vase, ca 1900*

mit Narzissenblüten in ausgesparter schwarzer Glasur auf der Schauseite. // with narcissi in reserve on black glaze on the principal side.
Bemalung // Painting Astrid Ewerlöf
H 12 cm
3 Kronen-Marke und · E · in grüner Farbe // *3 coronets mark* and · E · in green

146 *Vase, ca 1900*

mit Mohnblüten und -blättern in ausgesparter schwarzer Glasur. // with poppy flowers and foliage, in reserve on black glaze.
Bemalung // Painting Algot Eriksson
H 11 cm
3 Kronen-Marke und *AE* in grüner Farbe, blind *12* // *3 coronets mark* and *AE* in green, blind-stamped *12*

147 *Vase, ca 1900*

mit blühender Tulpe in ausgesparter schwarzer Glasur. // with tulip in full bloom in reserve on black glaze.
Bemalung // Painting Algot Eriksson
H 20 cm
3 Kronen-Marke und *AE* in grüner Farbe, blind *JL* (Jane Lindberg?) und *22* // *3 coronets mark* and *AE* in green, blind-stamped *JL* (Jane Lindberg?) and *22*

148 Vase, ca 1902

mit Hüllblättern und durchbrochenem Reliefdekor aus kleinen Pilzen.
// with husks and pierced relief decoration consisting of small mushrooms.
Modelliert // Modelled **Waldemar Lindström**; Bemalung // Painting
Karl Lindström
H 13 cm
3 Kronen-Marke und *KL* in grüner Farbe, blind • *WL* • (ligiert),*12593*
und *J3* // *3 coronets mark* and *KL* in green, blind-stamped • *WL* •
(monogram), *12593* and *J3*

Die Künstler, die Signaturen
Artists, Signatures

Alphabetisches Künstler-Verzeichnis // *Artists listed in alphabetical order*

Kurzbiografien von Keramikern und Künstlern, die während der Jugendstil Epoche (zwischen 1895 und 1915/20) bei Rörstrand in einem festen Beschäftigungsverhältnis oder in freier Mitarbeit tätig waren. Daneben arbeitete hier eine große Anzahl von Formern und Porzellanmalern, die in unterschiedlichem Maße auch Kunstporzellan fertigten.

// Brief biographies of ceramicists and artists who worked for Rörstrand during the Jugendstil/Art Nouveau era (between 1895 and 1915/20), either as employees on a permanent basis or as freelancers. In addition, a large number of repairers and porcelain painters worked for Rörstrand, who, to a varying extent, also made art porcelain.

Die Rörstrand-Fabrikmarke // *The Rörstrand-Factory mark*

Die verschiedenen Künstler-Signaturen kommen in der Regel zusammen mit der Fabrikmarke von Rörstrand vor, d.h. „Rörstrand" in Kursivschrift mit den drei Kronen, die 1884 eingeführt worden war. Sie erscheint aufgedruckt in Blau, Blaugrün, Schwarz oder Rot; die Bedeutung der jeweiligen Farbgebung ist noch unbekannt. Von einigen Künstlern wurde die Marke auch eigenhändig auf das gerade bearbeitete Stück aufgetragen, gewöhnlich in blaugrüner Farbe.

// The signatures of the various artists are usually encountered together with the Rörstrand factory mark, i.e. 'Rörstrand' in italics with the three coronets introduced in 1884. This mark occurs imprinted in blue, blue-green, black or red; the significance of using the different colours is not known. Some artists personally applied the mark on the piece they were working on, usually in blue-green.

ADELBORG, LOUISE (1885 – 1971)
Kunsthandwerkerin, Textil und Keramik
// Craftswoman working in textiles and ceramics

1909 Ausbildung an der Technischen Schule (HKS) in Stockholm. Seit 1915 an Rörstrand gebunden und gemeinsam mit Eva Jahnke-Björk und Edward Hald verantwortlich für die Beteiligung von Rörstrand an der Heimausstellung 1917 in der Kunsthalle Liljevalch mit einer neuen Kollektion von Kunst- und Gebrauchskeramik unter dem Motto „Schönere Alltagsdinge". 1915 erste Versuche einiger Tassen und Untertassen mit plastischen Dekoren (Trollslända/Zauberland, Mistel) in Alf Wallanders Geist, jedoch angepasst an neuere Tendenzen mit Rückgriffen auf die bäuerliche Tradition. Bis 1926 bei Rörstrand fest angestellt, später auch in Göteborg und Lidköping tätig. Ihre künstlerisch bedeutendsten Leistungen fallen in die 1920er und 1930er Jahre, u. a. mit dem *Nationalservice Swedish Grace* (Schwedische Anmut) von 1930.
// In 1909 trained at the School of Technique and Applied Arts, Stockholm (HKS). From 1915 linked with Rörstrand and, together with Eva Jahnke-Björk and Edward Hald, responsible for Rörstrand taking part in the household trade fair in 1917 at Liljevalch Art Hall with a new collection of art and utilitarian ceramics under the motto 'More beautiful everyday things'. In 1915 first attempts at making cups and saucers with sprigged decoration (Trollslända/*Magic Land*, Mistletoe) in the spirit of Alf Wallander yet adapted to more recent trends with a reversion to the rural tradition. Until 1926 employed at Rörstrand on a permanent basis, later also worked in Göteborg and Lidköping. Her most remarkable achievements date to the 1920s and 1930s, including the *Swedish Grace* national service (1930).

Signatur(e): *L A-g* (gemalt, geritzt // painted, incised)

ALMSTRÖM, HARALD (1870 – 1944)
Keramiker, Verwaltungsdirektor
// Ceramicist, administrative director

1890 – 93 als Zivilingenieur an der Königlich Technischen Hochschule (KTH) in Stockholm ausgebildet. 1893 bei Rörstrand angestellt; arbeitete ab den späten 1890er Jahren als Verwaltungsdirektor. Übernahm die Leitung des Werks zusammen mit seinem Bruder Knut Almström nach dem Tod des Vaters Robert Almström. 1893 Studienreise u. a. nach England. Um 1900 zahlreiche Ziervasen im Geiste von Wallander; datierte Objekte gibt es von 1896 bis 1901. Teilnahme an den Ausstellungen in Stockholm 1897 und in Paris 1900 mit jeweils mehr als 10 Vasen.

// From 1890 to 1893 trained as a civil engineer at the Royal Technical High School (KTH) Stockholm. In 1893 hired by Rörstrand; from the late 1890s administrative director. Became co-director of the factory with his brother, Knut Almström, on the death of their father, Robert Almström. Went to England and other countries on a study tour in 1893. About 1900, he made numerous decorative vases in the Wallander manner; dated objects are known from 1896 to 1901. Participation with more than ten vases each at the 1897 Stockholm exhibition and the 1900 Paris Exposition.

Signatur(e): *H. Almström* + Jahr // year (gemalt // painted)

ALMSTRÖM, KNUT (1873 – 1955)
Keramiker, Technischer Direktor
// Ceramicist, technical director

1892 – 1895 als Zivilingenieur an der Königlich Technischen Hochschule (KTH) in Stockholm ausgebildet. 1895 angestellt in Rörstrand; arbeitete seit Ende der 1890er Jahre als Technischer Direktor. Zwischen Juli und Dezember 1895 umfassende Studienreisen, teilweise gemeinsam mit Algot Eriksson, zur Besichtigung von Porzellanfabriken in Deutschland, Frankreich und England. Nach dem Tod des Vaters Robert Almström übernahm er 1910 zusammen mit seinem Bruder Harald Almström die Leitung der Fabrik. Schon seit 1893 hatte er mit verschiedenen Glasuren an eigenen und fremden Modellen oder den Standardmodellen der Fabrik experimentiert und brannte auch Steinzeug, das in Paris 1900 gezeigt wurde. Er signierte seine Arbeiten wohl nicht.

// From 1892 to 1895 trained as a civil engineer at Royal Technical High School (KTH) Stockholm. In 1895 hired at Rörstrand; worked from the late 1890s as technical director. Between July and December 1895 extensive study tours, accompanied on some by Algot Eriksson, to visit porcelain factories in Germany, France and England. On the death of his father, Robert Almström, he became co-director of the factory with his brother, Harald Almström, in 1910. From 1893 experiments with different glazes on his own and others' models or the standard factory models. He also fired fine stoneware, which was shown at the 1900 Paris Exposition. He probably did not sign his own work.

Signatur(e): nicht bekannt // not known

ANDERBERG, MELA (PAMELA) (1865 – 1927)
Porzellanmalerin, Keramikerin
// Porcelain painter, ceramicist

Tochter des Werkmeisters Anders W. Anderberg. Gegen Ende der 1880er Jahre bei Rörstrand angestellt; 1891 als künstlerische Porzellanmalerin in Göteborg erwähnt; Signaturen bekannt seit 1897. Sie beteiligte sich mit eigenen Arbeiten an der Ausstellung 1897 in Stockholm und 1900 an der Weltausstellung in Paris und erhielt dort eine lobende Erwähnung. 1912 wurde sie als Nachfolgerin von Algot Eriksson Vorstand der Abteilung Unterglasurmalerei und behielt diese Funktion bis ca. 1920. Sie trat mit fein abgestimmten kleineren Objekten hervor; für einige Jahre gab es eine engere Zusammenarbeit mit Hilma Persson.
// Daughter of foreman Anders W. Anderberg. Hired by Rörstrand towards the close of the 1880s; in 1891 mentioned as a painter of art porcelain in Göteborg; signatures known since 1897. She showed her own work at the 1897 Stockholm exhibition and the 1900 Paris World Exposition, where she was given an honourable mention. In 1912 she became successor to Algot Eriksson as head of the underglaze painting division and remained in that position until ca 1920. She was known for finely nuanced, rather small objects; for some years she collaborated quite closely with Hilma Persson.

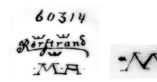

Signatur(e): *MA, .M.A.* (gemalt // painted)
Siehe Seite // see page: 92, 143, 172, 183

ANDRÉASEN, CH. (ca 1865 – ca 1930)
Keramiker, Porzellanmaler
// Ceramicist, porcelain painter

1889 – 1901 bei Rörstrand für Bemalung und Dekoration angestellt; 1901 – 26 mit entsprechenden Arbeitsaufgaben in der Porzellanfabrik Göteborg.
// From 1889 to 1901 employed at Rörstrand for painting and decoration; from 1901 to 1926 with similar work at the Göteborg Porcelain Manufactory.

Signatur(e): nicht bekannt // not known

ASPLUND, JOHAN GEORG (1873 – ca 1930)
Porzellanmaler, Keramiker
// Porcelain painter, ceramicist

Ausbildung unbekannt. Von Mitte der 1890er Jahre bis 1910 bei Rörstrand angestellt. Entwarf Kachelöfen, Kacheln und Ziergegenstände. Einige Entwürfe für Vasen und das berühmte Seerosen-Piedestal von 1895 sind erhalten. In den Lohnlisten von 1900 und 1910 wird er mit besonderem Lohnzuschlag erwähnt. Verbirgt sich wahrscheinlich hinter der Signatur .G. auf mehreren Vasen im Stil der Fabrik von 1900 bis 1910. 1911 an der Porzellanfabrik in Gävle angestellt; er entwarf dort u.a. einige zeittypische Servicemuster. Um 1917 schied er in Gävle aus. Es ist wahrscheinlich, dass er in der Folgezeit noch einmal für Rörstrand tätig war; Objekte mit einer varianten G-Signatur könnten ihm zugeordnet werden.
// Nothing is known about his education. Employed at Rörstrand from the mid-1890s to 1910. Designed tiled stoves, tiles and ornamental objects. Some designs for vases and the famous 1895 water lily pedestal have survived. He is mentioned in the 1900 and 1910 payrolls as receiving exceptional extra pay. Is probably concealed behind the signature .G. on several vases in the style associated with Rörstrand from 1900 to 1910. From 1911 to 1917 employed at the porcelain factory in Gävle; there his activities included designing some patterns for services in the style of the time. He probably worked again for Rörstrand after that; objects with a variant of the G signature have been attributed to him.

Signatur(e): (gemalt // painted) *JGA* (Monogramm // monogram 1895), *.G., G.* (in Rörstrand)
Siehe Seite // see page: 96, 97, 100, 176, 188, 196

BOBERG, ANNA, geb. // née SCHOLANDER (1864 – 1935)
Malerin // Painter

Tochter des Architekten Fredrik Wilhelm Scholander, verheiratet mit dem Architekten Ferdinand Boberg. Begann ihre Tätigkeit bei Rörstrand vor der Ausstellung 1897. Signaturen sind von 1897 bis 1902 nachweisbar. Am bekanntesten ist die große „Pfauenvase" von 1897, die in fünf Exemplaren hergestellt wurde; ein Exemplar in voller Farbigkeit ist im Museum Malmö erhalten, eine mild hellblau glasierte Variante (aus L. Hanssons Sammlung) befindet sich in Rörstrands Museum. Daneben existieren noch mehrere Ziervasen im Stil der Zeit.
// Daughter of the architect Fredrik Wilhelm Scholander, married to Ferdinand Boberg, also an architect. Began to work at Rörstrand before the 1897 exhibition. Signatures verifed from 1897 to 1902. The best known piece of hers is the large 1897

'Peacock Vase', of which five were made; one example in the full colour scheme is in the Malmö Museum, a variant glazed in soft light-blue (from L. Hansson's collection) is in the Rörstrand Museum. Several other ornamental vases in the style of the period have survived.

Signatur(e): *AB* (gemalt // painted), *.AB.* (in der Regel ligiert geschrieben // usually written as a ligatured monogram), auch // also *Anna Boberg*
Siehe Seite // see page: 91, 96, 97, 118, 138, 139

BOBERG, FERDINAND (1860 – 1946)
Architekt, Musterzeichner
// Architect, pattern draughtsman

Verheiratet mit Anna Boberg. 1897 – 1898 und 1900 bei Rörstrand angestellt; neue Kachelofen-Modelle und einzelne Kunstwerke, u. a. große Blumenkübel (Übertöpfe) und einzelne Service. Auch später noch als freier Mitarbeiter für Rörstrand tätig; gestaltete die Messestände 1902, 1908, 1909 und 1914 sowie 1915 ein für Gustav V. bestimmtes Service. 1909 und 1914 lieferte er auch Entwürfe für Gustavsberg.
// Married to Anna Boberg. From 1897 to 1898 and 1900 employed at Rörstrand; new tiled stove models and individual objets d'art, including large *caisses à fleurs* (cachepots) and occasionally services. Later also freelanced for Rörstrand; designed the Rörstrand trade fair stalls in 1902, 1908, 1909 and 1914 and, in 1915, a service destined for Gustav V. Also submitted designs to Gustavsberg in 1909 and 1914.

F. BOBERG

Signatur(e): *F. Boberg, Ferdinand Boberg*

ERIKSSON, ALGOT (1868 – 1937)
Porzellanmaler, Keramiker
// Porcelain painter, ceramicist

Aufgewachsen in Rörstrand; 1882 – 1889 und 1894 – 1895 Studien an der Technischen Schule (HKS) Stockholm; 1886 – 1912 bei Rörstrand angestellt. 1895 Studienreisen u. a. nach Dänemark, Deutschland und Frankreich. Arbeitete frühzeitig mit Unterglasurmalerei in der Nachfolge der dänischen Fabriken gemeinsam mit Hugo Hörlin (1893) und später stark beeinflusst von Alf Wallander. Er entwarf mehrere Service, darunter *Gröna blad* (= grünes Blatt, 1900) und *Alpviol* (= Alpenveilchen, 1901), betei-

ligte sich an der Rörstrandabteilung der Ausstellungen in Göteborg 1891 und Chicago 1893 und war 1897 in Stockholm und 1900 in Paris mit Prunkvasen und Servicen vertreten. Seit dem Ende der 1890er Jahre war er Vorstand der Abteilung für Unterglasurmalerei. 1912 – 1917 arbeitete er an der Porzellanfabrik Lidköping (u. a. Kunstkeramik) und später für die Porzellanfabriken in Gävle (1917) und Karlskrona (1918 – ca. 1930).
// Grew up in Rörstrand; from 1882 to 1889 and from 1894 to 1895 studied at the School of Technique and Applied Arts, Stockholm (HKS); from 1886 to 1912 employed at Rörstrand. In 1895 study tours abroad included visits to Denmark, Germany and France. Worked from an early date with underglaze painting following the Danish porcelain factories, collaborating with Hugo Hörlin (1893) and later noticeably influenced by Alf Wallander. Eriksson designed several services, including *Gröna blad* (Green Leaf, 1900) and *Alpviol* (Alpine Violet, 1901), participated in the Rörstand show at the 1891 Göteborg and the 1893 Chicago exhibitions and showed *Prunkvasen* [show vases] and services in Stockholm in 1897 and at the 1900 Paris Exposition. From the late 1890s he was head of the underglaze painting division. Between 1912 and 1917 he worked at the Lidköping Porcelain Manufactory (his work included art ceramic) and later for the porcelain factories in Gävle (1917) and Karlskrona (1918 – ca 1930).

Signatur(e): *A.E.* (gemalt // painted, mitunter *AE* ligiert // occasionally AE as a ligatured monogram, ausnahmsweise + Jahreszahl // rarely + year)
Siehe Seite // see page: 90, 100, 105, 117, 124, 129, 148, 159, 163, 171, 180, 182, 197, 199, 200, 201

ERIKSSON, GUSTAF (ca 1860 – ca 1930)
Keramiker, Modelleur
// Ceramicist, modeller

Zwischen 1892 und 1904 für Gustavsberg tätig. Seit 1897 sind signierte Vasen mit plastischem Dekor in Wallanders Stil nachweisbar. 1905 – 1920 Tätigkeit an der Göteborger Porzellanfabrik, auch hier mit Arbeiten im Rörstrand-Stil. Vermutlich auch vorübergehende Mitarbeit bei Rörstrand und Göteborg.
// Worked for Gustavsberg between 1892 and 1904. Verified signed vases with sprigged decoration in the Wallander manner since 1897. From 1905 to 1920 worked at the Göteborg Porcelain Manufactory, there too in the Rörstrand style. Believed to have worked temporarily at both Rörstrand and Göteborg.

Signatur(e): *GE*

EWERLÖF, ASTRID (1876 – 1927)
Porzellanmalerin, Keramikerin
// Porcelain painter, ceramicist

1899 Studienabschluss an der HKS (Högre Konstindustriella Skolan) in Stockholm. Danach Tätigkeit für Rörstrand. Ihre unter dem Einfluss von Wallander entstandenen Arbeiten zeichnen sich durch vorwiegend leicht reliefierte florale Dekore mit feinem Gefühl für Farbnuancen aus.
// In 1899 completed studies at the Higher Industrial Art School (HKS) in Stockholm. Subsequently worked for Rörstrand. Influenced by Wallander, her pieces are distinguished primarily by floral decoration in low relief revealing sensitivity to colour nuances.

Signatur(e): *E.*, *.E.* (gemalt // painted)
Siehe Seite // see page: 91, 107, 113, 129, 139, 146, 147, 162, 170, 183, 188, 189, 196, 201

GRAVENSTEIN, MATHILDA (geb. // born ca 1865)
Porzellanmalerin
// Porcelain painter

Vielleicht auch Formerin bei Rörstrand. In den Lohnverzeichnissen 1900 als besser qualifizierte Mitarbeiterin erwähnt. Signierte Vasen im Stil der Fabrik können eventuell mit ihr in Verbindung gebracht werden. Es sind nur wenige (gemalte und entworfene) Stücke bekannt.
// May also have worked as a repairer at Rörstrand. Entered in the 1900 payrolls as a worker with higher qualifications. Signed vases in the Rörstrand style can possibly be linked with her. Only a few (painted and designed) pieces known.

Signatur (e): *.MG.*

HALD, EDWARD (1883 – 1980)
Maler, Keramiker, Glaskünstler
// Painter, ceramicist, artist in glass

1916 – 1924 bei Rörstrand angestellt. Teilnahme u. a. an der Heimausstellung 1917 in Liljevalch und in Paris 1925 mit neuer Kunst- und Gebrauchskeramik zum Thema „Schönere Alltagsdinge". Einige bekannte Steingutservice, darunter *Turbin* 1917, *Halda* 1919, *Stilleben*, *Moln* und *Korg* (= Wölkchen und Korb), alle verbunden mit dem o. g. Thema. 1924 wechselte er zur Porzellanfabrik Karlskrona, wo er bis 1933 blieb. Seit 1917 auch im Glaswerk Orrefors tätig, 1933 – 1944 als Direktor.

// From 1916 to 1924 employed at Rörstrand. Exhibitions at which he showed his work included the 1917 domestic exhibition in Liljevalch and the 1925 Paris exposition, where his work addressed the 'More beautiful everyday things' theme. Some well known services in lead-glazed earthenware, including *Turbin* 1917, *Halda* 1919, *Stilleben* (Still life), *Moln* and *Korg* (Cloudlets and Basket), all associated with the above theme. In 1924 he transferred to the Karlskrona Porcelain Manufactory, where he stayed until 1933. He had also worked for the Orrefors glassworks since 1917, between 1933 and 1944 as director.

Hald

Signature: *Hald, E.H* (gemalt // painted)

HJORTZBERG, OLLE (1872 – 1954)
Maler, Professor an der Königlichen Kunsthochschule
// Painter, professor at the Royal Art Academy

Entwarf 1914 zu den Baltischen Ausstellungen einige Objekte für Rörstrand.
// Designed some objects for Rörstrand for the Baltic Exhibitions in 1914.

Signatur(e): nicht bekannt // not known

HOLCK, HELENE (1867 – 1922)
Porzellan- und Miniaturmalerin, Kunsthandwerkerin
// Porcelain painter and miniature painter, craftswoman

Studium 1879 – 1880 in Dresden und 1881 – 1887 an der Technischen Schule (HKS) in Stockholm. Unterrichtete in Göteborg und ab 1892 in Stockholm. Bis 1903 eigenes Atelier gemeinsam mit ihrer Schwester, der Textilkünstlerin Ingeborg Holck, danach ansässig in Lund. 1895 Studienreise nach London. Ab 1890 entstanden Arbeiten für Rörstrand, insbesondere 1896/97 für die Stockholmer Ausstellung. Beteiligte sich mit eigenen Arbeiten (Porzellan mit Aufglasurmalerei und Fayence) in Göteborg 1891, Stockholm 1897, Helsingborg 1903 und im Museum Malmö 1904.
// Studied in Dresden from 1879 to 1880 and from 1881 to 1887 at the School of Technique and Applied Arts, Stockholm (HKS). Taught in Göteborg and from 1892 in Stockholm. Until 1903 shared a studio with her sister, the textile artist Ingeborg Holck, then settled in Lund. In 1895 study tour to London. From 1890 produced pieces for Rörstrand, notably in 1896/97 for the Stockholm exhibition. Showed work of her own (porcelain with

overglaze painting and faience) in Göteborg in 1891, Stockholm 1897, Helsingborg 1903 and at the Malmö Museum in 1904.

Signatur(e): *Helene Holck* (gemalt // painted), *H Holck* (Monogramm // monogram; auch Namenszug kommt vor // cursive signature also occurs)

HÅRDSTEDT, JOHN (1878–1942)
Porzellan- und Dekormaler und Graveur
// Porcelain and decoration painter as well as engraver

1892–1941 bei Rörstrand angestellt. Arbeitete gemeinsam mit einigen Formgestaltern.
// From 1892 to 1941 employed at Rörstrand. Collaborated there with mould designers.

Signatur(e): *J. Hårdstedt* (gemalt // painted), *J. H-dt* (zeitweise auch + Jahreszahl // occasionally also + year)

HÖRLIN, HUGO (1851–1894)
Architekt, Musterzeichner
// Architect, patterns draughtsman

1879–1894 Oberlehrer an der Technischen Schule in Stockholm, wo er zum Vorstand der von ihm aufgebauten HKS wurde. Unterrichtete u.a. in Keramik und richtete 1888 den ersten Ofen an der Hochschule ein. Herausgeber von „Svensk Konstslöjd" 1888–1889 und 1891. 1888 als künstlerischer Berater und Mitarbeiter bei Rörstrand verpflichtet, u. a. zu den Ausstellungen in Paris 1889, Göteborg 1891 und Chicago 1893; bis zu seinem Tod dort tätig. Entwarf Muster für Fayencegeschirr und Serviceporzellan, dazu Vasen in glasiertem Ton, d. h. in Majolika „nach venezianischem Glas". Er soll die moderne Unterglasurmalerei in der Rörstrander Produktion eingeführt haben.
// From 1879 to 1894 teacher at the School of Technique and Applied Arts, Stockholm, where he established the HKS. Taught ceramics and other subjects and set up the first kiln at the Institute in 1888. Publisher of *Svensk Konstslöjd* 1888–1989 and 1891. In 1888 hired by Rörstrand as an artistic consultant and employee, working for the exhibitions in Paris 1889, Göteborg

1891 and Chicago 1893; remained at Rörstrand until his death. Designed patterns for faience tableware and porcelain services as well as vases in glazed pottery, i.e. majolica 'as per Venetian glass'. He is believed to have introduced modern underglaze porcelain painting at Röstrand.

Signatur(e): nicht bekannt // not known

JAHRL, KARL DAVID (geb. // born 1874)
Maler, Bildhauer, Zeichner und Grafiker; Modelleur
// Painter, sculptor, draughtsman and graphic artist, modeller

Studien an der Technischen Schule (HKS) in Stockholm, 1904 in Berlin, 1904/05 in Paris an der Académie Colarossi und der Académie Julian. Verheiratet mit Agnes Ståhle. Ab ca. 1900 bei Rörstrand als Modelleur beschäftigt; malte auch stimmungsvolle Landschaftsmotive.
// Studied at the School of Technique and Applied Arts, Stockholm (HKS), 1904 in Berlin, 1904/05 in Paris at the Académie Colarossi and the Académie Julian. Married to Agnes Ståhle. From about 1900 employed as a modeller at Rörstrand; also painted evocative landscape motifs.

Signatur(e): nicht bekannt // not known

JANCKE-BJÖRK, EVA (1882–1978)
Keramikerin, Malerin, Textilkünstlerin
// Ceramicist, painter, textile artist

1909 Technische Schule (HKS) in Stockholm. 1915–1921 bei Rörstrand und 1921–1925 bei St. Eriks Tonwarenfabriken angestellt, wahrscheinlich vorwiegend freischaffend. Arbeitete abschließend bis 1956 für BO Fayence in Gävle. Danach eigene Werkstatt in Mölndal. Unterrichtete an der HDK in Göteborg und arbeitete auch mit Textil und anderen Werkstoffen. Teilnahme u. a. an der Heimausstellung 1917 auf Liljevalch mit Kunst- und Gebrauchskeramik zum Thema „Schönere Alltagsdinge".
// In 1909 School of Technique and Applied Arts, Stockholm (HKS). From 1915 to 1921 employed at Rörstrand and from 1921 to 1925 at St. Eriks Pottery Factory in Uppsala, probably on a temporary freelance basis. Subsequently worked until 1956 for BO Fayence in Gävle. Then she had a workshop of her own in Mölndal. Taught at the HDK in Göteborg and also worked in textiles and other materials. Showed art ceramics and utilitarian ceramics related to the 'More beautiful everyday things' theme at the 1917 Liljevalch household wares exhibition.

Signatur(e): *EJB*, *EB* (gemalt // painted)

JOHANSSON, CARL JOHAN (1855 – 1930)
Porzellanmaler, Dreher
// Porcelain painter, turner

Ca. 1870–1926 bei Rörstrand angestellt. Qualifizierter Porzellanmaler. Kleinere Ziervasen, vorwiegend in traditionellen Stilarten. Erwähnt u.a. im Rahmen der Ausstellungen in Göteborg 1891, Mitarbeit in Stockholm 1897 und Paris 1900 mit ornamentalen Dekoren und Bemalung auf Servicen und Ziervasen. Steht für das letzte 1926 bei Rörstrand in Stockholm gebrannte Stück (ein Cremekännchen 1926 28/10).
// Employed at Rörstand from around 1870 to 1926. Qualified as a porcelain painter. Quite small ornamental vases, chiefly in traditional styles. Mentions include the exhibitions in Göteborg 1891, participation in Stockholm 1897 and Paris 1900: ornamental decoration and painting on services and ornamental vases. Stands for the last piece (a cream jug 1926 28/10) fired at Rörstrand in Stockholm in 1926.

Signatur(e): C.J.J. (gemalt // painted)

KAMPH, BORGHILD
Gastspiel in Rörstrand
// Guest at Rörstrand

Schale oder Tasse mit plastischer Handhabe in Gestalt einer Frau, signiert an der Seite „B Kamph 1906". Weitere Einzelheiten sind nicht bekannt.
// Bowl or cup with applied handle in the shape of a woman, signed on the side "B Kamph 1906". Nothing else is known about her.

Signatur(e): B Kamph

KARDELL, MARIA KAROLINA (1856 – 1940)
Dekorentwerferin mit eigenem Atelier
// Decoration designer with a studio of her own

1879 – 1884 Ausbildung an der HKS (Högre Konstindustriella Skolan) in Stockholm, danach dort Lehrtätigkeit bis 1926, insbesondere für Porzellan- und Fayencemalerei. 1888 stellte sie Keramik von Rörstrand (Flaschen, Schüsseln, Kannen und Krüge) in der HKS aus. Bezeichnete sich um 1890 als Porzellanmalerin. Keine Produktion für Rörstrand bekannt, dagegen Teilnahme an der Ausstellung in Malmö 1914 mit Steingutschalen und Schüsseln, die in Höganäs produziert worden waren.

// From 1879 to 1884 trained at the School of Technique and Applied Arts, Stockholm (HKS), subsequently instructed there until 1926, specifically porcelain painting and faience painting. In 1888 she exhibited ceramics from Rörstrand (flasks, bowls, tankards and jugs) at the HKS. About 1890 she called herself a porcelain painter. Not known to have made anything for Rörstrand although she did show lead-glazed earthenware dishes and bowls produced in Höganäs at the 1914 Malmö exhibition.

Signatur(e): keine aus Rörstrand bekannt // none known from Rörstrand

LARSSON, HUGO
Porzellanmaler
// Porcelain painter

In der ersten Hälfte des 20. Jahrhunderts eventuell auch Former bei Rörstrand. Verzeichnet in den Lohnlisten 1900 als höher qualifizierter Arbeiter. Keine Stücke bekannt, möglicherweise kann ihm eine mit . L. signierte Schale zugewiesen werden.
// During the first half of the twentieth century possibly also a repairer at Rörstrand. Entered in the 1900 payrolls as a workman with higher qualifications. No pieces of his known; a dish signed . L. might possibly be attributed to him.

Signatur(e): . L.

LINDBERG, EMMA (1871 – nach // after 1930)
Porzellanmalerin
// Porcelain painter

1890 – 1926 bei Rörstrand angestellt. Erwähnt bei den Ausstellungen in Stockholm 1897 und Paris 1900 sowie als höher qualifizierte Malerin in den Lohnlisten von 1900. Nur wenige Stücke bekannt.
// From 1890 to 1926 employed at Rörstrand. Mentioned in connection with the 1897 Stockholm and 1900 Paris exhibitions and entered in the 1900 payroll as a painter with higher qualifications. Only a few pieces of hers known.

E.L.

Signatur(e): E.L., E.L. (gemalt // painted)
Siehe Seite // see page: 133

LINDBERG, JANE (geb. // born 1867)
Porzellanmalerin und Dreherin
// Porcelain painter and turner

1900 und 1910 bei Rörstrand, erwähnt in den Lohnverzeichnissen unter den höher qualifizierten Malern. Nur wenige Stücke bekannt, darunter eine Vase, ca. 1903, bez. *JL* zusammen mit dem gemalten Monogramm *KL* (für Karl Lindström).
// In 1900 and 1910 at Rörstrand, entered in the payrolls under painters with higher qualifications. Only a few pieces of hers known, including a vase, ca 1903, marked *JL* along with the painted monogram *KL* (for Karl Lindström).

Signatur(e): *JL*

LINDSTRÖM, KARL (1865 – 1936)
Porzellanmaler, Keramiker
// Porcelain painter, ceramicist

Vetter von Waldemar Lindström. Einer der hervorragendsten Mitarbeiter bei Rörstrand. Angestellt seit 1878 und tätig bis 1931. Erwähnt u. a. bei den Ausstellungen in Göteborg 1891 und Chicago 1893; nahm mit Kunstobjekten in Stockholm 1897 und in Paris 1900 teil. Auf vielen unterschiedlich gestalteten Vasen mit plastischem Dekor kommen ein geritztes *WL* und ein gemaltes *KL* vor, woraus sich ergibt, dass Waldemar Lindström für die plastische Ausformung verantwortlich zeichnete und Karl Lindström für den malerischen Dekor zuständig war. Erwähnt in den Lohnlisten 1900 und 1910 unter den höher qualifizierten Malern.
// Cousin of Waldemar Lindström. One of the most outstanding employees at Rörstrand. Employed there from 1878 and active until 1931. Mentioned *inter alia* in connection with the 1891 Göteborg and 1893 Chicago exhibitions; showed objets d'art in Stockholm in 1897 and Paris in 1900. An incised *WL* and a painted *KL* occur on many vases of varying design with sprigged decoration, which means that Waldemar Lindström moulded the vase and Karl Lindström executed the painted decoration. Entered in the 1900 and 1910 payrolls under the heading of painters with higher qualifications.

Signatur(e): *KL, Karl Lindström*
(gemalt // painted)
Siehe Seite // see page: 88, 106, 110, 113, 119, 129, 133, 138, 146, 147, 150, 160, 167, 168, 171, 175, 177, 182, 187, 197, 202

LINDSTRÖM, WALDEMAR (1875 – 1941)
Keramiker // Ceramicist

1891 – 1897 Technische Schule, 1898 HKS. Sohn des Werkmeisters Axel Lindström und Vetter von Karl Lindström. 1897 – 1941 bei Rörstrand angestellt. Vor allem bekannt für seine vielen Tierfiguren und seine Vasen mit plastischem Dekor, die er gemeinsam mit Karl Lindström gestaltete. Tätig als Formgeber, seit 1917 Werkmeister in Rörstrand, ab 1926 Werkstattleiter in der Göteborger Fabrik.
// From 1891 to 1897 School of Technique and Applied Arts, Stockholm, 1898 HKS. Son of foreman Axel Lindström and cousin of Karl Lindström. From 1897 to 1941 employed at Rörstrand. Known chiefly for his many animal figurines and for vases with sprigged decoration, which he designed in collaboration with Karl Lindström. Worked as a mould designer, from 1917 foreman at Rörstrand, from 1926 workshop foreman at the Göteborg Factory.

Signatur(e): *WL, W Lindström, Waldemar Lindström* (gemalt // painted); *WL, .W.L., W Lindström, Waldemar Lindström* (geritzt // incised)
Siehe Seite // see page: 102, 110, 113, 133, 159, 167, 168, 171, 177, 179, 202

LUNDSTRÖM, NILS EMIL (1865 – 1960)
Maler, Porzellanmaler, Keramiker, Textilkünstler
// Painter, porcelain painter, ceramicist, textile artist

1885 – 1889 Studium in Düsseldorf und 1889 – 1892 an der Kunstakademie in Stockholm; hielt sich 1892 – 1894 in Berlin auf. 1896 bei Rörstrand angestellt, tätig bis 1935. Viele bedeutende Arbeiten, u. a. Servicemuster und viele Vasen, oft mit „Gemälde-Motiven". Steuerte auch zahlreiche Kunstobjekte zu den Ausstellungen in Stockholm 1897 und Paris 1900 bei. Ab ca. 1910 arbeitete er auch mit Scharffeuerglasuren und stellte eine größere Kollektion in der Stockholmer Herbstausstellung 1915 vor. Trat in den 1920er und 1930er Jahren mit Kunstobjekten im Zeitgeschmack hervor.
// From 1885 to 1889 studied in Düsseldorf and from 1889 to 1892 at the Royal Art Academy in Stockholm; lived in Berlin between 1892 and 1894. In 1896 hired by Rörstrand, where he worked until 1935. Many important works, including patterns for services and numerous vases, often with 'motifs taken from paintings'. Also contributed numerous objets d'art to the 1897 Stockholm exhibition and the 1900 Paris Exposition. From about 1910 he also worked with high-fired glazes and showed

quite a large collection at the 1915 Stockholm autumn exhibition. Known for objets d'art in the contemporary style during the 1920s and 1930s.

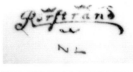

Signatur(e): *NL, NEL* (gemalt // painted) manchmal // at times *NLE* (Monogramm // monogram)
Siehe Seite // see page: 87, 90, 91, 95, 100, 106 – 109, 118, 119, 129, 132, 134, 140, 144, 150, 152, 155, 162, 163, 170, 182 – 184, 192, 196, 197, 199

NERPIN, HENRIK (1834 – 1908)
Maler, Dekorationsmaler, Bildhauer
// Painter, decoration painter, sculptor

Schüler an der Technischen Schule, studierte in den 1860er Jahren in Paris. 1858 – 1902 Oberlehrer an der Technischen Schule für Ornamentzeichnen und Modellierung. Hatte in Stockholm ein eigenes Bildhaueratelier mit vielen öffentlichen Aufträgen. Zeitweise für Rörstrand tätig, u. a. in den 1860er und 1870er Jahren, für die Ausstellung 1897 und dann noch einmal in den Jahren um 1900. Dekorierte und bemalte größere Prunkvasen und Ausstellungsobjekte.
// Attended the School of Technique and Applied Arts, Stockholm, studied in Paris in the 1860s. From 1858 to 1902 instructor at the School of Technique and Applied Art, where he taught ornament drawing and modelling. Had his own sculpture studio in Stockholm and received many public commissions. Worked occasionally for Rörstrand, in the 1860s and 1870s, for the 1897 exhibition and then again in the years before and after 1900. Decorated and painted quite large *Prunkvasen* [show vases] and exhibition objects.

Signatur(e): nicht bekannt // not known

NERPIN, THOR (1868 – 1957)
Bildhauer // Sculptor

Sohn von Henrik Nerpin; 1884 – 1887 ausgebildet an der Technischen Schule in Stockholm. Führte zu Beginn des Jahrhunderts einzelne Arbeiten für Rörstrand aus.
// Son of Henrik Nerpin; from 1884 to 1887 trained at the School of Technique and Applied Arts, Stockholm. Executed individual commissions for Rörstrand in the early twentieth century.

Signatur(e): nicht bekannt // not known

NEUMANN, ADOLPH (1849 – 1938)
Maler, Dekorationsmaler, Glasmaler
// Painter, decoration painter, glass painter

1878 – 1888 in Rörstrand angestellt, später weitere Aufträge. Dekorierte oft große Ziervasen mit Motiven von verschiedenen bekannten Künstlern. Einzelne Prunkvasen zu den Ausstellungen 1897 und um 1900. Betrieb gemeinsam mit Anton Josef Vogel eine Firma für Glasmalerei und Glasfenster, die an mehreren Ausstellungen erfolgreich teilnahm.
// From 1878 to 1888 employed at Rörstrand, later more commissions. Decorated ornamental vases, which were often large, with motifs taken from the works of famous artists. One-off *Prunkvasen* [show vases] for the exhibitions in 1897 and around 1900. Together with Anton Josef Vogel ran a glass painting and glass window company, which successfully participated in several trade fairs.

Signatur(e): *A Neumann, AN* (gemalt // painted)

NORDIN-TENGBOM, HJÖRDIS (1877 – 1967)
Bildhauerin, Malerin
// Sculptor, painter

1897 – 1900 Technische Hochschule (HKS); 1900 – 1901 Kunstakademie in Stockholm; 1901 – 1906 Studien in Paris. Mehrere Plastiken und Büsten usw., auch Silberschmuck und Beleuchtungsarmaturen in Kupfer. 1906/07 bei Rörstrand angestellt, 1913/14 Ausführung von Einzelarbeiten. Zeigte in der Abteilung des Gewerbevereins Malmö 1914 „*Mädchenstatuetten aus Schonen in feldspatechter Unterglasurtechnik von Rörstrand"*.
// From 1897 to 1900 School of Technique and Applied Arts, Stockholm (HKS); 1900 to 1901 Royal Art Academy in Stockholm; 1901 to 1906 studies in Paris. Several pieces of sculpture and busts, etc., also silver jewellery and light fixtures in copper. In 1906/07 hired at Rörstrand, 1913/14 executed one-off pieces. Showed *Statuettes of Girls from Schonen in Genuine Feldspathic Underglaze from Rörstrand* at the Malmö Trade and Commerce division in 1914.

Signatur(e): nicht bekannt // not known

ÖBERG, THURE (1871 – 1935)
Keramiker // Ceramicist

Ausgebildet an der Technischen Schule in Stockholm, Sohn von Axel Öberg, Modellmeister bei Rörstrand. Bei Rörstrand einige Jahre nach 1890 tätig, wechselte später in das Tochterunternehmen Arabia in Finnland und war dort von 1896 bis 1932 als führender Keramiker und künstlerischer Leiter tätig.

// Trained at the School of Technique and Applied Arts, in Stockholm; son of Axel Öberg, master modeller at Rörstrand. Worked at Rörstrand for some years after 1890, later transferred to Arabia, the Rörstrand subsidiary in Finland, where he was employed from 1896 to 1932 as head ceramicist and artistic director.

Signatur(e): keine aus Rörstrand bekannt // not known for Rörstrand; *T Öberg, T.Ö.* (+ Jahreszahl, bei Arabia // + year, at Arabia)

PERJE, HERBERT (1890 – 1981)
Graveur // Engraver

Seit 1904 Ausbildung und erste Anstellung bei Rörstrand; 1910 Wechsel in das Porzellanwerk Gävle, dort bis zu seinem Ausscheiden 1955 tätig.
// From 1904 training and first employment at Rörstrand; in 1910 transferred to the Gävle porcelain works, where he worked until he retired in 1955.

Signatur(e): nicht bekannt // not known

PERSSON-HJELM, HILMA (1877 – 1953)
Porzellanmalerin, Keramikerin, Formgestalterin
// Porcelain painter, ceramicist, mould designer

1899 – 1900 Ausbildung an der Technischen Schule (HKS) Stockholm. Reiste 1903 nach Dänemark, Deutschland, England und Frankreich. 1900 – 1906 bei Rörstrand angestellt; ihre in dieser Zeit entstandenen Arbeiten entsprechen dem von Alf Wallander bestimmten Erscheinungsbild der Rörstrand-Porzellane. Häufig entwarf sie die Formen, während andere (oft Mela Anderberg) die Objekte bemalten. Sie dekorierte Rörstrands erste Weihnachtsteller (1904 – 1907) und modellierte auch Figurinen in Volkstrachten. Weihnachten 1906 zog sie in den Familienwohnsitz nach Rackstad, richtete dort ihr eigenes Atelier ein und heiratete 1909 den Keramiker Rolf Hjelm.
// From 1899 to 1900 trained at the School of Technique and Applied Arts, Stockholm (HKS). Visited Denmark, Germany, England and France in 1903. From 1900 to 1906 employed at Rörstrand; the pieces she produced at that time match the appearance prescribed for Rörstrand porcelain by Alf Wallander. She often designed moulds while others (often Mela Anderberg) painted the objects. She decorated the first Rörstrand Christmas plates (1904 – 1907) and also modelled figurines in folkloric dress. At Christmas 1906 she moved to her family home in Rackstad, where she set up a studio for herself and married the potter Rolf Hjelm in 1909.

Signatur(e): *HP, H Persson*

PETTERSSON, ANNA EUGENIA MATHILDA (1864 – 1948)
Porzellanmalerin // Porcelain painter.

1876 – 1912 bei Rörstrand durch Eugène Bonnerue ausgebildet und angestellt; danach eigene Schule für Porzellan- und Seidenmalerei in Stockholm; Mitarbeit bei den Ausstellungen in Stockholm 1897 und Paris 1900 mit Blumenmalerei auf Vasen und Servicen.
// From 1876 to 1912 trained at Rörstrand by Eugène Bonnerue and hired; subsequently established a school for porcelain painting and silk painting in Stockholm; contributed to the 1897 Stockholm exhibition and the 1900 Paris Exposition with flower painting on vases and services.

Signatur(e): *AP* (ligiert // monogram, ligatured)

PETTERSSON, ANSELM JOHAN WILHELM (1858 – 1902)
Porzellanmaler, besonders Emailmalerei
// Porcelain painter, notably enamel painting

Von 1870 bis zu seinem Tode bei Rörstrand angestellt. Arbeitete u. a. mit ornamentalen Dekorationen auf Servicen und Prunkvasen; vertreten auf den Ausstellungen in Kopenhagen 1888 und Göteborg 1891, auch in Stockholm 1897 und Paris 1900. Sohn des Dekorateurs Johan Pettersson bei Rörstrand.
// Employed at Rörstrand from 1870 until his death. Worked *inter alia* on ornamental decoration on services and *Prunkvasen* [show vases]; showed work at the 1888 Copenhagen exhibition and at Göteborg in 1891 as well as Stockholm in 1897 and Paris in 1900. Son of the Rörstrand decorator Johan Pettersson.

Signatur(e): nicht bekannt // not known

PETTERSSON, MARIA (geb. // born 1861)
Porzellanmalerin und Dreherin
// Porcelain painter and turner

1900 und 1910 in den Lohnlisten von Rörstrand mit besonderem Lohnzuschlag erwähnt. Um 1905 Vasen im Stil der Fabrik.
// In 1900 and 1910 entered in the Rörstrand payrolls with mention of extra pay. Vases in the Rörstrand style ca 1905.

Signatur(e): *MP* (gemalt // painted)
Siehe Seite // see page: 95, 129, 147

PETTERSSON, SELMA

Bei Rörstrand angestellt ca. 1895 – ca. 1920; tätig in der Gießerei und in anderen Bereichen. War beteiligt an der Ausformung von Figurinen, Vasen usw.
// Employed at Rörstrand ca 1895 – ca 1920; worked in the foundry and other areas. Collaborated on moulding figurines, vases, etc.

Signatur(e): *SP* (geritzt // incised)

POST, VICKEN (HEDWIG) VON,
verh. // married name BÖRJESSON (1886 – 1950)
Bildhauerin, Keramikerin
// Sculptor, ceramicist

1904–1908 Kunstakademie; studierte auch bei Gerhard Henning. Von Sommer 1915 bis 1921 bei Rörstrand angestellt; modellierte ca. 30 Figurinen für die Ausführung in der Fabrik, u. a. *Prinzessin, Pierrot, Nymphe, Romantisches Paar* etc. Erste Ausstellung in NK Stockholm im Spätherbst 1915.
// From 1904 to 1908 Art academy; also studied with Gerhard Henning. Employed at Rörstrand from summer 1915 until 1921; modelled approx thirty figurines for the exhibition at the Rörstrand factory, including *Princess, Pierrot, Nymph, Romantic Couple*, etc. First exhibition at NK Stockholm in late autumn 1915.

Signatur(e): *V v Post, V.v. Post-B-n*
(gemalt // painted)

PRINZ EUGÉN (EUGÉN BERNADOTTE) (1865 – 1947)
Künstler, Maler // Artist, painter

Sohn von König Oscar II. Betätigte sich in geringem Maße auch als Kunsthandwerker, u. a. in Silber und in einigen Fällen auch mit keramischen Arbeiten, darunter einzelne Prunkvasen und der berühmte Blumenkübel von 1913/14. 1905 entwarf er für sein Haus Waldemarsudde ein Tafelservice, das bei Rörstrand ausgeführt wurde. Schon in den 1880er Jahren soll er Tassen und Teller bei Rörstrand dekoriert haben, die als Geschenke für seine Verwandtschaft vorgesehen waren.
// A son of the king Oscar II. Worked to some extent as a craftsman, including silversmithing, and produced some ceramics, including one-off *Prunkvasen* [show vases] and the celebrated

caisse à fleurs of 1913/14. Designed a table service made at Rörstrand for his home Waldemarsudde in 1905. As early as the 1880s is believed to have decorated cups and plates at Rörstrand, which were intended as presents for his relatives.

Signatur(e): *Eugen*

RISING, RUBEN (1869 – 1929)
Bildhauer, Keramiker
// Sculptor, ceramicist

Seit Mitte der 1890er Jahre bei Rörstrand angestellt. Signierte Vase 1898. Verzeichnet in den Lohnlisten von 1900 und 1910 als Porzellanmaler und Dreher mit Sonderlohnzulage. Mitarbeit bei der plastischen Ausformung von Vasen in der Serienproduktion und der Dekoration in Unterglasurmalerei im Stil der Fabrik.
// Employed at Rörstrand from the mid-1890s. Signed vase in 1898. Entered in the 1900 and 1910 payrolls as a porcelain painter and turner with extra pay. Worked on moulding vases for serial production and decorating in underglaze painting in the Rörstrand style.

Signatur(e): *RR* (gemalt und gewöhnlich geritzt // painted and usually incised)
Siehe Seite // see page: 91, 106 – 108, 113, 118, 129, 144, 146, 162, 163, 175 – 177, 180, 184, 189, 195

TRYGGELIN, ERIK HUGO (1846 – 1924)
Architekt, Keramiker
// Architect, ceramicist

1872 in Rörstrand angestellt als „Chefdessinateur", tätig bis 1910. Entwarf Modelle für Prunkvasen und Service und die Mehrzahl von Rörstrands Kachelöfen. Ausführung und Dekoration von bemalten Vasen, Wandfontänen u.a. Verantwortlich für die Produktion von Kachelöfen und die Porzellandekoration. Entwarf u. a. die berühmte Maurische Fontäne, die Krönung der Rörstrand-Abteilung auf der Ausstellung in Göteborg 1891 und Chicago 1893. Er entwarf und bemalte auch einige Ziervasen im neuen Stil um 1900 und war auch für die Planung von einigen der neuen Werkstattgebäude und Wohnhäuser auf dem Fabrikgelände verantwortlich.
// Hired at Rörstrand as *chefdessinateur* [head designer] in 1872, worked there until 1910. Designed models for *Prunkvasen* [show vases] and services as well as most of the Rörstrand tiled stoves.

Executed and decorated painted vases, wall fountains, etc. Responsible for the production of tiled stoves and porcelain decoration. His designs included the famous Moorish Fountain, the highlight of the Rörstrand section of the 1891 Göteborg and the 1893 Chicago exhibitions. Around 1900 he also designed and painted some ornamental vases in the new style and was in charge of planning some of the new workshop buildings and employee housing on the factory premises.

Signatur(e): *E H T-n, HT., .H.T., EHT* (Monogramm // monogram), *E H Tryggelin*
Siehe Seite // see page: 112, 127, 198

VOGEL, ANTON JOSEF (1859 – 1935)
Lehrer für Porzellanmalerei
// Teacher porcelain painting

Kam 1883 nach Schweden und war als Lehrer für Porzellanmalerei bei Rörstrand tätig. Führte auch eigene Arbeiten in den 1880ern und 1890ern aus; bekannt ist eine signierte Tonvase von 1885, außerdem einige Arbeiten um 1900. Später gemeinsam mit Adolph Neumann Inhaber der Firma Neumann & Vogel, die u.a. Glasmalerei betrieb.

// Went to Sweden in 1883 and taught porcelain painting at Rörstrand. Also executed pieces of his own in the 1880s and 1890s; a signed pottery vase dated 1885 and some works done ca 1900 are extant. Later co-proprietor with Adolph Neumann of Neumann & Vogel, whose goods and services included glass painting.

Signatur(e): *Ant. Vogel*

WALLANDER, ALF (1862 – 1914)
Maler, Keramiker, Kunsthandwerker
// Painter, ceramicist, craftsman

1878–1880 Schüler der Technischen Schule (HKS), 1880–1885 Kunstakademie Stockholm, 1885–1889 Paris. 1894 erster Kontakt mit Rörstrand, 1895 als Nachfolger von Hugo Hörlin dort eingestellt, von 1896 bis 1914 in wechselndem Umfang dort tätig; in diesen Jahren Rörstrands führender Künstler, verantwortlich für eine Reihe von Neuheiten im künstlerischen Bereich, sowohl für skulpturale Kunstwerke in Feldspatporzellan mit Unterglasurmalerei als auch in Steingut und Steinzeug. Mehrere Speiseservice (u.a. *Liljor/Iris* 1897, *Tulpan/Tulpe* 1897, *Fjäril/Schmetterling* 1911) sowie Tee- und Kaffeeservice (*Iris* 1899, *Trollslända/ Libelle* 1908). Einige Entwürfe für die Serienproduktion von künstlerischem Steinzeug. Wallander war auch verantwortlich für sämtliche Beiträge Rörstrands zu den Industrieausstellungen

zwischen 1898 und 1914. Er betrieb eigenverantwortlich die Aktiengesellschaft „Schwedische Kunstgewerbeausstellung S. Giöbel" 1898–1914 (Möbel, Textilien u.a.m.) und lieferte auch Entwürfe für Glas (Rejmyre, Kosta), Schmuck, Bucheinbände u. a.

// From 1878 to 1980 pupil at the School of Technique and Applied Arts, Stockholm (HKS), 1880 to 1885 the Royal Art Academy in Stockholm, 1885 to 1889 Paris. In 1894 initial contact with Rörstrand, hired in 1895 as a successor to Hugo Hörlin, worked there from 1896 to 1914 to a varying extent; during those years was the leading Rörstrand artist, responsible for many innovations in the artistic sector, both for sculptural objets d'art in feldspar porcelain with underglaze painting and lead-glazed earthenware and ordinary stoneware. Several tableware services (including *Liljor/Iris* 1897, *Tulpan/Tulip* 1897, *Fjäril/Butterfly* 1911) as well as tea and coffee services (*Iris* 1899, *Trollslända/ Dragon fly* 1908). Some designs for art stoneware in serial production. Wallander was also responsible for all Rörstrand contributions to trade fairs between 1898 and 1914. On his own responsibility he ran the Swedish Artistic Crafts Exhibition S. Giöbel, a private company 1898–1914 (furnishings, textiles and much more) and also submitted designs for glass (Rejmyre, Kosta), jewellery, bookbindings, etc.

Signatur(e): *AW, Alf Wallander* (gemalt // painted); *AW, A Wallander* (geritzt // incised); *DESSIN ALF WALLANDER, Dessin Alf Wallander, DESSIN WALLANDER* (gemalt oder gestempelt // painted or stamped)
Siehe Seite // see page: 84, 98, 112, 114, 120, 122, 123, 130, 137, 152, 156, 164, 168, 176

ZIELFELDT, GERDA AMALIA (1893 – 1947)
Malerin // Painter

Verheiratet mit Karl Frithiof Wistedt. Arbeitete von 1913 bis 1921 als Malerin bei Rörstrand, studierte anschließend bis 1926 an der Kunstakademie in Stockholm und war eine Zeitlang Schülerin von Carl Wilhelmson (1866 – 1928), der seinerseits Schüler von Carl Larsson (1853 – 1919) war.

// Married to Karl Frithiof Wistedt. Worked as a painter at Röstrand from 1913 to 1921 before studying until 1926 at the Royal Art Academy in Stockholm; was for a while a pupil of Carl Wilhelmson (1866 – 1928), who had studied with Carl Larsson (1853 – 1919).

Signatur(e): *.Z.*
Siehe Seite // see page: 138

Rörstrand bei wichtigen Ausstellungen (1889 – 1917)
Rörstrand at important Exhibitions (1889 – 1917)

1889   Kopenhagen // Copenhagen
Nordisk Industri-, Landtbrugs- og Kunst- Udstilling.
Skandinavische Ausstellung. Rörstrand nahm teil in der Abteilung des Schwedischen Gewerbevereins und erhielt einen Preis. Arabia nahm teil. // Scandinavian trade fair. Rörstrand took part in the Swedish Chamber of Trade and Commerce and was awarded a 1st prize. Arabia participated.

1889   Paris
Exposition Universelle.
Goldmedaille für Rörstrand. Arabia nahm teil. // Gold medal for Rörstrand. Arabia participated.

1891   Göteborg // Gothenburg
Allgemeine Kunst- und Industrieausstellung. // Universal Art and Industrial Exhibition.
Teilnahme von Rörstrand in der Industrieabteilung und in der Kunstgewerbeausstellung der Gesellschaft „Der Funke", u. a. mit Arbeiten von H. Tryggelin und H. Hörlin. Rörstrand erhielt einen Großen Preis und zwei Goldmedaillen. // Rörstrand participated in the industrial division and in the applied arts exhibition of 'Der Funke' society, showing work *inter alia* by H. Tryggelin and H. Hörlin. Rörstrand was awarded a Grand Prix and two gold medals.

1893   Chicago
The World's Columbian Exposition, The White City.
Teilnahme von Rörstrand in der Industriehalle mit Arbeiten von u. a. H. Hörlin und A. Eriksson (Unterglasurarbeiten). Rörstrand erhielt eine „Ehrenmedaille". Arabia nahm teil. // Work showed by Rörstrand in the industrial hall included pieces by H. Hörlin and A. Eriksson (underglaze painting). Rörstrand was awarded an honorable mention. Arabia participated.

1894   San Francisco
California Midwinter International Exposition.
Rörstrand erhielt eine Goldmedaille. // Rörstrand was awarded a gold medal.

1894   Antwerpen // Antwerp
Exposition internationale d'Anvers.
Rörstrand nahm teil. // Rörstrand participated.

1896   Stockholm
Gebäude des Schwedischen Gewerbevereins. // Swedish Chamber of Trade and Commerce Building.
Debütausstellung von Alf Wallander. // Alf Wallander made his debut at this trade fair.

1896–1904 Paris
Galerie L'Art Nouveau S. Bing.
Kunstporzellane von Rörstrand (A. Wallander, A. Eriksson u. a.) wurden seit 1896 in Siegfried Bings berühmter Galerie angeboten und blieben wahrscheinlich bis zu deren Schließung 1904 im Angebot. // Art porcelain by Rörstrand (A. Wallander, A. Eriksson, *et al*) was sold at the celebrated Siegfried Bing gallery from 1896 and probably continued to be sold there until the gallery closed down in 1904.

1896   Göteborg // Gothenburg
Kunst- und Industrieausstellung. Gesellschaft „Der Funke". // Art and Industrial Exhibition. 'Der Funke' Society.
Rörstrand nahm teil. A. Wallander stellte unter eigenem Namen in der Abteilung für Objets d'art der Kunstausstellung aus. // Rörstrand participated. A. Wallander showed work under his own name in the objets d'art division of the art section.

1896   Malmö
Nordische Industrie und Gewerbeausstellung in Malmö. // Nordic Industrial and Applied Arts Exhibition in Malmö.
Rörstrand nahm in der Industrieabteilung teil, u. a. mit Kunstkeramik von A. Wallander und A. Eriksson. Der Beitrag wurde mit einer Goldmedaille ausgezeichnet. // Rörstrand participated in the industrial section, with exhibits including ceramics by A. Wallander and A. Eriksson. Rörstrand was awarded a gold medal.

1896   Berlin
Berliner Kunstgewerbeausstellung. // Berlin Applied Arts Exhibition.
Rörstrand nahm teil, u. a. mit Kunstkeramik von A. Wallander. // The work shown by Rörstrand included art ceramics by A. Wallander.

1897   Stockholm
Allgemeine Kunst- & Industrieausstellung in Stockholm 1897. // Universal Art and Industrial Exhibition in Stockholm 1897.
Rörstrand beteiligte sich in der Industriehalle mit Serviceporzellan und Kachelöfen sowie mit Kunstkeramik von A. Wallander, A. Boberg, A. Eriksson, N. Lundström, K. und W. Lindström u. a. In der Kunsthalle zeigte A. Wallander 19 keramische Objets d'art. Goldmedaille für Rörstrand. // In the industrial hall Rörstrand showed porcelain services and tiled stoves as well as art ceramics by A. Wallander, A. Boberg, A. Eriksson, N. Lundström, K. and W. Lindström, *et al.* In the art hall A. Wallander showed nineteen ceramic objets d'art. Gold medal for Rörstrand.

1897   Nashville
The Tennessee Centennial Exposition.
Silbermedaille für Rörstrand. // Silver medal for Rörstrand.

1897   Brüssel // Brussels
Exposition internationale de Bruxelles.
Rörstrand nahm teil. // Rörstrand participated.

1897   Kopenhagen // Copenhagen
Kunstindustrimuseet Ausstellung über „Englische Papiertapeten, keramische Arbeiten aus Rörstrand, Bronzen von Ville Wallgren, Paris". // Kunstindustrimuseet exhibition of 'English wallpapers, ceramics from Rörstrand, bronzes by Ville Wallgren, Paris'.
Eine Spezialausstellung mit Kunstwerken aus Rörstrand, u. a. von A. Wallander, A. Eriksson, N. Lundström. Der Disponent Robert Almström schenkte nach der Ausstellung dem Museum eine reichhaltige Kollektion. // A special exhibition with art works from Rörstrand, including pieces by A. Wallander, A. Eriksson, N. Lundström. Robert Almström, an expediter, donated a rich collection to the museum after the exhibition.

1898   Berlin
Moderne Keramik im Kunstgewerbemuseum. // Modern Ceramics at the Applied Arts Museum.
Ausstellung von moderner Keramik aus der Kgl. Porzellanfabrik Kopenhagen, von Bing & Grøndahl, von Rörstrand, der Kgl. Porzellanmanufaktur in Berlin, Muller & Cie. aus Ivry bei Paris und einzelnen Steinzeugkünstlern. Rörstrand u. a. mit Arbeiten von A. Wallander. // Exhibition of modern ceramics from the Royal Copenhagen Porcelain Manufactory, Bing & Grøndahl, Rörstrand, The Royal Porcelain Manufactory in Berlin, Muller & Cie. from Ivry near Paris and individual artists working in fine stoneware. Artists representing Rörstrand included A. Wallander.

1898   Wien // Vienna
Winterausstellung des Österreichischen Museums für angewandte Kunst. // Winter Exhibition at the Austrian Museum for Applied Art.
Rörstrand war vertreten. // Rörstrand was represented.

1900   Stockholm
Nationalmuseum. // National Museum.
Die Kollektionen von Rörstrand und Gustavsberg für die Weltausstellung in Paris. // The Rörstrand and Gustavsberg collections for the 1900 Paris World Exposition.

1900   Paris
L'Exposition Universelle.
Teilnahme von Rörstrand mit Serviceporzellan und Kunstporzellan, u. a. von A. Wallander, A. Boberg, A. Eriksson, N. Lundström, K. und W. Lindström in der Industrieabteilung und im Schwedischen Pavillon. Die Fabrik nahm den Grand Prix entgegen, einige der Künstler auch Goldmedaillen und Ehren-Erwähnungen. Arabia erhielt eine Goldmedaille. // Porcelain services and art porcelain shown by Rörstrand included work by A. Wallander, A. Boberg, A. Eriksson, N. Lundström, K. and W. Lindström in the industrial section and the Swedish Pavilion. Rörstrand received a Grand Prix and some of the Rörstrand artists were awarded gold medals and honourable mentions. Arabia won a gold medal.

1900   Paris
Exposition Internationale de Céramique.
Ehrendiplom für Rörstrand. // Rörstrand received an honourable mention certificate.

1900   Stockholm
Warenhaus Joseph Leja. Weihnachtsausstellung von Kunstgewerbe. // Joseph Leja Department Store. Christmas Applied Arts Fair.
Kunstkeramik aus Rörstrand (vor allem A. Wallander). // Art ceramics from Rörstrand (notably A. Wallander).

1901   Gävle
Industrie- & Gewerbeausstellung in Gävle. // Industrial and Applied Arts Trade Fair in Gävle.
Teilnahme von Rörstrand in der Industrieabteilung (außer Konkurrenz). // Rörstrand showed work in the industrial section (*hors concours*).

1901   St. Petersburg
Baltische Kunst- & Industrieausstellung. // Baltic Art and Industrial Trade Fair.
Teilnahme von Rörstrand mit Service- und Kunstporzellan. Grand Prix. // Rörstrand showed porcelain services and art porcelain. Grand Prix.

1902   Göteborg // Gothenburg
Skandinavische Kunstausstellung. // Scandinavian Art Exhibition.
Rörstrand nahm teil u.a. mit Arbeiten von A. Wallander, A. Boberg, A. Eriksson, N. Lundström, K. und W. Lindström. // Exhibits featured by Rörstrand included work by A. Wallander, A. Boberg, A. Eriksson, N. Lundström, K. and W. Lindström.

1902   Turin
Esposizione Internazionale di Arte Decorativa Moderna.
Rörstrand nahm teil in der Schwedischen Abteilung u. a. mit Arbeiten von A. Wallander, A. Boberg, A. Eriksson, N. Lundström, K. und W. Lindström. Grand Prix für Rörstrand. // Work shown by Rörstrand in the Swedish section included pieces by A. Wallander, A. Boberg, A. Eriksson, N. Lundström, K. and W. Lindström. Grand Prix for Rörstrand.

1903   Helsingborg
Industrie-, Gewerbe- und Kunstausstellung in Helsingborg. // Industrial, Applied Arts and Fine Art Exhibition in Helsingborg.
Teilnahme von Rörstrand (außer Konkurrenz) in der Industrieabteilung mit Kachelöfen, Service- und Kunstporzellan. // Rörstrand showed (*hors concours*) tiled stoves, porcelain services and art porcelain in the industrial section.

1904   Malmö
Keramische Ausstellung, 14. April – 12. Mai 1904. // Ceramics Exhibition, 14 April–12 May 1904.
Sonderausstellung im Malmö Museum mit u. a. Rörstrand (A. Wallander, A. Eriksson, A. Boberg. K. und W. Lindström, N. Lundström) und Gustavsberg und Helene Holck. Die dänischen Fabriken werden von Bing & Grøndahl, der Kgl. Porzellanfabrik, Aluminia, Herman A. Kähler und P. Ipsens Witwe vertreten. (Die norwegischen Fabriken hatte die Teilnahme abgelehnt). // Special exhibition at Malmö Museum including work from Rörstrand (A. Wallander, A. Eriksson, A. Boberg, K. and W. Lindström, N. Lundström) as well as Gustavsberg and Helene Holck. Danish factories were represented by Bing & Grøndahl, the Royal Copenhagen Porcelain Manufactory, Herman A. Kähler and P. Ipsen's widow (Norwegian porcelain factories did not wish to participate).

1904   St. Louis
Louisiana Purchase International Exhibition.
Rörstrand nahm teil in der Industrieabteilung und im Schwedischen Pavillon („Schwedisches Landhaus"). Goldmedaille für Rörstrand. // Rörstrand showed work in the industrial section and the Swedish Pavilion ('Swedish Country House'). Gold medal for Rörstrand.

1905   Liège
Exposition Universelle et Internationale.
Teilnahme von Rörstrand in der Industrieabteilung mit Service- und Kunstporzellan. Grand Prix. // Rörstrand showed porcelain services and art porcelain in the industrial section. Grand Prix.

1906   Mailand // Milan
Espozione Internazionale
Rörstrand nahm teil. // Rörstrand participated.

1906   Norrköping
Kunst- & Industrieausstellung in Norrköping. // Art and Industrial Exhibition in Norrköping.
Rörstrand nahm teil (außer Konkurrenz) in der Industrieabteilung mit Serviceware, Kachelöfen und Kunstporzellan. // Rörstrand showed (*hors concours*) porcelain services, tiled stoves and art porcelain in the industrial section.

1907   Lund
Kunst- & Industrieausstellung in Lund. // Art and Industrial Exhibition in Lund.
Rörstrand nahm außer Konkurrenz teil. // Rörstrand showed work *hors concours*.

1908   St. Petersburg
Baltische Kunst- & Industrieausstellung. // Baltic Art and Industrial Exhibition.
Rörstrand nahm teil in der Industrieabteilung mit Serviceware, Kachelöfen und Kunstporzellan. Goldmedaille. // Rörstrand showed services, tiled stoves and art porcelain in the industrial section. Gold medal.

1909   Stockholm
Allgemeine Schwedische Ausstellung für Kunsthandwerk und Kunstindustrie. // Universal Swedish Exhibition for Applied and Industrial Art.
Rörstrand nahm teil in der Industrieabteilung mit Serviceware, Kachelöfen und Kunstporzellan. // Rörstrand showed services, tiled stoves and art porcelain in the industrial section.

1910 Brüssel // Brussels
Exposition Universelle et Internationale.
Rörstrand nahm teil in der Industrieabteilung mit Servicen, Kachelöfen und Kunstporzellan. Goldmedaille. // Rörstrand showed services, tiled stoves and art porcelain in the industrial section. Gold medal.

1910 Wien // Vienna
„Künstlerbund Hagen", Schwedische Kunst und Kunstindustrie. // *Künstlerbund Hagen*, Swedish Art and Industrial Art.
Keramik von A. Wallander. // Ceramics by A. Wallander.

1911 Prag // Prague
„Manes", Schwedische Kunst und Kunstindustrie. // *Manes,* Swedish Art and Industrial Art.
Rörstrand nahm teil mit Keramik von A. Wallander. // Rörstrand showed ceramics by A. Wallander.

1912 Gent // Ghent
Industrieausstellung. // *Industrial Exhibition.*
Rörstrand nahm teil. // Rörstrand participated.

1914 Malmö
Baltische Ausstellung. // *Baltic Exhibition.*
Teilnahme von Rörstrand in der Industrieabteilung mit Servicen, Kachelöfen und Kunstporzellan. // Rörstrand showed services, tiled stoves and art porcelain in the industrial section.

1915 San Francisco
San Francisco World's Fair (The Panama-Pacific International Exposition).
Teilnahme von Rörstrand in der Industrieabteilung. // Rörstrand showed work in the industrial section.

1915 Stockholm
Warenhaus Nordiska Kompaniet, NK. // *Department Store Nordiska Kompaniet, NK.*
Ausstellung von Rörstrand mit Arbeiten von N. Lundström, V. von Post u. a. // Rörstrand exhibition showed work by N. Lundström, V. von Post, *et al.*

1917 Stockholm
„Heimausstellung", Ausstellung der Schwedischen Gewerbevereinigung von Einrichtung für Kleinwohnungen in der Kunsthalle Liljevalchs. // *'Home Exhibition'*, exhibition mounted by the Swedish Trades Association of furnishings for small flats at the Liljevalchs Art Hall.
Teilnahme von Rörstrand u.a. mit Arbeiten von E. Hald, L. Adelborg, N. Lundström. // Exhibits from Rörstrand included work by E. Hald, L. Adelborg, N. Lundström.

Literatur
(in Auswahl)
Literature
(a Selection)

Allmänna svenska utställningen för konsthandtverk och
    konstindustri i Stockholm 1909, S./p. 132–140.

Almström, Harald. 1915
    Porslin och glas. In: Baltiska utställningen i Malmö 1914.
    Offizieller Bericht S./p. 493–545.

Almström, Robert. 1899
    Kakelugns-, fajans- och porslintillverkningen på
    utställningen. In: Allmänna Konst- & Industriutställningen
    i Stockholm 1897. Offizieller Bericht, Teil II,
    S./p. 626–651.

Almström, Robert. 1904
    Lervarorna och deras tillverkning.

Arabia 100 år. 1973
    In: Keramik och glas. 1973 (Jubiläumsnummer).

Bæckström, Arvid. 1930
    Rörstrand och dess tillverkningar 1726–1926.

Becker, Ingeborg (red.). 2005
    „Schönheit für alle". Jugendstil in Schweden. Bröhan
    Museum Berlin 2005.

Berge, August. 1925
    Chemische Technologie der Tonwaren.

Borrmann, Richard. 1902
    Moderne Keramik.

Bröhan, Karl H. 1998
    Porzellanfabrik Rörstrand, Stockholm. In: Porzellan.
    Kunst und Design 1889 bis 1939. Vom Jugendstil zum
    Funktionalismus. II, S./p. 205–255 (u. a. K. Lindström,
    W. Lindström, N. E. Lundström, A. Wallander).

Cramér, Margareta. 1991
    Den verkliga kakelugnen. Fabrikstillverkade kakelugnar i
    Stockholm 1846–1926.

Dahlbäck Lutteman, Helena. 1980
    Svenskt porslin. Fajans, porslin och flintgods
    1700–1900.

Dahlbäck Lutteman, Helena. 1985
    Svensk 1900 – talskeramik. Stengods, porslin, flintgods.

Ekerot, Gunnar. 1899
    Rörstrands Porslinsfabrik. In: Svenska Industriella Verk
    och Anläggningar. 1899: I, S./p. 1–12.

Ericsson, Anne-Marie. 1989
    Konstindustri och konsthantverk. In: Baltiska utställningen
    1914, S./p. 139–170 (Keramik och glas S./p. 159–163).

Ericsson, Anne-Marie. 2002
    Keramiken. In: Signums Svenska Konsthistoria. Konsten
    1915–1950. Lund.

Folcker, Erik G. 1892
    En svensk konstslöjd. In: Ord & Bild 1892,
    S./p. 423–426.

Folcker, Erik G. 1896
    Konstnärlig keramik. In: Ord & Bild 1896, S./p. 379–384.

Folcker, Erik G. 1897
    Våra porslinsfabriker. En utställnings studie. In: SSF:M
    1897, II, S./p. 52–61.

Formens rörelse. 1995
    Svensk form genom 150 år (Red. Kerstin Wickman).

Fredlund, Jane. 1997
    Gammalt porslin. Svenska serviser 1790–1990.

Frick, Gunilla. 1986
    Rörstrand. In: Konstnär i industrin, S./p. 33–76.

Friedl, Hans. 1984
    Warum? Weshalb? Wieso? 100 Fragen aus dem Gebiet der
    Keramik.

Friedl, Hans. 1986
    Warum? Weshalb? Wieso? 100 Fragen über Porzellan.

Fuchs, W. 1941
    Über die Zusammensetzung des Porzellans und seiner
    Abarten. Die Naturwissenschaften, Band 29, Nr. 2, Januar
    1941, S./p. 18ff.

Hård af Segerstadt, Ulf. 1976
    Keramik. Sekelskifte till sjuttiotal.

Hecht, Hermann. 1923
    Lehrbuch der Keramik.

Herlitz-Gezelius, Anne Marie. 1989
    Rörstrand.
Jaennicke, Friedrich. 1900
    Geschichte der Keramik.
Jakó, Géza. 1928
    Keramische Materialkunde. Beschreibung der Masse-,
    Glasur- und Brennmaterialien sowie der Farbstoffe, durch-
    gesehen und mit einem Originalbeitrag über: Die Technik
    der vernünftigen Kalkulation keramischer Mineralien
    von R. Jäger.
Kerl, Bruno. 1907
    Handbuch der gesammten Thonwaarenindustrie.
    Bearbeitet von Eduard Kramer und Hermann Hecht.
    3. Auflage.
Kretschmer, Winfried. 1999
    Geschichte der Weltausstellungen.
Lagercrantz, Bo. 1960, 1996
    Iris, Vineta och Gröna Anna. Rörstrandsserviser
    1869–1960 (desgl. mehrere spätere Auflagen).
Lehnhäuser, Werner. 1959
    Glasuren und ihre Farben.
Levering, Gustav. 1921
    Porzellanmalerei. Geschichte und Technik.
Lundgren, Bertil, Lundgren, Kristian & Stenberg, Peter. 1996
    Rörstrands dekorer. Rörstrands porslinsfabrik.
Neuwirth, Waltraud. 1974
    Österreichische Keramik des Jugendstils.
Nyström, Bengt. 1967
    Alf Wallander och Rörstrand. In: Fataburen 1967,
    S./p. 93–108.
Nyström, Bengt. 1982
    Konsten till industrin. Alf Wallander och Gunnar
    Wennerberg som konstindustriella formgivare.
Nyström, Bengt. 1996
    Rörstrand Porcelain. Art Nouveau Masterpieces.
Nyström, Bengt. 1998
    „Une fée du Nord…" Jugendporslin från Rörstrand. In:
    Jugendporslin från Rörstrand, en amerikansk privatsam-
    ling. Prins Eugens Waldemarsudde. Katalog Nr. 46:
    1998, S./p. 18–57.
Nyström, Bengt. 2000
    Keramiken. In: Signums Svenska Konsthistoria. Bd 10.
    Konsten 1845–1890, S./p. 647–672.
Nyström, Bengt. 2001
    Keramiken. In: Signums Svenska Konsthistoria. Bd 11.
    Konsten 1890–1915, S./p. 440–473.
Nyström, Bengt. 2003
    Svensk Jugend Keramik.
Nyström, Bengt. 2005
    Alf Wallander – enthusiastisch und vielseitig, In:
    „Schönheit für alle". Jugendstil in Schweden (Bröhan
    Museum Berlin 2005).

Nyström, Bengt & Ankarberg, Carl-Henrik. 2007
    Rörstrand i Stockholm. Tegelbruk, fajansmanufaktur och
    keramisk storindustri i Stockhohn 1270–1926.
Nyström, Bengt & Brunius, Jan. 2007
    Rörstrand. 280 år med fajans och flintgods, porslin och
    stengods.
Nyström, Bengt. 2008
    Svensk keramik under 1900-talet. Keramiker, fabriker,
    signaturer.
Palme, Per & Nordensson, Eva. 1965
    Svensk keramik.
Pukall, Wilhelm. 1922
    Grundzüge der Keramik.
Ring, Herman A. 1900
    Paris och världsutställningen 1900.
Rörstrand. 1900
    Stockholm (Imprimérie Centrale) 1900.
Rörstrand. 1986
    Design made in Sweden … seit 1726.
Hänisch, Lutz. 1984
    Skandinavisches Porzellan des Jugendstils aus der
    Sammlung der Familie Hänisch. Essen.
Stavenow-Hidemark, Elisabet. 1964
    Svensk Jugend.
Stavenow-Hidemark, Elisabet. 1995
    Förändringarnas vind. In: Formens rörelse. Svensk form
    genom 150 år, S./p. 25–43.
Thieme-Becker. 1992
    Allgemeines Lexikon der bildenden Künstler. Nachdruck.
Thorson Walton, A. 1994
    Ferdinand Boberg – Architect. The complete work.
Upmark, Gustaf (d. J.). 1910
    Keramik, glas och stenindustri. In: Det svenska konst-
    handtverket 1909.
Vingedal, S. E. 1982
    Porslinsmärken.
Vollmer, Hans. 1992
    Allgemeines Lexikon der bildenden Künstler des
    20. Jahrhunderts. Nachdruck.
Watz, Birgitta (red). 1982
    Form och tradition i Sverige.
Weimarck, Ann-Charlotte och Hans. 1969
    Höganäskeramik. Konst- och brukföremål 1832–1926.
Wickman, Kerstin (red). 1995
    Formens rörelse. Svensk form genom 150 år.
Widman, Dag (red). 1967
    Svenskt konsthantverk från sekelskifte till sextiotal.
    Årsbok för svenska statens konstsamlingar XIV.
Widman, Dag. 1975
    Konsthantverk, konstindustri, design 1895–1975. Konsten
    i Sverige.

Namens-Register
Index of Names

Impressum // Imprint

© 2011 ARNOLDSCHE Art Publishers, Stuttgart und die Autoren
// and the Authors

Autor // Author
Dr. Bengt Nyström

Vorwort // Preface
Johannes Busch
Hans Schmidts

Übersetzung // Translation
Dr. Gesine Schulz-Berlekamp (Swedish/German)
Joan Clough (German/English)

Korrektorat // Editorial Work
Wendy Brouwer (English)

Grafische Gestaltung // Layout
Silke Nalbach, nalbach typografik, Mannheim

Bildnachweis // Photo Credits
Alle Objekt-Fotos sind von // All object-photos by von Uslar fotodesign,
Irene von Uslar, Bielefeld.
Bei den Text-Abbildungen ist der jeweilige Fotograf genannt, andernfalls
sind sie vom Autor geliefert. // For the illustrations, the photographer is credited
next to each picture, otherwise they are by the author.
Für die Abdruckgenehmigung wurden die jeweiligen Rechteinhaber kontaktiert,
einige konnten jedoch nicht ausfindig gemacht werden. Der Verlag bittet in
solchen Fällen um Kontaktaufnahme. // We have contacted the owners of rights
to the images for their permission; however, in some cases they could not be
identified. In such cases we ask that the owners contact us.

Offset Reproduktion // Offset reproductions
Schwabenrepro GmbH, Stuttgart

Druck // Printed by
Leibfarth + Schwarz, Dettingen

Gedruckt auf PEFC-zertifiziertem Papier. Dieses Zertifikat steht europaweit
für nachhaltige und sozialverträgliche Waldbewirtschaftung.
Printed on PEFC certified paper. This certificate stands throughout Europe
for long-term sustainable forest management in a multi-stakeholder process

Bibliografische Information der Deutschen Nationalbibliothek
Die Deutsche Nationalbibliothek verzeichnet diese Publikation in der Deutschen
Nationalbibliografie; detaillierte bibliografische Daten sind im Internet über
http://dnb.d-nb.de abrufbar.
Bibliographic information published by the Deutsche Nationalbibliothek
The Deutsche Nationalbibliothek lists this publication in the Deutsche
Nationalbibliografie; detailed bibliographic data are available in the Internet at
http://dnb.d-nb.de.

ISBN 978-3-89790-341-8

Made in Germany, 2011

ARNOLDSCHE art books are available internationally at selected bookstores
and from the following distribution partners:

USA
ACC USA, New York, NY, sales@antiquecc.com
CANADA
NBN Canada, Toronto; lpetriw@nbnbooks.com
UK + FRANCE + SOUTH AMERICA + SOUTH AFRICA
ACC GB, Woodbridge, Suffolk, sales@accdistribution.com
BENELUX
Coen Sligting Bookimport, Alkmaar, sligting@xs4all.nl
SWITZERLAND
OLF S.A., Fribourg, information@olf.ch
SCANDINAVIA
Elisabeth Harder-Kreimann, Hamburg, elisabeth@harder-kreimann.de
SOUTHERN EUROPE
Joe Portelli, Bookport Associates, Corsico, bookport@bookport.it
EASTERN EUROPE
Josef Kolar, josefkolar@aon.at
RUSSIA
MAGMA, Moscow, magmabooks@mail.ru
ASIA
Ralph & Sheila Summers, formtone@dircon.co.uk
CHINA
Benjamin Pan, benjamin.pan@cpmarketing.com.cn
JAPAN
Yasy Murayama, yasy@yasmy.com
THAILAND
Paragon Asia Co., Bangkok, paragonasia@gmail.com

For general questions, please contact ARNOLDSCHE Art Publishers directly at
art@arnoldsche.com, or visit our homepage at www.arnoldsche.com for further
information.

Die vorliegende Publikation erscheint anlässlich der Ausstellungs-Reihe:
// The present publication is published on the occasion of the exhibition series:

Internationales Keramik-Museum, Weiden
Zweigmuseum der Neuen Sammlung – The International Design Museum Munich
16. 10. 2011 – 22. 1. 2012

Museum Huelsmann, Bielefeld
28. 10. 2012 – 24. 3. 2013

weitere Ausstellungen in Skandinavien folgen. // further exhibitions in
Scandinavia will follow.